The Pyramid under the Cross

Franciscan Discourses of Evangelization
and the Nahua Christian Subject
in Sixteenth-century Mexico

Viviana Díaz Balsera

The University of Arizona Press | *Tucson*

The University of Arizona Press
© 2005 The Arizona Board of Regents

∞ This book is printed on acid-free, archival-quality paper.
Manufactured in the United States of America
10 09 08 07 06 05   6 5 4 3 2 1

Library of Congress Cataloging-in-Publication Data
Díaz Balsera, Viviana, 1958–
    The pyramid under the cross : Franciscan discourses of evangelization
and the Nahua Christian subject in sixteenth-century Mexico / Viviana
Díaz Balsera.
        p. cm.
    Includes bibliographical references (p.   ) and index.
    ISBN 0-8165-2380-0 (cloth : alk. paper)
    1. Nahuas—Missions—Mexico—History—16th century. 2. Nahuas—
Religion. 3. Indian Catholics—Mexico—History—16th century. 4.
Franciscans—Missions—Mexico—History—16th century. 5. Christianity
and other religions—Mexico—History 6. Christianity and culture—Mexico—
History—16th century. 7. Mexico—History—16th century—Sources. I. Title.
F1219.73.D55 2005
972'.02'00497452—dc22
                                                                    2004023857

Contents

Acknowledgments vii

Introduction: Franciscans, Nahuas, and Colonialism 3

PART I | *The Christian Word Comes to Anahuac*

1. The *Colloquios y doctrina cristiana* and the Emergence of the Nahua Christian Subject in Sixteenth-century Mexico 15

PART II | *Nahua Theater of Evangelization in Sixteenth-century Mexico*

2. Introduction to Some Cultural Performance Practices in Medieval Spain and Pre-Hispanic Mexico 53

3. Performing the Limits of Colonialist Power: Evangelization, Irony, and Resistance in the *Neixcuitilli Final Judgment* 65

4. A Judeo-Christian Tlaloc or a Nahua Yahweh? Domination, Hybridity, and Continuity in the Nahua Evangelization Theater 81

5. Performing Otherness and Identity in *The Fall of Our First Parents* 97

PART III | *Confession, Acculturation, and Resistance in Sixteenth-century Mexico*

6. Confession in the Old and New Worlds 117

7. Molina's *Confessionario mayor* and the Impossible Nahua Christian Subject 125

8. Juan Bautista's *Advertencias para los confesores de los Naturales* and the Malaises of Domination 147

PART IV | *Falling Back Into History*

  9. *Historia eclesiástica indiana* or Writing the Crisis of
  Providentialism   *161*

  Conclusion: The Pyramid under the Cross   *203*

  Notes   *213*

  Works Cited   *247*

  Index   *263*

Acknowledgments

WRITING IS ALWAYS A JOURNEY, and the acknowledgments section in every book is a recollection of significant moments along the way. My first acknowledgment goes to the University of Miami for generously subsidizing parts of this journey with two Orovitz research awards, as well with as a summer grant for the study of Nahuatl. My thanks to my colleagues in the Department of Foreign Languages and Literatures, especially Barbara Woshinsky and Ralph Heyndels, who read sections of my manuscript and whose sound advice contributes to the book's more successful pages. Asunción Lavrin deserves particular mention for all her encouragement and practical traveling advice as I first ventured into my research topic in Mexico. I still keep the tokens of good luck she gave me to safeguard my trip, a trip that bound me spiritually and intellectually to the subject of my book in a very special and meaningful way. Her readings of early drafts of my chapters were always ever so helpful. Another significant moment of my journey was having met Barry D. Sell, who graciously shared with me his vast knowledge of Nahuatl and things Franciscan. I am grateful to José Rabasa for reading parts of the manuscript and for his suggestions and enthusiastic endorsement, and to Raquel Chang-Rodríguez for encouraging me to publish an excerpt in *Colonial Latin American Review.* My special thanks to Patti Hartmann, acquisitions editor at the University of Arizona Press, and to the anonymous readers for the excellent suggestions that helped to improve the book.

I recollect with gratitude the support I received from my family while writing this book. I thank my sister, Maria Elena Díaz, also in academe, for her sharp and careful comments on my manuscript, and my mother for her faith in me. Many, many thanks to my husband, Alberto Jorge Carol—who knows this book by heart—for patiently reading its many versions, for enduring hours of discussion, and for sustaining me with his love. His gifted drawing for the book jacket expresses so well one of the deepest meanings of this work. The last mention of gratitude goes to my son Dylan Carol, who unexpectedly came into the world as I labored with my intellectual offspring. He made the remaining steps to the completion of this journey—and everything else in my life—full to the very brim.

The Pyramid
under the Cross

Franciscans, Nahuas, and Colonialism

As many critics of former Western colonialism have observed, although imperial relations were usually established by force, they were largely maintained by discourse, textuality (Tiffin and Lawson, 3), representation, and other semiotic devices. The natives were conceptualized, inscribed, and addressed from within the colonizer's cultural system, thereby thinking and making the former think about themselves through the eyes of the intruder. The position grosso modo allotted to the native was that of lacking and/or lessening difference: half-child, half-wild, of barbaric practices or of hardly any practice at all, or if having an undeniable degree of civilization, of perplexing customs and beliefs revealing an inherently deficient use of reason and great ignorance of truth. Ironically, the imagined inadequacies and differences of the native would be among his most coveted traits for the European colonizer of the early modern period. Such constructed deficiencies were instrumental in catapulting the colonizer at the end of the fifteenth century from his historical marginality into a central position in the world. They triggered in the European the imagination of a universal subjectivity that was heightened by the actual, empirical experience of the confines of the planet. Spain was the driving force in this early period of European expansionism, as she assumed the role of ecumenical, Catholic subject. The present book deals with a chapter in the first century of this Spanish-led expansionism that has to do much with the political and economic subordination of the native subaltern, but even more with the attempt to possess his soul. The book will tell a story about this zealous endeavor and about how it fragmented, transformed, and left unchanged the desiring European self and the coveted other in ways sometimes unforeseen by both.

On 13 August 1521, after being placed under siege for seventy-five days, Tenochtitlan, the capital city of the Mexica empire, fell into the hands of the Spaniards, their masterful but implacable captain Hernán Cortés, and their indispensable allies the Tlaxcalans. Eight months later, in the bull *Exponi Nobis*, Pope Adrian VI consented to Cortés's petition to send missionaries to the newly conquered territories and gave them extraordinary privileges to evangelize, because no organized church was in place in the new lands. Finally in 1524, Hernán Cortés received the first Franciscan missionaries, known as "the Twelve," to start the difficult and most arduous task of reshaping an alien, frightening, yet profoundly devout and extraordinarily disciplined culture, in order to make it fit into the universal and ecumenical world of Christianity.

The drama of evangelization started as soon as the Twelve set foot in Veracruz. The number twelve, of course, carried all the evocative force of apostlehood that the Western imagination could muster. Just as the twelve apostles had gone into the world to preach the word of Christ, the newly arrived Franciscans had come into a new world in order to illuminate it with the holy word. Lest someone think they were moved by the desire of worldly possessions, the friars performed their first feat of piety walking barefoot from Veracruz to Tenochtitlan. They stopped for a couple of days in Tlaxcala where the *tlatoani*, or dynastic ruler, feeling sorry for these miserably clad Spaniards who kept bawling and pointing up to heaven, ordered that they be fed (Muñoz Camargo, 162).

It was not until they reached the capital of New Spain that the first spectacle of the power of the missionaries occurred. Accompanied by all the Spanish gentlemen and *indios principales* (Nahua noblemen) gathered for the occasion, Hernán Cortés, the new, feared, and encumbered lord of Tenochtitlan, "yendo de rodillas abatido por el suelo" [dragging himself on his knees][1] (Muñoz Camargo, 241) kissed one by one the hand of the twelve friars in rags. After him, all his captains, soldiers, and gentlemen did the same. Then, having watched attentively the whole scene, the indios principales, who commanded utmost respect and authority over the masses, followed suit. According to Gerónimo de Mendieta, paintings depicting the event were commissioned and spread all over New Spain in eternal memory of the glorious deed the Holy Spirit had performed through the haughty and proud Cortés, so as to lay a firm base for the Word (Mendieta, HEI, 211).[2] By performing this foundational act of subjection of the mighty warriors to the impoverished friars, or what Pauline M. Watts calls "a transmutation of the ancient Roman ceremony of the *adventus*" ("Languages," 144),[3] Cortés and his soldiers indeed empowered the strange newly arrived to become protagonists in the reconstruction of the public sphere of New Spain. From that point on, the feeble twelve-member contingent would lay the foundations, invent the strategies, and establish the guidelines for carrying out the formidable task of incorporating one of the most densely populated areas in the world, heretofore unknown, into the Catholic community of Christianity.

This book will examine sixteenth-century texts written by the Franciscan spiritual colonizers in their efforts to produce Christian subjects out of the Nahuas,[4] as well as some of the collaborative textual production of the latter. The process of evangelization was indeed one of discipline, punishment, and force; but because Catholic Christianity implies the intricate issues of consent and free will, it also mandated negotiation with the Christian subject-to-be. The Nahua theater of evangelization, sponsored by the Franciscans but represented and often even written by Nahuas for a Nahua audience, is a particularly exemplary case of the cultural negotiation involved in the evangelization process in Mexico, especially during the sixteenth century. Simply stated, the Christianization of the Nahuas would demand to some extent the Nahuatization of Christianity; for in spite of their asymmetrical and clearly uneven power locations, seldom could the discourses of the colonizer be all-powerful machines of domination rolling down one-way streets. Postcolonial critic Homi Bhabha's figure of hybridity will be particularly relevant here because it insists on the fact that colonizing discourses can never reproduce themselves in the cultural contexts of the colonized without becoming to some extent what they desire to transform. No matter how powerful the colonizer's discourse may be, it is never powerful enough to control all the ways and modes of its circulation as it is exercised over an alien but also alienating other.

In the book I will explore then not only (some of the many) moments of imposition of a Eurocentric worldview and culture upon the Nahua, but also the hybridization of such a view as the spiritual colonizer attempted to encompass the new non-Western constituency. I will also examine moments of ambivalence, disruption, and anxiety in his discourses of domination produced by the confrontation with a half-acquiescing, yet never entirely containable other. The latter, in turn, was also irreversibly contaminated by what he had to adopt, resist, appropriate, circumvent, and/or mimic from the colonizer.[5] All of these heterogeneous and even contradictory discursive and subjective relations constitute the intricate and sometimes chaotic picture of the colonial encounter in sixteenth-century Mexico.

The principal reason motivating my choice of a mainly Franciscan, sixteenth-century textual corpus is that the Friars Minor in New Spain can be considered the founders of the early Mexican Church.[6] Being the first missionary order to arrive, they occupied the most important political and social centers of the Valley of Mexico, including Tenochtitlan, Tetzcoco, and Tlatelolco. They set the strategies for evangelization that other missionaries would follow, particularly in the pivotal role they gave to the learning of indigenous languages. Harboring millenarian hopes for the new Indian Church that they led, the Franciscans were accused by their numerous enemies of having secessionist aspirations during this period. Although clearly agents of acculturation, the Franciscans nonetheless would frequently oppose the crown's and episcopal church's policies toward the last quarter of the sixteenth century. Hence, many of their discursive productions may be thought of as cleaving Spanish imperialism while promoting Western epistemologies and sometimes even as blurring the divide between colonizer and colonized in their harsh critiques of some colonial practices. It is not entirely surprising that many of the texts produced at the height of the Franciscan order's prestige and power in the sixteenth century were prohibited and/or confiscated by Philip II. In 1585, the Third Mexican Provin-

cial Council decreed that the spiritual conquest had been already completed and that the Franciscans, Dominicans, and Augustinians had to submit to
the secular clergy. The "golden" age of the church of friars (Poole, 213)
was coming to a close. However, this did not occur without bitter struggle,
with the Franciscans among the most vocal opponents. The resulting frag-
mentation and opposition within the camp of the colonizer should dispel the
idea that it formed a monolithic front unified by its concerted efforts to dominate the colonized. On the contrary, as Rolena Adorno observes, one of
the outstanding characteristics of sixteenth- and seventeenth-century Spanish American voices and perspectives is precisely their disputatious thrust
vis-à-vis the subjects of legitimacy and power ("Reconsidering," 143).

My primary sources will consist of a variety of texts written by
renowned Franciscan figures such as Motolinía, one of the Twelve, Fray
Bernardino de Sahagún, Fray Alonso de Molina, Fray Juan Bautista, and
Fray Gerónimo de Mendieta, as well as by Nahua grammarians Antonio
Valeriano, Alonso Vegerano, Martín Jacobita, and Andrés de Leonardo,
and other anonymous indigenous authors. Some of these texts have been
widely known since the sixteenth century and have had several editions
since. The publication of others was prohibited during the three-centuries-
long Spanish domination, and thus they did not see the light until the post-
Independence period. Other texts were simply forgotten. In any case,
although most of the primary sources I will use in my book have been available to modern scholarship since the early twentieth century, even those
most widely read by students of the Latin American colonial period have not
received the critical attention they deserve.

The book will be organized into four parts, some subdivided into chapters. In the first part of the book, I will examine Fray Bernardino de Sahagún
and his Nahua aides' rendition of *Colloquios y doctrina cristiana*. These *Colloquios* reconstruct the first conversations in which the Twelve Franciscans
supposedly engaged Nahua priests and statesmen in 1524. Written (or
rewritten) in 1564 and published finally in 1924, the text is significant
because it represents a civil and polite debate between the two camps
defending their religious beliefs. Although the Nahuas are ultimately represented as willing to accept the Christian faith, many moments in the text

suggest that their disposition is conditioned more by the similarities that the conversations disclose between the new colonial god and the Nahuas' own deities than because of the truths that the friars' arguments may have expounded. Moreover, at the time Sahagún undertook the production of the *Colloquios,* his own ethnographic fieldwork had belied a full conversion to Christianity as it uncovered that many pre-Hispanic cults and practices were still in place. It will be my contention that in this reconstruction of the very first evangelizing attempt of the Franciscans, we can locate the specific Nahua Christian subject that emerged in the Mexican highlands, for whom the memory of the pre-Hispanic supernatural would never be erased completely.

I then analyze two dramatic pieces of the Nahua theater of evangelization (*The Last Judgment* and *The Sacrifice of Isaac*), as well as Fray Toribio Motolinía's renowned account of the 1538 performance of *The Fall of Our First Parents* in his *History of the Indians of New Spain* in the first part of the book. Until very recently, this theater had traditionally been considered a spectacle of domination in which the narratives of the colonizer were presented to the Nahua audience in order to set examples to follow. And yet, it may also be thought of as a theater of self-legitimation (Burkhart, *Holy,* 48) in which the Nahuas displayed the uncanny power of their culture to commerce with, placate, and/or even incorporate the alterity of the European. Ultimately, in this theater both Franciscans and Nahuas experimented with new cultural identities, forms, and possibilities, providing an important and rich moment of both cultural collaboration and riposte in the history of colonial Mexico.

"Confession, Acculturation, and Resistance in Sixteenth-Century Mexico" is the title of the third part of the book. The first chapter in this part discusses confession and the second chapter focuses on Molina's *Confessionario mayor.* The *Confessionario mayor* (1569) is a bilingual manual to guide the Spanish confessor in administering the sacrament properly, as well as to help literate Nahuas prepare for receiving it. The *Confessionario* is an invaluable document of the colonialist attempt to impose a universal Christian subjectivity upon the (discursively) defaced Nahua. Nevertheless, this confessional manual also opens and avows the possibility of resistance to colonial power, if only because the onerous, disconcerting freedom and full agency attributed to the Nahua penitent ironically negates his/her spiritual infancy, which was one of the "deficiencies" most frequently invoked to justify the Spanish colonial presence. The third chapter of this part is entitled "Juan Bautista's *Advertencias para los confesores de los Naturales* and the Malaises of Domination." This manual, written in 1600 also for confessors of natives, presents a different Nahua subject from the one posited by Molina's demanding manual. Fray Juan Bautista's *Advertencias* purports to console the now disenchanted and less zealous Franciscan missionaries for the failure of their pastoral efforts, as well as to urge them not to abandon their native flock.

Finally, the fourth and last part of the book will be dedicated to Fray Gerónimo de Mendieta's little studied *Historia eclesiástica indiana* (HEI), finished in 1596 but unpublished until 1870. Silenced by the very hegemonic powers it was supposed to reproduce, this text, along with many others prohibited by Philip II in his 1577 decree to Viceroy Martín Enríquez, occupies a precarious position in the field of colonialist discourses.[7] This part of the book is entitled "Falling Back Into History." My choice of the HEI is motivated, among other things, by the exemplary clarity with which the tribulations of the colonizer are represented. The ambivalent voice of the censuring, marginalized colonizer that emerges in this poignant yet beautiful text serves as further evidence that even though the dichotomies of colonizer/colonized, domination/resistance, European self/other, cannot be dismissed in the analysis of Spanish-American colonial experience, they are nonetheless insufficient to account for its specificities, contradictions, and multiplicities.

Although the selection of texts is obviously limited by the constraints of time and space, they do give an idea of the complexity of the epistemological clashes, discourses, negotiations, ruptures, and forms of violence at work in the Franciscan missionary enterprise and in the emergence of the Nahua Christian subject in sixteenth-century Mexico.

Before delving into the texts, a few words about method and critical location are called for. As an academic trained in the discipline of literature, my framework will be, not surprisingly, textual and discourse analysis. I will thus give more weight to the production of signification and to the discursive constrictions of the ever-malleable signifier than to other equally important aspects of the colonialist equation such as political, social, and economic history. Closely related to my literary training and as it may be already apparent to the reader, the field of postcolonial studies is an important influence in this study. I recognize the difficulties of working with a current of thought that emerged as a result of the post–World War II demise of British and French nineteenth- and twentieth-century colonialism, in order to conceptualize, represent, and question Spanish colonialism of the early modern period. As Walter Mignolo, Hernán Vidal, Jorge Klor de Alva, Aníbal Quijano, and many others have pointed out, an unreflective use of postcolonial theory to address the Latin American colonial experience and its legacies could be considered yet another instance of intellectual dependency.[8] In one way or another many of the key issues theorized by postcolonial studies such as "the subaltern subject, cultural translations, oral and written traditions, margin-center relations" (Castro-Klarén, "Writing," 230) have been on the front burner in Latin America since the nineteenth century, if not in the colonial period itself, as the work of the friar-ethnographers and many indigenous writers attest. To suggest or imply, when engaging colonialism in Latin America, that the cultural and political issues brought up by postcolonial studies are new subjects of interest would indeed be an untenable position.

Nevertheless, as some of these very same Latin American critics recognize, even though nationalist discourses in Latin America have been manifestly anticolonial since the postindependence period, they have never been able to break away completely from colonialist modes of exclusion and subordination regarding their own so-called traditional, non-European populations. In their bids for modernization, these national discourses have often reproduced internally the privileging of Western knowledges and forms of thought over indigenous ones, deeming the latter backward and frozen in time. Armed with the prestige of a theoretical framework inherited from poststructuralism, with great lucidity about the political implications of its practice and with an emancipatory thrust, postcolonial studies have offered powerful strategies for decolonizing knowledges and for rethinking the very concept of the nation and the dynamics of colonialism all around the world. As Santiago Castro-Gómez and Eduardo Mendieta have observed, for better or for worse, the deterritorialization brought about by the seemingly irreversible processes of globalization demands a concomitant change in the way of conceptualizing Latin America (Introduction to *Teorías sin disciplina*, 7), and we would add, any other world region. However, we should not think that globalization can or will have an equal impact in all locations. The most plausible scenario is one in which the global is localized (Castro-Gómez and Mendieta, 12), and the local accedes to the global, leaving its imprint on it too. By thinking about the Latin American colonial (and present neocolonial) period through postcolonial theory, the latter is opened up by new geographies and temporalities, and issues of the Latin American colonial legacies are updated and revitalized.

Taking the above into account, it will be my position in this book that it would be limiting for the scholar of Latin American studies to dismiss or privilege intellectual insights just because they have been produced elsewhere (or in some specific place). The Latin Americanist critic, like the Derridean *bricoleur*, needs to make use of any intellectual discipline that has yielded valuable knowledge about Latin America, whether produced inside or outside a particular region, continent, or even way of thought. Thus, I envision my study on Franciscan discourses of colonization and the emergence of the Nahua Christian subject in sixteenth-century Mexico to be situated in an intersection between postcolonial studies and the more traditional disciplines of history, ethnography, cultural anthropology, cultural criticism, and, of course, literature. Speaking from a postcolonial critique of colonial domination, I will engage some forms of riposte from the colonized-to-be in the very discourses and practices promoted by the missionaries. I will explore how those discourses at times produced unexpected reversals of meaning and also occasions in which they split the colonizer and made him other to himself. But at the same time, I will consider and take seriously the manifest intentionality of the Franciscan spiritual colonizers and particularly their awareness of the contradictions and serious flaws of the colonizing enterprise. In order to be able to imagine, see, and represent these forces, deeply involved in and transformed by the processes of hybridization in the contact zones of the colonial past, I cannot help but draw from the knowledges produced by history, ethnography, and cultural anthropology. And even though these knowledges are "the undeniable progeny of modernism" (Comaroff and Comaroff, *Of Revelation*, 15) and thus "they cannot escape the epistemological horizons that continue to enclose mainstream western social thought" (ibid.), the same limitation may apply to not a few of the theoretical "post" locations from where so many of us currently think: poststructuralism, postmodernism, post-Marxism, and postcolonial studies, especially as they increasingly institutionalize themselves in the First World academy.[9] I will listen and question those very ethnocentric, modern Western knowledges that have constructed, documented, and recorded the other with the expectation that at some point I may in fact hear his or her voice between the lines. But most importantly, seeking to understand better the complex and difficult Latin American colonial past, my study will tap into its grand hybrid legacy. It will go to the source of Spanish and Amerindian writers, historians, playwrights, performers, preachers, philologists, and proto-ethnographers, who began four centuries ago to contend with the cultural heterogeneities that lie deep within the fabric of whosoever we may be.

PART I | *The Christian Word Comes to Anahuac*

1

The *Colloquios y doctrina cristiana* and the Emergence of the Nahua Christian Subject in Sixteenth-century Mexico

The *Libro de los Colloquios* or "Book of the Colloquies" is a foundational text in the colonial literature pertaining to the saga of Franciscan evangelization in the Mexican highlands. The *Colloquios* recreate the first speeches by the Franciscan missionaries expounding on the imperative to accept the Christian god as the one and only deity and the polite reply of Nahua lords and priests about why they must refuse to do so. I will argue in this chapter that the cultural interaction seen in the *Colloquios* can be conceived as a paradigm of the hybridizing dynamics of the Spanish spiritual colonization in the Mexican highlands. The text reconstructs both in Spanish and in Nahuatl one of the very first attempts to produce a Christian subjectivity in Mexico and the specific type of resistance that it engendered.

Although several distinguished studies have been dedicated to the *Libro de los Colloquios* and in spite of the fact that it is often mentioned in manuals and histories of colonial textual production, the work has not received the critical attention that it merits. There are several reasons why this may have been the case. The fragmented state of the extant text, the indeterminable historicity of its discursive events, and the puzzle of its Franciscan (co-) author's intentions in undertaking its composition, and later perhaps in refusing its publication, have enveloped the *Colloquios* in a veil of obscurity that may have limited scholarly inquiry. Given all these unknown variables, much of what may be said about this text can only be conjectural. It will be my contention, however, that regardless of the uncertainty surrounding the

Colloquios, its study will yield invaluable insights about the dynamics of spiritual colonization and its resistance in Mexico. I should add that I am well aware that since the text was written at least forty years after the narrated events occurred, it does not pretend to be an account or report of what went on in 1524 and must not be read as such. Nonetheless, I have placed the *Colloquios* as the first text to be analyzed in my book because its status as the reconstructed if not fictive origin of the Franciscan evangelization enterprise in Mexico is to my mind the best introduction to the specific hybridized Christian subject that emerged in the lands of Anahuac, or "the place near the water."

The putative author of the Spanish part of the *Libro de los Colloquios* is none other than Fray Bernardino de Sahagún (1499–1590), one of the outstanding figures of the Spanish colonial period. His work has not only been key in preserving important aspects of Nahua pre-Hispanic culture for future generations, but on many occasions, in spite of Sahagún's Christian epistemology, he reveals a modernity in dealing with the knowledge and practices of the other that would be pivotal in the invention of the social sciences of non-Western subjectivities, particularly anthropology and ethnography. This modernity has to do with a descriptive narrative distance in which the speaker's own subjectivity is made present only through the seemingly transparent act of gazing.

Sahagún arrived in Mexico in 1529, five years after the arrival of the quasi-mythical contingent of the first twelve Franciscan missionaries.[1] He understood quickly that in order to transform the other into (an image of) a Christian self, the first thing to be done was to learn his language and culture so as to find out who he was. This is the origin of Sahagún's best-known work, the monumental protoethnographic *Historia general de las cosas de la Nueva España*, known also as the *Florentine Codex*. In the prologue to book 1 of the *Historia* he declares that doctors cannot cure their patients or apply medicines adequately if they do not know the root of the malady. The missionaries are doctors of the soul and thus "it is good that they have practical knowledge of the medicines and spiritual ailments" (Sahagún, *Florentine*, 1:45).[2] The *Historia* will offer confessors knowledge and experience of the "malady," namely, the pre-Hispanic idolatrous past, by describing and documenting its practices, discourses, rites, and beliefs. Sahagún's innovative methodology is well known: the use of native informants, Nahua aides and translators trained in the Colegio de Tlatelolco,[3] and the corroboration of data by comparing input from different informant sources and groups. Equally well known is the fate of Sahagún's exhaustive study: it was confiscated by the Council of the Indies in 1577 after Philip II's prohibition of writing about the pre-Hispanic past of the Amerindians, lest their idolatrous practices should be preserved in historical memory. No part of Sahagún's extensive production was published during his lifetime, except the *Psalmodia cristiana*, a collection of hymns written in Nahuatl to be sung on different religious occasions. Most of his unique and pioneering work would see the light only after Mexican Independence.[4]

The original plan of *Libro de los Colloquios* suggests it to be a logical sequence to the *Historia general*. Following book 12 of the *Historia*, in which the fall of Tenochtitlan (and thus the end of the Mexica culture described in the previous eleven books) is narrated from the perspective of the vanquished, the first book of the *Libro de los Colloquios* is a representation of the starting point of the evangelization campaign in the Mexican highlands, as mentioned above. The conversations that marked this beginning must have been held in Tenochtitlan, shortly after the Twelve arrived.

The second book of the *Colloquios*, still lost, presupposes the acceptance of Christianity as represented in the first book. It is a *Doctrina cristiana*, or the things the people need to know and believe when accepting to practice the Christian faith. The third book was to be a history of what happened during the first six years of evangelization and the final part a *Postilla*, or collection of exegeses to the epistles and gospels corresponding to each Sunday of the year. When confronted with the length of the book, Sahagún decided not to undertake the third part, because Fray Toribio de Benavente or Motolinía (the Nahuatl word for poor, miserable, disgraced) had already written a history about the missionary efforts of the first twelve Franciscans up to 1541.[5] The fate of the fourth book is uncertain. Sahagún scholars have identified it in several different manuscripts whose contents closely reflect those that the friar had announced in the foreword that the book would contain (León-Portilla, prologue to *Adiciones*, vi).

The extant version of the *Libro de los Colloquios* was lost until 1924. The specific circumstances of the disappearance are also still unknown. The manuscript may have simply been shelved by an overly sensitive Council of the Indies in Spain, because in the 1583 license approving the publication of the *Psalmodia* in Mexico, there was also an authorization to print the *Colloquios* (Duverger, 35–41). Jorge Klor de Alva has argued that after Motolinía's death in 1569, Sahagún was able to confront openly the myth that surrounded the missionary deeds of the Twelve and the providential mass conversions effected through their agency. He must have changed his mind about publishing the *Colloquios*, considering that they perpetuated such a myth (Klor de Alva, "Sahagún's," 86–87), although just up to a point, as I will seek to show in this chapter. Be that as it may, in 1924, the Franciscan Pascual Saura discovered the first thirteen chapters of the Spanish version of the *Colloquios* and the first fourteen of the Nahuatl counterpart in the secret archives of the Vatican. As with the *Historia general*, Sahagún composed a Spanish version of the work. The Nahuatl version was first translated into German by Walter Lehmann (published posthumously in 1949), then into Spanish by Miguel León-Portilla in 1985 and into English that same year by Jorge Klor de Alva.[6]

The text of the *Colloquios* embodies in its sources, structure, content, and organization salient issues of bilingualism and cultural transposition. In the foreword to "the prudent reader," Sahagún alleges that in 1564 he had found some notes about these first conversations between the Twelve and the Nahuas in the Colegio de Santa Cruz de Tlatelolco (León-Portilla, *Coloquios*, 20).[7] Not explaining with what specific purpose in mind, he goes on to say that he took upon himself and four of the most outstanding Nahua grammarians of the colegio (Antonio Valeriano, Alonso Vegerano, Martín Jacobita, and Andrés Leonardo) the task of polishing the language and elaborating the notes into a full-blown rendition of the conversations in both Spanish and Nahuatl. Sahagún then briefly expounds the contents of the text.

Louise Burkhart has argued that the Spanish account is an abstract or summary of the Nahuatl ("Doctrinal," 65), while Ángel Garibay proposes that they may be considered a different text based on the papers and *memo-*

riales (memorials) that ended up in Sahagún's possession (*Historia*, 2:242). Miguel León-Portilla would not disagree with the latter position insofar as he has pointed out that in the Spanish version of the *Colloquios* Sahagún tried to make accessible to the contemporary Spanish reader the pre-Hispanic world and beliefs attested in the Nahuatl text ("Nota," 73). Several audiences are presupposed then by the presence of both versions of the *Colloquios*. One is a literate Spaniard of the sixteenth century, a "prudent reader" interested in the spread of Christianity in the New World and in Spain's role in the enterprise. The second, more difficult to discern and possibly more heterogeneous, may be a still not fully Christianized yet educated, literate Nahua, mirrored by the *tlatoque* (lords) and *tlamacazque* (priests) in the text. A third type of implied audience could have been composed of illiterate, still unconverted Nahuas who were being instructed in Christianity with the first arguments used to persuade the tlatoque and tlamacazque decades earlier.

Another important issue of bilingualism and biculturalism exemplified in the Spanish and Nahuatl versions of the *Colloquios* is the stylistic contrast between the correspondent literate and oral cultures. Although both versions represent an oral exchange between the Spanish friars and the Nahua lords and priests, they do so in notably different ways, to the point that Ángel Garibay proposed considering them separate texts, as we pointed out above. The Spanish version deploys an analytical, lineal distribution of thought with subordinate clauses reflecting carefully crafted connections of cause and effect. Consequently, the expression of ideas comes through as being more compact and direct. The Nahuatl rendition is like a notation of the linguistic oral performance of both the Franciscans and the Nahua tlatoque and tlamacazque. Thus it exhibits salient features of Nahua oral rhetoric such as the accumulation of metaphors and metonymies describing manifold aspects of a particular element, the constant *difrasismo* or "parallel expressions in which the same idea is repeated in different ways" (León-Portilla, *Literatura*, xxxi; translation is mine), identical phrases that open and close a specific theme, "a tendency to double, triple or quadruple every noun, verb, and larger phrase" (Lockhart, *The Nahuas*, 366). All these elements reveal a highly elaborate, formulaic, and redundant use of language characteristic of oral cultures that conveys a different way of representing experience and of relating to the world (Ong, 31–42). Hence, it could even be posited that concurrently with the colloquy going on between the friars and the Nahua lords and priests within the text, there is a deeper layer of conversation and debate going on between the worldviews embodied in the Spanish and Nahuatl languages of the two versions.

Another polemical aspect of the *Colloquios* has been their historicity. Some scholars like the Mexicans Zelia Nutall, who published the text in Mexico for the first time in 1927, and the *nahuatlato* León-Portilla are of the opinion that the *Colloquios* were a reconstruction of true historical events that took place at the arrival of the Twelve in 1524 (Nutall, quoted in León-Portilla, "Estudio," 23; León-Portilla, *Aztec*, 62–70). In his *Historia de la literatura náhuatl*, Ángel Garibay vehemently denounces the historicity of the text but argues that it is a document invaluable in insights about Nahua pre-Hispanic culture (2:240–46). In the most sophisticated and informed treatment of the problem to date, Jorge Klor de Alva contends that the *Colloquios* are indeed historical but that the temporality represented in the text is figurative. As Sahagún openly admits in the prologue, the indigenous aides reorganized, elaborated, and polished, if not translated into Nahuatl, the notes he found at the Colegio. This means that the Nahuatl version is depicted as an avowed reconstruction of the speech events,[8] not as a naively intended written record of them. Thus, the conversion in the text is fancied as having taken place in a matter of days. However, Klor de Alva argues that in order for such a conversion to have occurred in the way the *Colloquios* claim, it must have entailed many weeks if not months of extended conversations, preaching, and a much deeper knowledge of Mexican language and culture than the friars could have mastered upon their arrival at Tenochtitlan ("Historicidad," 57–58). He makes a similar point about the historicity of the text in 1988, in a second article about the *Colloquios*. In 1987, the French nahuatlato Christian Duverger argued that although the Spanish version was intended to be a historical record, the Nahuatl version gave evidence of a didactic end (51–52). Last but not least, Duverger rightly points out that the form of the *Colloquios* is an established literary genre (52), whose origin harks back to Plato (427?–237 B.C.), Cicero (106–43 B.C.), and Lucian (125–180 B.C.?). In sixteenth-century Spain, the genre flourishes from 1525 on, initially under the influence of Dutch humanist and reformer Erasmus of Rotterdam (1466?–1566) (Gómez, 152–53). Because Humanism was interested in pedagogy and the practical application of knowledge for the community, issues of all sorts, religious, philosophical, social, and the like, were cast in dialogues in order to make the arguments expounded more vivid, persuasive, and relevant for social civil life (Gómez, 199–206). All of this means that the *Colloquios* were also mediated by literary convention and thus further removed from a direct report of events, even if in fact they were conversations that actually took place.

Nonetheless, in spite of the more or less idealized temporality, the reconstruction of events, and the literary mediation that critics have proposed, the *Libro de los Colloquios* exhibits specific patterns of cultural contact, imposition, and hybridization that can be observed in many other texts produced in relation to the evangelization enterprise in sixteenth-century Mexico, including several of those studied in this book. Whether intentionally or not, the (religious) discourse of the Spanish colonizer in the *Colloquios*, embodied in the Twelve, shows crevices, contradictions, and insufficiencies that belie its claims to an indisputable, self-evident visibility of truth and authority. This discourse also shows overlaps with the religious practices and beliefs of the colonized-to-be that facilitated the assimilation of the new Christian god but also, in many ways, contributed to preserving the memory of the pre-Hispanic deities. Such assimilation to the new religion without ever fully giving up the old would inform the specific Christian subject that emerged in the Mexican highlands.

One of the things that strikes the reader of Sahagún's prologue to the *Colloquios* is the extent of the author's claims about what they depict. He alleges that the importance of the conversion of the Amerindians is for the Christian world second only to the primitive church (Sahagún, *Coloquios*, 72).[9] This notion circulated among the Franciscans associated with millenarianism. That is, the new Indian church, presided over by the mendicant orders, was seen by some prominent figures in the first generation of missionary

Franciscans in Mexico as a return to the more spiritual origins of the church, whose hallmark was the practice of evangelical poverty. St. Francis's *Imitatio Christi* or imitation of Christ had been a realization of this desire to return to the age of Christ, when the Church was still unburdened by its political hierarchy, wealth, and institutional power (Phelan, 42). It was not mere coincidence, as we said earlier, that the first contingent of Franciscans and Dominicans arriving in New Spain was composed of twelve friars, emulating the twelve apostles reaching out to the gentiles.

In addition, Sahagún adopts a full-blown providential discourse in his prologue. He claims that such a momentous conversion had taken place due to God's inscrutable designs, which had prescribed that knowledge of the "endless" lands of the New World and its inhabitants be withheld until the arrival of the Spaniards (*Coloquios*, 72). Sahagún asserts in the prologue and in the introductory note to the text of the *Coloquios* the myth of the indigenous mass conversions to Christianity brought about by the Twelve that later he would denounce as a delusion. It should be recalled that in several appendixes to his *Historia general* Sahagún raises the note of alarm that the Nahuas, while publicly assuming Christian practices and rituals, kept worshipping their pre-Hispanic deities and performing their rites in private.[10] For Klor de Alva, the fact that Sahagún sticks to the myth of the quasi-miraculous mass conversions in the *Coloquios* at a time when his ethnographic fieldwork had already rendered evidence to the contrary serves as proof of the faithfulness of the *Coloquios* to their historical sources, the scant notes supposedly written in 1524 about the event ("Sahagún's," 91–92). This, however, cannot be the case for the prologue, which is written in 1564 and openly expounds the myth through Sahagún's own voice. The issues of what this means in terms of the friar's textual production, his intentionality in rewriting the *Coloquios*, and perhaps in his later decision not to publish the work are indeed important to its understanding and interpretation. However, it must be admitted that these issues may not be fully answerable, at least at this point in the text's scholarship.

As part of the myth of the miraculous mass conversions, Sahagún alludes in the prologue to the Holy Spirit as having guided the friars when laying the foundations of their arguments to convert the Nahuas (*Colo-*

quios, 73). What is remarkable about the allusion to the Holy Spirit is that it may be read as a reference to the tripartite schema of history conceived by the controversial twelfth-century theologian Joachim di Fiore. In this schema, the last age of history would be governed by the third person of the Holy Trinity, when "all men would attain quasi-angelic perfection" (Phelan, 42). During this era the Holy Ghost would effect a spiritualization of the world, or at least of its religious leaders, that went hand in hand with the practice of evangelical poverty or the renunciation of the material and worldly aspects of the post-Constantine church. It may be hypothesized, then, that the friars' speeches are represented in the prologue as having been directly inspired by the Holy Ghost and thus are regarded as a manifestation of the *plenitudo intellectis* (full understanding) that the Third Person would have elicited from the most spiritual sectors of humankind (Reeves, 13).

Another aspect of the miraculous, according to Sahagún, is the fact that Cortés, having conquered the great, civilized Mexican nation, immediately notified his emperor about this feat, and the emperor, in turn, the Pope (*Coloquios*, 72). That is, it was a miracle that the political sphere would so promptly and willingly subject itself to the spiritual. This is precisely what was supposed to happen in the third age of the world. [11]

Needless to say, the insistence on the divine, if not miraculous underpinnings of the Conquest and colonization works to satisfy the colonizer's need for self-legitimation. However, there is a performative element related to this insistence that puts high stakes on the depiction of the friars' linguistic demeanor. The burden of the text is to represent to a Spanish and Nahua audience that the tlatoque and the tlamacazque are being persuaded, not by speech crafted by the friars, but by speech coming directly from the Holy Spirit Thus, in order to convince the implied audiences that this is the case, the words of the Twelve must sound worthy of the divinity that supposedly speaks through them. Every moment in the text in which the friars address the Nahua lords and priests can conceivably be read against this high standard.

The divinely inspired Twelve open their colloquies with the other in the first extant chapter claiming that they have been sent as ambassadors of the Pope. In the Spanish version the defining trait of papal authority is his spiritual jurisdiction over all who live on Earth (Sahagún, *Coloquios*, 79), but in the Nahuatl rendition it is his magnificent speech. The Pope is usually referred to as "the great speaker of divine things" (Klor de Alva, "Aztec," 59). Such an emphasis is evidently a cultural translation because Nahua rulers and important political figures were defined as tlatoque: those who speak. Not surprisingly then, most figures of authority in the Nahuatl version are referred to as "speakers." This would likely elicit a positive response from the Nahua audience, both within and outside the text, meeting their expectations about power and authority. Hence, in representing themselves as the envoys of the commanding figure of the Pope, the friars themselves are depicted throughout the Spanish and Nahua versions as well-bred, wise speakers who choose their words carefully. Following Nahua linguistic protocol, they address their indigenous audience in a very endearing mode, and they make sure to declare that their motives for coming to meet the Nahuas were not for "jade, divine excrement [gold], nor quetzal plumes" (Klor de Alva, "Aztec," 65) but only out of desire that the Indians be saved; that is, only for love.

Shortly into the very first conversation, however, the speakers of love declare that they had witnessed the Nahuas' ignorance of the true God, and how they had angered Him with their acts.[12] Thus, He had sent the Spaniards "to punish and afflict" them (Sahagún, *Coloquios*, 81). This is a paradigmatic moment of epistemic violence recurrent in the Spanish colonialist discourse in the Americas. The Spanish military conquest is represented as the fulfillment of God's desire to hurt the Nahuas because of their wrongful behavior. An appalling aspect of this punishment is the fact that it was inflicted upon unknowing people. That is, the Nahuas are told that they have to believe they were breaking boundaries and transgressing when they thought that they were rightly serving their gods. The powerful Christian divinity had been angered by such transgressions and had thus showered disgrace and affliction on them.

The casting of the Spanish conquest as divine retribution evidently works both as a strategy of legitimation and as an epistemological imposition. But it also openly acknowledges the terrible suffering that it brought upon the Nahuas. In both the Spanish and Nahuatl versions, this acknowledgment and the framing of the conquest as punishment cancels out all possible political arguments about lawful military self-defense, the right to demand subjection to Charles V, and even the (convenient) rationale of the *requerimiento*. The latter, we should recall, conferred on the Spaniards the right to wage war on the indigenous people if they opposed the preaching of Christianity in their lands and/or refused to recognize the Spanish Kings as their rightful sovereigns.[13] The conquest then was an atrocious punishment for something that had been done before the arrival of the Spaniards. Thus, according to the *Colloquios* (and contrary to the claims of Hernán Cortés in his *Relaciones*, to López de Gómara, and to Bernal Díaz del Castillo in their respective histories of the Conquest of Mexico), there could not have been an appropriate reaction to the military presence of the Spaniards in the Mexican highlands that could have prevented the destruction of the Nahuas.[14]

Equally significant is the irony that the epistemic violence perpetrated by the justification of the destruction of the Nahuas as retribution also could have facilitated an approximation to the indigenous concept of the relationship between humans and gods, as the Nahua audience could certainly identify with the notion of afflictions brought upon unknowing humans by angry deities. For them, divine anger was usually triggered by human transgressions, many of which were perpetrated by pollution, filth, or *tlazolli*. It is precisely in the contagious aspect of filth and tlazolli that the notion of defilement independent from intentionality can be appreciated. The emanations from people in a state of filth could bring about the pollution of many around them and could be offensive to the gods (Burkhart, *Slippery*, 96–97). A bad ruler could bring filth and thus affliction to his city (ibid., 97). Contaminated people could then suffer the impact of divine anger due to a defilement that they had not originated.

Similarly, certain aspects of the concept of *tlatacolli* or "something damaged" (Burkhart, *Slippery*, 28) could also relate to this notion of a defilement separate from the will. Tlatlacolli could be caused by improper sexual conduct, by stealing, by intoxication but also by unintentional acts that spoiled something (Burkhart, *Slippery*, 28). All of the above sins were forms of disruptions of order that destabilized and upset the delicate cosmic balance. These disruptions, in their turn, could cause the "anger" of the gods or the uncontrolled unleashing of their influences, which could be harmful to the individual and to his or her community. Taking all the above into consideration, it can be posited that the Nahua audiences could have been able to relate to the harsh representation of the Spanish Conquest as punishment for behaviors that had polluted them without their knowledge. Even though such identification may have, in fact, subjected the Nahuas into giving up their religious beliefs, it also made the new, angry, avenging Christian god not entirely other to the Nahua pre-Hispanic deities that He had sent the missionaries to displace. Also, much like the Nahua pre-Hispanic priests who were in charge of staging and managing to the most minute detail the complex array of rituals to placate the deities (Nicholson 433), the missionaries represent themselves in the Nahuatl version as having been sent to instruct the Nahuas "how to cool the heart / of He by Whom All Live, so He will not completely destroy you" (Klor de Alva, "Aztec," 72). According to this statement, the missionaries were, like the Nahua priests, the knowers of the right way to service the supernatural powers in order to appease them.

But perhaps the most remarkable approximation between Christianity and pre-Hispanic religious practices prompted by the effort to impose the former is the fact that both in the Spanish version, and more openly in the Nahuatl one, the Twelve are represented as using the very same modifiers to describe the Christian god that the Nahuas attributed to their deities: "He by Whom All Live" (*ipalnemohuani*); "the True Speaker" (*nelli tlatoani*); "Possessor of the Near, Possessor of the Surrounding" (*tloque nahuaque*); "Possessor of Heaven, Possessor of Earth" (*ilhuicahua tlalticpaque*). These phrases and epithets were used by the Nahuas to address Tezcatlipoca, their most powerful divine entity. Thus, even while defining all Nahua gods as devils, including Tezcatlipoca, a "subtle identity" (Burkhart, "Doctrinal," 70) between him and the Christian deity was nonetheless established in order to facilitate a cultural translation. As Louise Burkhart points out, "The audience may more easily understand the new god by thinking of him in comparison to Tezcatlipoca" (ibid., 70).

This cultural translation is a two-way street, however. By representing the Christian god in Nahua terms, Western notions of truth and divinity were indeed made comprehensible to the Nahuas. The objective of supplanting and displacing indigenous beliefs became in this way more feasible. But on the other hand, as Walter Lehmann rightly pointed out in 1949 (albeit in very Eurocentric fashion), Nahuatl expressed Christian theological terms with great precision (Lehmann, 111n1). The German scholar was astonished by Nahuatl's ability to account for Western notions of divinity: Nahuatl has the conceptual sophistication to produce an adequate representation of the Christian god. Moreover, by using Tezcatlipoca's epithets to articulate the highest truths of the Christian god, the latter was actually being Nahuatized or defined in Mesoamerican terms. Regardless of how false the Nahua deities were accused of being, the fact that their attributes were deemed appropriate to name the Christian god ultimately entailed an acknowledgment of the Nahuas' language, conception, and capacity to imagine the power of a supreme divinity. This is a key issue in the *Colloquios* that will recur in the discourses and textual production engaging the colonial religious dynamics in the Mexican highlands.

Because—according to the prologue to the *Colloquios*—the foundational arguments of the Twelve were inspired by the Holy Spirit, the friars are depicted in both the Spanish and Nahuatl versions as disclosing the visible superiority of the truth of the Christian deity and the consequent falsity of those whom the Nahuas regarded as gods. The arguments demonstrating such falsity were that the pre-Hispanic deities are "not only one but very many"; they are "carved in stone, in wood"; they "are invented." They ridicule and trick the people, they have no pity, they send numberless afflictions and diseases, and the people insult them when they are angry. In addition, these gods are extremely cruel: they demand blood and hearts. They are revolting, they vomit on people (Klor de Alva, "Aztec," 82–84).

Of these ten arguments, four can be applied also to the Christian deity. Although the Nahuas indeed had manifold gods whom they worshipped and whose feasts they kept, they did have major deities and a god who reigned supreme over others, such as Tezcatlipoca. The latter "was [a] virile, ever-youthful, omnipotent, omnipresent, omniscient deity, before whom all creatures were completely helpless. It was the ascription to Tezcatlipoca of total power, which, above all, characterized this remarkable deity" (Nicholson, 412). Equally important is that the densely populated Nahua pantheon could masquerade as saints, who also wielded supernatural powers and had specific domains of influence in Christianity. True, sixteenth-century Christians did not see saints as lesser deities, and consequently the Twelve may be represented in good faith as establishing the truth of their god on the grounds of His uniqueness (in spite of the baffling concept of the Holy Trinity that posited three persons who were both separate and one at the same time).[15] However, wittingly or unwittingly, the Catholic Christian system had loopholes that facilitated the substitution. According to Lockhart, the cult of saints was the aspect of Christian religious practices that had the greatest impact on the lives of colonial Nahuas because they could relate saint cults to their collective pre-Hispanic beliefs (*The Nahuas*, 236).

Without moving outside the text, however, there is a representation of a multiplicity of beings in the Christian supernatural. In chapter twelve of both versions, the supreme Christian god is depicted as conferring to nine orders of angels specific powers and domains of influence:

> "You seraphims, / I give you / great love for the people/ You cherubims, / I give you great knowledge of things/ You thrones, / I bestow on you / great strength. / You dominations, / I give as personal property to you / the command.... You powers, / I have a task for you, / by which you will confront the devils, / you will obstruct them / so that they will not damage it, / the earth." (Klor de Alva, "Aztec" 165–66)[16]

Although it is made clear that God is the supreme power because he is the one conferring the different potentialities and tasks on the angels, and that the latter represent quite different forces from what the pre-Hispanic deities stood for, arguably the Nahua audience could have related the *multiplicity* of angelic, supernatural beings to the specific powers of their own lesser deities.

The arguments that the practice of carving sacred beings in wood and stone, the diseases with which the Nahua gods afflicted the people, and the fact that the people when angry would insult their gods were all proof of the falsity of such gods are weak, if not specious. It did not take too analytical a missionary mind to realize that the very same things could be predicated of Catholic Christianity. As is well known, Catholicism also encouraged the representation of the sacred in stone and wood as the many images in churches, cathedrals, and monasteries attested (and attest) and even more so the extended institutionalized worship of images supposedly endowed with miraculous powers. The Christian god constantly tested and even punished people with diseases (as the Nahuas themselves were supposed to be experiencing), and blasphemies were the Christian counterpart to the verbal offenses the Nahuas would perpetrate against their deities when the latter did not favor them as expected. Thus, whether intentionally or not, these particular arguments reveal, especially for a Spanish reader, a failure to establish real differences between the true Christian god and the false Nahua deities and/or a biased evangelization strategy based on partial representations of Christianity.

But difference there was. The moral aspect of the Christian god and His acolytes was absent in the Nahua deities. Mexica deities had split personalities and many identities (Read, 15). One and the same Nahua deity could have a beneficial or a destructive influence depending on the occasion. Or, under a different name and manifestation, a deity could exert a nefarious or favorable impact. Consequently, it was not entirely wrong to say, although certainly tendentious, that Nahua gods were tricksters. Because they did not behave according to moral patterns, it was difficult to anticipate their behavior or to secure their favor. In fact, one of the attributes of Tezcatlipoca was his capriciousness. He promoted chaos everywhere. He sowed discord and trouble both among and within opposite parties (Sahagún, *Florentine*, 2:2). He could give people great wealth and then take it away for no reason except his whim (ibid.). He would punish his worshippers for the very transgressions he incited (Burkhart, *Slippery*, 92). In addition, he was "an archsorcerer, associated with darkness, the night and the jaguar" (Nicholson, "Religion," 412). The friars could indeed claim that such traits put human beings in a more vulnerable and uncertain position than that of Christians vis-à-vis their god.

Another significant difference between the Nahua deities and the evidence of the falsity of the former, as construed by the Twelve, was that they demanded to be fed human blood and hearts. We know that the cultural practice of human sacrifices was the point of greatest distance from the European. Calendrical rituals and sacrifices were celebrated according to the Mesoamerican solar year of eighteen months of twenty days. In every month a specific ritual and feast was celebrated to honor, commemorate, and conjure up the corresponding deity or deities. Most of these rituals involved human sacrifice, and many of them, heart extraction from the victim in order to offer it to the honored god. An *ixiptla* or "deity impersonator" (Smith, 224) for each god in question could be sacrificed in order to bring forth, albeit not in an identical fashion, the powers generated in mythical time through his/her divine immolation. According to some scholars, human sacrifices were a way or repaying the gods for their self-sacrifices in order to create humans and the world (Matos Moctezuma, 148; Román Berrelleza, 135; Smith, 221). Others maintain that these human sacrifices were conceived more specifically as food for hungry gods (Nicholson, 402; Clendinnen, *Aztecs,* 73–77; Read, 123–55; Bernand and Gruzinski, 97–98) who, despite the fact that they possessed greater powers than human beings,[17] could not or would not survive independently from the humans' acts, at least in the same shape and form. The relationship between gods and humans was much more interdependent than in the Christian mode, which was completely asymmetrical. The nourished gods were expected to reciprocate humanity with a benevolent or at least manageable manifestation of their power, because human beings could not exist without the animals, plants, and natural phenomena the gods animated and unleashed. Thus, because of their hunger and dependence on humans, the Nahua gods could indeed be perceived by the friars to be cruel and demanding.

The Twelve are also depicted as attempting to prove to the Nahuas the falsity of the pre-Hispanic deities because of their commerce with filth: "Their images, their witchcraft are very black, very dirty...they vomited on people" (Klor de Alva, "Aztec," 87). Once again Tezcatlipoca, as the perpetrator of chaos, was associated with pollution. According to Sahagún in the *Florentine Codex*, the skunk was one of his images or ixiptla (6:171). Mictlantecuhtli and Mictecacihuatl, deities of death and of the underworld, had contact with filth and dirt in their grisly abode. They ate the putrid corpses of people and all sorts of excrement and refuse from those on earth and in heaven (Read, 136). There was even a dirt deity called Tlazolteotl, who in another (not entirely negative) manifestation was known as the "Eater of Foul Things" because she removed filth from people in confession (Burkhart, *Slippery*, 92).

Although the Twelve do point out important differences between the pre-Hispanic deities and the Christian god by bringing up the issues of dependence, human sacrifices, and the involvement of the gods with filth, it does not follow that these differences are clear-cut evidence of falsity. They only attest to another conception of divinity and a world that is not Christian. Thus, a significant part of the proof of the perversion and untruth of the Mexica divinities presented by the friars in this colloquy was circular: in order to be efficacious it required that the party being persuaded would share the same cultural system and values as the persuading party.

The friars then proceed to represent their god to the Nahuas as the very opposite of the pre-Hispanic deities: He does not mock anyone, does not hate, envy, or desire anything that is dirty (Klor de Alva, "Aztec," 88–89), he is entirely good and loving of his creatures; but most of all, he excels in compassion and mercy, for he became human, he adopted human nature and "likewise, for us, He came to die, He came to shed His precious blood for us, by it He came to save us" (ibid., 89). As was argued above, the friars do present real contrasts between their God and the pre-Hispanic deities. Nevertheless, the acts that are portrayed as the embodiment of the attributes that best exemplify the difference of the Christian god ironically blur this distinction, because pre-Hispanic deities were believed to have done similar things. Although invisible, many pre-Hispanic gods occasionally also took human shape. In book 12 of the *Florentine Codex*, for instance, it is narrated how Tezcatlipoca appeared to Montezuma's messengers as a drunkard in order to show them a vision of the imminent fall of Tenochtitlan (13:33–34). The goddess Cihuacoatl appeared dressed as a courtesan, and sometimes carried with her a crib, which she abandoned in the market (Sahagún, *Historia*, 1:39–40). But more importantly, "the need for the death of all of the gods to make possible the existence of the world of humans was made clear in the ancient Nahua myths" (López Austin, *Tamoanchan*, 18). One of the most poignant and best known of these was the birth of the fifth and present sun. In this myth, Nanahuatzin and Tecciztecatl sacrificed themselves in front of the assembled gods at Teotihuacan. The diseased but valiant Nanahuatzin, resolutely leaping into the fire, was transformed into the fifth sun. The rich Tecciztecatl, who hesitatingly followed suit, was transformed into the moon as a result of his cowardice. Because the newly created sun would not move, the assembled gods offered themselves up in sacrifice at sunrise in order to feed it (Nicholson, "Religion," 402; López Austin, *Tamoanchan*, 18; Read, 48–60).[18]

Similarly, the creation of mankind also entailed a great deal of hard work from the gods. Quetzalcoatl was the god appointed to go down to Mictlan to collect bones and ashes of the previous, deceased generation of men. After many hurdles he was finally able to present his precious bone cargo to the gods assembled in Tamoanchan. The bones were ground into fragments by a goddess, at which point the rest of the assembled gods proceeded to bleed themselves or to perform self-sacrifice so that life could spring forth from the bone mass (Nicholson, "Religion," 400). Thus, because of their own pre-Hispanic religious myths, the Nahua lords would have been able to assimilate well the notion of the merciful Jesus Christ shedding His blood for the benefit of humankind. But once again this assimilation entailed the erasure or at least the attenuation of difference, as it was the similarity between their gods and the friars' god, and not their contrast, which enabled the understanding. Such attenuation, on the other hand, undermined the friars' attempt to establish the undeniable visibility of the truth and superiority of the Christian god.

The Nahua lords and priests' reply to the Twelve's not so persuasive arguments is perhaps the most moving part of the *Colloquios*. Significantly, the pathos of this reply comes through both in the Spanish and Nahuatl versions. As we know, the use of language in pre-Hispanic Mexico was characterized by extreme urbanity and courtesy. Such politeness is inscribed in the very meaning of Nahuatl as "those who speak well," and in the language's ubiquitous reverential apparatus, which can transform almost all parts of speech into honorific expressions.[19] It is significant in this respect that, as has been already discussed, the dynastic ruler of the *altepetl*, or town, was called *tlatoani*, or speaker (Lockhart and Karttunen 37). Moreover, in Nahua rhetoric and in the very speech of the tlatoque in the *Colloquios*, words are constantly compared to highly valued objects. And indeed, the tlatoani who comes forth to respond to the friars greatly ponders their words and compares them to "all sorts of precious stones, very pure, resplendent, with no stain or defect, thick and round, sapphires, emeralds, rubies and pearls; you have shown us new, rich feather work, of great value" (Sahagún, *Coloquios*, 86). [20]

The implication of these similes and metaphors is that language is held in the highest esteem. Beautifully and rightly spoken words can cause feelings of well-being like those produced by the sight of precious jewels and feather work. Thus, words can appease anger and fend off its disruptive effects. Arguably, this is not totally unlike sixteenth-century Western conceptions of eloquence and rhetoric, which also derived their persuasive power from the beauty of linguistic form. However, while humanistic rhetoric usually intended to persuade the audience about something or to move the will to emulate the speakers' values, Nahua rhetoric may have sought first and foremost to placate. [21] In a world where the sacred was amoral and unpredictable, powerful and meager, creative and destructive, Nahua reverential eloquence could have been imagined as a way of avoiding breaches and ensuring order.

The Nahua lord proceeds with his reply to the friars' demands of repudiating the pre-Hispanic deities by invoking the strong hierarchical and specialized character of Mexica society. Their priests, very wise and skilled, devote themselves to the different aspects of the cult. The tlatoani describes some of the specialized functions of these priests and concludes his argument by saying that neither he nor the other lords are capable of responding adequately to the venerable friars, since their realms of competence are war, justice, and tributes. Finally, they say they will summon these priests, and they respectfully take their leave.

According to Klor de Alva, the Nahua lord's description of his functions and those of the priests are of "a remarkable realism" ("Historicidad," 164). And indeed, the priests mentioned by the tlatoani appear in the account of nearly forty types of priests in the appendix of book 2 of Sahagún's *Historia general*.[22] But more than the historical and ethnographic precision of the *Colloquios*, what is most relevant to our reading is that the image that emerges in the Nahua lord's address is that of a devout subject, with a coherent, highly organized worldview. Sahagún portrays the Nahua lord's reply to the Twelve in terms that are reasonable if not commendable for the Spanish implied reader. The former's courteous refusal to refute the friars and to bring his religious counterparts to do so is worthy of a prudent, disciplined governor, cognizant of his limits, his proper social place, and his jurisdiction. The culture of the other acquires in this way legitimacy and high standing for the Spanish reader. In addition, because of its depicted urbanity, the violence of the friars' exhortation to hate, despise, and spit on everything the Nahuas had considered divine, although understandable for the Spanish reader, may nonetheless appear less than fitting.[23] Whether Sahagún intended to denounce a certain harshness in the rhetorical mode of the Twelve is of course difficult to ascertain. But it is undeniable that the tlatoani is represented as very civilized, rational, and self-controlled, even as he declines to submit to Christianity.

Finally, the high priests enter the scene to take on the job of responding to the Twelve. Much like the tlatoani, a tlamacazqui comes forth and earnestly welcomes the friars as beloved lords and speakers. Significantly, as part of his *captatio benevolentiae* (capturing the good will of the audience), he declares that the Twelve had been sent by the true God so that the Nahuas could be governed. He further recognizes that because of his love for them, the Twelve have brought the Nahuas the book of the celestial words of God (Sahagún, *Colloquios*, 88). At this point Sahagún seems to represent the Nahua priest as starting his defense of the indigenous gods not by trying to refute the friars' discourse but by displaying his ability to mimic or reproduce it. This reading is supported by Lockhart's contention that the Nahuas did not refuse Christianity because the victory of the Spaniards was for the former a *"prima facie* evidence of the strength of the victor's god" (*The Nahuas*, 203). The tlamacazqui makes it very clear that he accepts and agrees with the friars' claims about the Christian deity.

The Nahua priest proceeds to declare to the Twelve aspects about the

Nahua gods that clearly overlap with the Christian conception of the divinity. The Nahua gods are the possessors of all wealth and enjoyment; they inhabit places of plenty and delight; they are the ones who confer on humans all honors, dignities, and worldly goods (Sahagún, *Coloquios*, 88). No one can remember when men started to serve them, because it was a long time ago. The stream of similarities with the Christian god is interrupted by the allusion to the plurality of Nahua divinities and by the mention of the sacred places where their cult originated: Tulan, Huapacalco, Tamoanchan, Teotihuacan, and other great cities of Mesoamerican antiquity, heretofore unknown to the Christian world. However, in spite of these undeniable marks of difference, the scope, power, and function of the supernatural realm in the tlamacazqui's speech does not come through as being essentially other to Christianity's domain.

The Nahuatl account is, however, closer to the pre-Hispanic worldview and not only because of the obvious reason that Nahuatl is used. The four Nahua grammarians who composed this version were already Christianized. Yet, according to Klor de Alva, the tlamacazqui's apology for the pre-Hispanic gods is "one of the most solemn and authentic [discourses] that exist in Nahuatl"("Historicidad," 165; translation is mine). The speech highlights the speaker's specialized knowledge about the pre-Hispanic religious system and his solidarity with the vanquished people ("Historicidad," 165). In addition, although the notes that the Twelve presumably left should have laid out the core of the tlamacazqui's argument, the tone, emotional charge, and linguistic elaboration are those of Valeriano, Vegerano, Jacobita, and Leonardo. This may lead us to think that the four Nahua grammarians inhabited at least two worlds and systems of thought, albeit in different locations from those of missionary-ethnographers like Sahagún. The grammarians wrote in impeccable Nahuatl a serious account of Mesoamerican knowledge and conceptions of the supernatural from the point of view of the Nahuas, while being proficient in and even professing the Christian faith. As Rolena Adorno points out, the resultant articulation of indigenous experience is not cultural syncretism or "the production of a harmonious whole" ("Cultures," 35). Rather, it is a new formation in which the diverse cultural parts coexist with more or less tension and sometimes contradiction (ibid., 35) and in which the multicultural elements interact, sometimes in unexpected ways, as they become contexts of each other.

In the Nahuatl version the friars are depicted by the high priest as ixiptla, or representatives of Tloque Nahuaque, Possessor of the Near, Possessor of the Surrounding. Thus, their representational quality was not at all Western, because the ixiptla were assumed to attract and actually embody the supernatural forces of the deities they represented (Clendinnen, *Aztecs*, 248–53). In most of the calendrical feasts that reenacted the original sacrifice of the gods during mythical time (López Austin, *Human*, 1:61–66), an ixiptla, or representative of the honored deity (or deities) in the feast, was sacrificed. The ixiptla died not as an individual person, or even as an individual representing the divine, but as the represented entity itself (Burkhart, *Holy*, 44). This may be an additional cultural context that may explain why, perhaps even beyond the usual Nahua linguistic protocol, the priests are depicted as treating the friars with so much reverence and politeness, why they want to avoid their anger as much as possible, and why they fear its inevitability since they cannot fully accept their words. This may also be the reason why they state that "He causes you to be the face, He causes you to be the ears / He causes you to be the lips / of the Possessor of the Near, Possessor of the Surrounding. / Indeed, here, thus, we see Him as a man, / here, we call to Him as to a man,..." (Klor de Alva, "Aztec," 116). That is, because the friars are represented as the Christian deity's ixiptla, the Nahuas can actually see Him embodied in human form, so to speak. It is as though Christ had become incarnate not only in Jesus but also in his ixiptla. Such a representation of the friars attests to an approximation of the colonizer's foreign notions, but only after having been processed, altered, and hybridized by understanding them through the cultural contexts of the indigenous audience. This cultural translation may have indeed facilitated an identification with the concept of the Incarnation of Christ and of the friars' relationship to Him. However, it also made it ever more difficult to inhabit these notions in a fully Western way, because it was an unorthodox way of understanding Christ's humanity and the friars' status as His representatives.[24]

Interestingly, however, much like in the Spanish version, the Nahua gods are Christianized in the tlamacazqui's reply to the Twelve. There is no representation in his speech of the dual character of the Nahua deities, only a passing allusion to their commerce with death, and no mention of their involvement with destruction and filth. The Nahua priest declares that their ancestors had taught them that their gods "by whose grace one lives, they merited us" (Klor de Alva, "Aztec," 121) and that the gods had given them everything they needed for their sustenance. The speaker in the Nahuatl version states in more detail than in the Spanish the things the people received from their gods,[25] which creates the effect of a heightened sense of appreciation for such goods. In both versions the tlamacazqui is depicted as believing that the Nahua people had not experienced scarcity or need, but quite the contrary: an abundance of things essential for their well-being on Earth. There was no reason then to forget or to repudiate the Nahua deities as they had been able to take care of the people and guarantee their survival. In a worldview that for most people meant that death was the extinction of the individual (Read, 109–14; Brundage, 189–91; López Austin, *Human,* 1:331–38), this was proof enough of the truth and functionality of their deities.

Although the arguments presented by the tlamacazqui in his reply are adequately captured in the Spanish, westernized version, there are subtle differences between the two renderings produced by the dynamics of cultural doubleness and translation. In the Spanish version, in order to convey to the Spanish audience the power of the Nahua resistance to the friars' demands to repudiate their pre-Hispanic deities, this resistance is constructed around the creation of similarities between the Nahua gods and the Christian god. In the Nahuatl version, although the differences between the Christian and Nahua gods are also blurred, the counter argument to the friars is based primarily on the claim about the willingness and capacity of the deities to nourish the people and guarantee their earthly sustenance, the highest goods obtainable in pre-Hispanic dealings with the sacred.

Also, there is more insistence in the Nahuatl version on the fact that "already our heart is this way" (Klor de Alva, "Aztec," 124); that is, the Nahuas already had an age-old way of conceiving divinity. The tlamacazqui thus pleads with the Twelve "to beware of doing something" that might unleash the anger of the gods against the people or that will turn them against the priests. In the context of the *Colloquios*, this "something" clearly points toward saying or claiming things unheard of by the people; in short, breaking with tradition. The Nahua priest wraps up his reply by saying that "our hearts are not able to be full" (Klor de Alva, "Aztec," 126); that is, they have not been persuaded, moved by the friars' words and demands. As in the Spanish version, after humbly subjecting themselves to the will of the "divine guardians," the high priest closes his reply by stating that with his response they have returned the precious breath and word of the Twelve. In both versions, then, the tlamacazqui shows that all of them clearly understand the friars' words and demands. The Twelve, however, fail to persuade them not of the fine attributes of the new Christian god, but of the need to give up their own deities.[26]

Faced with a lucid, clear, and well-thought rebuttal that "a speaker of Nahuatl made…[to] come out of his lips" (Klor de Alva, "Aztec," 114), that is, a translator, the Twelve resort to various rhetorical strategies in their counter reply to the tlamacazqui. First they attempt to prove that the Nahua gods are false by arguing that they were not ecumenical: "If the gods were truly real gods, / Perchance, would we not also regard them as gods? / . . . / And likewise, would they not everywhere on earth / be summoned, / be implored?" (ibid., 128–29). Indeed, the local character of many Nahua deities is invoked by the friars as evidence of their falsity. Except for gods such as Tlaloc, Tezcatlipoca, and Quetzalcoatl, who harked back to the ancient Mesoamerican pantheon, many deities were worshipped only by particular *altepetl*.[27] Even within the altepetl, there were the *calpolli*, or neighborhoods, composed of clusters of families, which also had their particular tutelar gods. This is a conspicuous aspect of Nahua religious conceptions that must have been readily noticed by the friars. However, the speciousness of the Twelve's argument of lack of universality as proof of falsity quickly becomes evident, at least to the Spanish audience, as soon as one considers the friars' own subject position in the *Colloquios*; that is, besides the fact that the Twelve knew very well that Christianity was not accepted all around the world (something that the Nahuas could not know), their very attempt to convert the Nahuas implies that Christianity was not universal either and that not everybody regarded Christ as God. If to this we add that by 1564 Sahagún's own ethnographic investigations revealed that the Nahuas were still serving many of their pre-Hispanic deities in secret, it was even more obvious that the Christian divinity was not being considered the one and only God throughout the world. The rhetorical deception of this argument again points toward the difficulty of consummating what the friars are portrayed in the prologue as being inspired by the Holy Spirit to do, namely, to demonstrate the truth of the visible superiority of Christianity to the Nahuas, who had never heard about it before. Could this rhetorical deception be read as a metaphor of Sahagún's later condemnation of the "tradition of the early optimistic literature portraying the conversion process as an unqualified success" (Klor de Alva, "Sahagún," 86)?

The Twelve then introduce one of their most powerful rhetorical weapons in full force: the claim to knowledge. They declare that they know who and how the Nahua deities are: "where, and in what manner they began, they commenced, who they were...and what sort is their being, their heart, their function, their will, and from where they came" (Klor de Alva, "Aztec," 129). The friars' assertion to wield truths about the Nahua deities that the Nahuas do not know themselves is the quintessential colonial gesture of epistemic domination, endemic to the absolutist and universalistic ideological system of Christianity and by derivation to the emerging Western subjectivity itself. Christianity was radically exclusive and asymmetrical: it ascribed to itself the power to speak truth about the non-Christian other's relation to the sacred while flatly rejecting that the other could do the same about the Christian self.[28]

By contrast, because of Nahua and even Mesoamerican religious conceptions that harked back to the ancient Olmecs, the people of what is today Mexico and Central America did not claim the same unique transcendental location for their divinities. Nahuas and Mesoamericans at large inherited old cult traditions to deities that embodied natural forces or personified "specific segments of the cosmic order; each segment or deity...[having] many manifestations" (Davies, 253). The Mexica had migrated from the north with their tutelary god, Huitzilopochtli, but they incorporated into their pantheon the old gods of the earliest civilizations in the Mexican highlands as well as all the tutelary gods of the Nahua groups living in the area (Krickeberg, 125–28; Nicholson, 395–446). The Mexica even "captured" the deities of the enemies and took them home to the *coateocalli*, "a special building in the great ceremonial precinct... assigned to house the captive religious paraphernalia and fetishes of conquered communities" (Townsend, 116). All of this shows that the Nahuas at large and the Mexica in particular would never claim that theirs were the only truthful and existing deities, although like the Christians, they could impose the cult of their principal gods on other people and destroy temples upon conquering territories to show the strength of their divinities.

In any case, the subjecting power of the friars' declaration about their knowledge of the one and only god is represented as not yielding the expected results. Thus, the Twelve are depicted as explaining their failure to persuade the Nahuas to hear the friars' truth about their gods as due to the fact that they had never heard or received the divine word. In the Nahuatl version, and this is a difference from the Spanish, the Twelve described such a word as being visible and painted in a book that they kept. It is notable that the friars are represented as portraying themselves as "guardians of the divine word" and using Nahua categories of writing to represent the Scriptures. According to Dennis Tedlock, both in Mayan languages and in Nahua the term for writing and painting is one and the same ("Introduction," 30). In the codices, made out of long strips of dried *amate* paper, the divine words were painted insofar as the glyphs could symbolize "abstract concepts regarding their [the Nahuas'] religious doctrines, myths, and juridical organization" (León-Portilla, *Literatura*, xix; translation is mine). Moreover, one of the tasks of the Nahua priests and wise men was to be "guardians" of the codices, keeping them under their power and interpreting them. In the *Códice Matritense de la Real Academia*, the *tlamatinime*, or wise men, are described as:

> *Those who*
> *Carried with them*
> *The black and red ink,*
> *The manuscripts and the pictures,*
> *Wisdom.* (León-Portilla, *Aztec*, 23)

Once again, the translation by the friars of the Scriptures into Nahua cultural categories surely helped to make the Christian world and teachings familiar to the Nahua subject and thus more readily acceptable. However, because of this very same familiarity, a confusion and/or non-differentiation between the two worlds also could have emerged. Insofar as the Twelve represented themselves as guardians of the ancient divine word of the Possessor of the Near and the Surrounding, which is "very properly real, properly upright, / properly that which is followed as true" (Klor de Alva, "Aztec," 130), they are not very different from the way the Nahua priests conceived of themselves. Therefore, the friars' represented attempt to convince the tlamacazque and the tlatoque to abandon their religious practices and beliefs by casting Christian practices and beliefs in terms not totally unlike those that had to be forsaken was not improbable to result in a rhetorical impasse.

Not surprisingly, the explanation as to why the friars' knowledge about the Nahua deities had been ineffective in moving their audience to give up their religious ideology is shown as not having achieved its intended persuasive effects either. Hence, the Twelve finally resort to a last rhetorical stratagem: discursive terror. They declare that the Nahuas had not been completely destroyed by the Christian god because they had not received his divine word, and thus they did not know they were not serving him appropriately. However, from that moment on, after knowing that such a word of total truth existed, if they refused to hear it, they would perish (Klor de Alva, "Aztec," 131–32).

The Nahua grammarians composing the Nahuatl version of the *Colloquios* represent the tlatoque and the tlamacazque as "imploring at once" that they want to hear the Christian truths about their gods (Klor de Alva, "Aztec," 133). This response is seemingly couched in a propitiatory way, as if the lords and priests wanted to appease the anger of the Twelve or ixiptla of the god of the victors, lest more destruction would befall upon them. In its analytical tenor, the Spanish version is less pathetic and more succinct. After the threat of destruction, the Nahua wise men simply reply that they would be glad to know from the friars who their gods are.[29]

The remaining chapters of the extant text of the *Colloquios* contain the representation of the friars' fulfillment of the indigenous request. Perhaps much like the Nahua wise men and priests when they had to give a "long performance" in which they told the story behind the glyphs of the codices that they guarded and carried with them everywhere, the Twelve will perform an account of the complete story of the book of Genesis.[30]

The friars start off their "long performance" by declaring or manifesting once again who their God is and what his attributes are. It must be pointed out that this part of the Twelve's speech is particularly eloquent. There is a notably elaborate use of language both in the Spanish and the Nahuatl versions. In Sahagún's rendering, there is a *copia* or abundance of qualities and things that are said in order to make monotheism representable to the Nahua audience. Some of these attributes are portrayed in a familiar Christian way for the Spanish reader: God is omniscient, eternal, glorious, and always blessed. He is all loving toward his creatures. Some other attributes are represented in direct contrast to the Nahua deities, such as the fact that He brought everything into being without laboring or that He created the sun, moon, stars, and the world itself for the service and benefit of humans. The friars' speech is delivered in crisp, dynamic statements, beaming with analytical clarity. Nothing seems to be missing or irrelevant. The collective voice of the friars is depicted as well tempered and in full possession of its discursive object. It is perhaps the moment in the text when the represented speech of the friars comes closest to performing the rhetorical claim laid out in the prologue of its divinely inspired origin.

The Nahuatl version is equally eloquent and powerful. What is remarkable about this is that, as was pointed out above, although it was Sahagún's assistants who composed the version in Nahuatl, the Christian god is represented from a Christianized, although not fully westernized viewpoint. Nevertheless, in Klor de Alva's opinion, some parts of the Twelve's "long performance" are among the finest and most beautiful passages ever written in Nahuatl ("Historicidad," 170). If this appreciation is correct, it would imply that the bicultural Nahua aides crafted a superb verbal representation that met Nahua standards in terms of religious language use in order to depict the new foreign god.

Because the Twelve's long performance is the telling of the complete story of the book of Genesis, they recount next the creation of heaven, of the angels, and the fall of Lucifer and his followers. This episode is of utmost rhetorical importance because the Nahua gods will be identified with the fallen angels. As Klor de Alva points out, the friars did not deny the existence of the Nahua gods; they accounted for them within a Christian ontology representing them as devils ("Historicidad," 169). Ironically, this identification contributed to the possibility of the pre-Hispanic deities inhabiting the new colonial present, albeit under a different guise.

The reason for the fall is Lucifer's desire to be like the Creator: "I will be equal to Him / this One Who completely surpasses things, God" (Klor de Alva, "Aztec," 147). Ironically, Lucifer's desire to displace monotheism (which is another way of conceiving idolatry) will not be punished by God Himself but by the archangel Saint Michael and a multiplicity of followers, the good angels. By bringing into the picture so many supernatural creatures of different hierarchies, the Twelve come through as either trying to ease the transition from the pre-Hispanic into the colonial pantheon or as not succeeding in differentiating them completely. Saint Michael finally defeats Lucifer and his followers, and they are cast into a dark place that resembled the Nahuas' conception of Mictlan, the place of the dead. The fallen angels then become devils, who are in turn identified as those whom the Nahuas call *tzitzimime*, fearsome night creatures "who could appear and devour human beings at the end of a cosmic age" (Sahagún, *Coloquios*, 173n6); *Tzontemoc*, "one name for Mictlanteuctli, the Lord of the Dead" (ibid., 173n7); and *Cuezal*, "which was a name for Xiuhteuctli, 'the Lord of Fire'" (ibid., 173n9). According to the friars, these "demonic" creatures were "very black ones, very dirty ones / . . . / very great mocker [*sic*] of anyone, / very furious ones / and very angry-hearted ones" (Klor de Alva, "Aztec," 151).

It is possible that by identifying the Nahua deities with Lucifer and the fallen angels, the dualistic-minded friars could have induced their audience to think about the latter in a new, Christian way: namely as *exclusively* evil creatures and great enemies of the people. As was mentioned earlier, in the Nahua pre-Hispanic conception of the world the gods unleashed both positive and negative forces, depending on the particular time and form of their manifestation.[31] The deities constantly changed attributes and identities, for it was understood that harmony and disharmony, order and chaos, life and death were fundamental, inescapable aspects of existence (Burkhart, *Slippery*, 37; Read, 146–47). Thus, it is also conceivable that because the devils were represented by the friars in the *Colloquios* as doing things that did not differ much from what the Nahuas believed many of their gods did at least part of the time, the audience may not have been persuaded that the devils were the utterly despicable figures that the Twelve claimed had to be forsaken. For instance, two of Tezcatlipoca's negative attributes were his mockery of the people and his anger.[32] These were characteristics that the friars used to describe the devils in the text (Klor de Alva, "Aztec," 151). However, as was discussed above, other epithets of Tezcatlipoca were also applied by the friars in the *Colloquios* to the Christian god, creating "a certain ambiguity" (Burkhart, "Doctrinal," 70) between the two. Hence, it is not far-fetched to suggest that this ambiguity, insofar as it may have produced the effect of confusing or even merging the identities of the Christian god and Tezcatlipoca, may have confirmed the Nahua audience in their resistance to see the latter as exclusively evil and deserving to be forsaken.

As Burkhart points out, because the *Colloquios*' principal concern is to persuade the Nahua lords and priests that their gods are the Christian devils, the emphasis of the text is on Lucifer's jealousy and on his repeated efforts to disconcert the people and move them to injure "the precious heart, / of He by Whom All Live, God, Speaker" (Klor de Alva, "Aztec," 180). Thus, in recounting the fall of the first couple, hardly any attention is given to the moral aspect of their behavior. Rather, the emphasis will be on the devil's deception (Burkhart, "Doctrinal," 74–75). The same can be said about Cain's assassination of Abel, the emergence of idolatry, and the tower of Babel, the other three great offenses depicted in the text as having been perpetrated against God before Christ's Incarnation to save the world from sin.

Although the Christian god is greatly insulted by the people's induced transgressions, never is He shown to destroy them completely. In fact, sinners like Cain have copious offspring. The practice of idolatry or "the act of following things as gods" is initiated by his children (Klor de Alva, "Aztec," 183). After the deluge, represented as a punishment of Cain's descendants, humankind multiplies again quickly. Shortly after, it will be once again tempted or "disconcerted" by the devils—Nahua gods—to injure the heart of He by Whom All live. It is significant that in the Nahuatl version the injury was to try to climb to heaven by building up a "high mountain" (ibid., 187) or pyramid. Clearly, the Nahua grammarians made a cultural translation in terms of the buildings erected as the human attempt to reach the godhead and for which they were punished. The extant text is cut off at the moment at which the friars lament that those devils who have harmed humanity so badly were taken as gods by their audience (Klor de Alva, "Aztec," 188).

It is quite possible that the tlatoque and tlamacazque could have detected some familiarity in the account of the successive destructions and generation of humans and the role of their gods/devils in it. As is well known, the idea of successive creations that were destroyed because of their imperfections was widespread in Mesoamerica and very ancient. Depending on the region, the number and sequence of creations would vary. In some records, such as the *Popol Vuh*, there were four creations. In *The Legend of the Suns*, whose full text appears in the sixteenth-century *Codex Chimalpopoca*, there were five creations or "suns." The canonical sequence of these creations in Tenochtitlan appears in the "Stone of the Five Suns," or Mexica Calendar, and in the "Coronation Tablet of Motecuhzoma II" (Townsend, 127). The first era was extinguished when a jaguar ate the giants who roamed the earth at that time. According to López Austin the sins of these giants (arrogance, sexual promiscuity, and drunkenness) unleashed the anger of the gods, provoking their destruction (*Human*, 1:239). The subsequent eras also ended in cataclysms with their beings transformed into monkeys, then birds, and later fish. López Austin points out that it is not clear whether these beings were conceived merely as precursors of mankind, which would finally emerge in the last and most perfect sun, the fifth and present era, or whether as the inhabitants of the previous eras, they were regarded as true (yet inferior) human[s] (*Human*, 1:239–40). In any case, it has been argued that like the Judeo-Christian concept Nahua cosmogony had "a moral history" (Burkhart, *Slippery*, 74). Transgressions and incompetence were causes of destruction and may be found at the origin of every era. Thus, even in the most perfect of them all, the fifth, the god Quetzalcoatl stumbled when bringing from the underworld the bones from which

humans would be made. This slip would "affect the race of humans he...
[was] about to create from the troubled fifth sun" (Burkhart, *Slippery*, 76).

Nevertheless, as Kay A. Read contends, there was also an amoral element of natural (dis)order, schedule, and sequence in these cataclysms.
Because beings were never totally destroyed but appeared transformed in the
next era, "each sun perished in order that the next one could begin" (Read,
69). That is, destruction was not total ruin in the first four eras insofar as it
always marked a new beginning. The end of the fifth sun, the era of the
true human species, would occur not only due to the people's immoral conduct or their ritual negligence, but also because of its geographical, culminating position at the center of the world. Five was the number and symbol
of excess (Burkhart, *Slippery*, 74; Nicholson, 418), and it would eventually
lead to the exhaustion of "the seed of earth" (Sahagún, *Florentine*, 6:37).
After the fifth, there was no further position in the terrestrial plane for
another sun (López Austin, *Human*, 1:240; Burkhart, *Slippery*, 74).

There are then several parallels that the Nahua audience could have seen
between the Twelve's "long performance" of the Christian narrative of origins and their own indigenous myths of creation. Because—according to the
friars—at least three of the offenses induced by the devils/pre-Hispanic
deities led to catastrophic ends (albeit not total extinction), the Nahua audience may have found some similarity between such punished transgressions and their own four suns with their respective demises. Even though the
text is cut off after the episode of Babel, the extant summary of contents
indicates that Christ's worldly kingdom is discussed shortly thereafter.
Thus, it may be speculated that the Nahuas could have seen some similarities between the Incarnation of Christ and their present fifth sun, because
the Incarnation could be interpreted as the beginning of a new, more perfect era, also destined to end because of the people's great sins.

Regarding the Twelve's representation of the pre-Hispanic gods/devils
as the culprits for the cataclysms suffered by humanity, it is important to
recall that in both the Spanish and Nahuatl versions the Christian god had
been represented in earlier conversations [chapter nine] as omnipotent,
omniscient, and omnipresent: "Always, eternally He sees / all that is visible
and what is not visible/Everything is thus in the palm of His hand /.../

Being all powerful / no matter what it is He desires for Himself, / at once it is done / no one hinders Him / nothing obstructs Him" (Klor de Alva, "Aztec," 139–40).[33] Taking this representation into account, the (represented) emphasis of the Twelve on the devils' success in damaging God's creation (Burkhart, "Doctrinal," 74–78) had logically to imply his sanction. In other words, it is difficult to reconcile the idea of God's omnipotence with that of acts from the devil that resulted in God's offense and, ultimately, in a series of cataclysms in His creation that He did not desire. If no one could hinder or obstruct Him as the friars preached, then the devils/pre-Hispanic gods could not have acted entirely against the Godhead's omnipotent will. No matter how jealous and malevolent, they could not have been God's real foes. Their destructive agency could not be altogether separated from His absolute goodness and power. Thus, not totally unlike the Mesoamerican view of the universe, the agency of the gods/devils in the friars' speech performance could have been construed by the Nahua audience as part of a cosmic economy or scheme of things where death, trickery, damage, and destruction were not the opposites of life, but their inevitable and inescapable complements. In this sense, the friars' argument that the devils/pre-Hispanic gods had caused so much harm and pain to humankind and thus deserved to be scorned and repudiated may have not sounded very compelling to the Nahua audience since the Christian god himself had taken some part in the destruction, if only by consenting to it. Not unlike the pre-Hispanic deities, who were capable of producing both positive and negative effects, the Christian god procured the negative by allowing his creatures, the devils, to wreak havoc.[34]

In any case, according to the extant Spanish summary of the *Colloquios*, we may surmise that the friars were not represented as having fully succeeded in converting the Nahua priests and statesmen with this part of their "long performance." The next chapter, according to the table of contents, is dedicated to explaining once again who the Nahua gods were. The argument that finally seems to turn things around is that the Nahua gods had not been powerful enough to save the Indians from the Spaniards, whereas the Christian god always protected his worshippers.[35] As Sahagún states in the prologue, the foundation, order, and distribution of the Twelve's arguments had been animated by the Holy Spirit. However, it could be argued that their triumphant argument may have worked not only because of the friars' divinely inspired eloquence, but also because the reasoning was compatible with the Mesoamerican long-standing cultural practice of adopting the gods of the conquerors (Lockhart, *The Nahuas,* 203; Duverger, 204–05).

Finally, the tlatoque and the tlamacazque are represented in the summary as having disowned their gods in chapter 21 and as having been "satisfied" and "pleased" by what the Twelve had said in chapters 22 and 26. Because we do not have the text of any of these chapters, it is difficult to know how the execration and the acceptance were represented. Be that as it may, in the last chapter of the *Colloquios* the Nahua lords are said to have finally brought to the friars their idols as well as their women and children. With these acts, Christianity would seem to have triumphed at the close of the first book of the text.

By the time Sahagún finished editing the *Colloquios,* he must have been already of the opinion that if the triumphal conversion of the Nahua elite by the Twelve had indeed been historical, it had certainly had a less than felicitous sequel. The ethnographic information that he had been gathering since the late 1540s for his monumental *Historia general de las cosas de la Nueva España* showed that while practicing Christianity, the Nahuas did not give up completely the religious beliefs and practices of their forefathers.[36]

It is then very hard to ascertain Sahagún's intentionality in composing a text whose triumphal claims he could hardly accept. It is less difficult to argue, however, that the extant text, including the summary of contents, does not do what the prologue says. For in spite of having been inspired by the Holy Spirit to construct their arguments in the way and order that they did, as Sahagún declares in the prologue, the Twelve do not come across as having made their truths that visible and irrefutable for the Nahua audience in the text or even for the implied Western reader. In more than a few cases the arguments of the Franciscans cannot escape circularity. Namely, the truth of the beliefs that they seek to manifest to their audience is demonstrated by invoking arguments and having recourse to authorities (such as the Holy Scriptures) that only believers would accept. In other cases their evidence is upheld by statements that the friars and the Spanish readers knew very well to be false. In still other moments, such as the fall of the angels, the expulsion from Paradise of Adam and Eve, Noah's ark, and the tower of Babel, the Christian narratives do not seem to be inherently any more rational, coherent, or persuasive than the Nahuas' stories of creation. This last point, of course, most probably would have been inaccessible to Sahagún's Euro-Christocentric episteme, or way of understanding, categorizing, organizing, and obtaining knowledge from the world.

But the lingering memory of the pre-Hispanic supernatural would be due not only to the friars' failure to demonstrate and prove rationally the absolute and self-evident superiority of Christianity. There were also enough intersections between the Christian and the pre-Hispanic religious systems so as to be able to accommodate to the former without having to give up the latter completely. In the summary of contents, the triumphal argument that seems to overpower all others (namely, that the Nahua gods had been unable to protect their believers from perishing at the hands of the Spaniards) can be located in both Christian and Nahua cultures. It may be argued, then, that the acceptance of Christianity in the *Colloquios* was achieved not only because of the friars' ability to prove to the Nahuas that they should repudiate their idolatrous pre-Hispanic past, but also because of the similarities that Christianity had with such a past. The Franciscans would appropriate these similarities on more than one occasion in their evangelization endeavor. This pattern of interaction in the *Colloquios* is paradigmatic of the specific religious, cultural dynamics that informed the emergence of the Nahua Christian subject in sixteenth-century Mexico. We will see such a pattern recur, wittingly or unwittingly, in the analysis of three extant pieces of the Nahua theater of evangelization and in Gerónimo de Mendieta's *Historia eclesiástica indiana*. In addition, we will see that much like naming the Christian god with the attributes of Tezcatlipoca, as well as redefining the pre-Hispanic deities as fallen supernatural beings who had enormous powers of destruction, the intersections between Christianity and the pre-Hispanic past worked in an ambivalent way: they helped with the assimilation of Christianity, yes, but they also guaranteed that the presence of the Mesoamerican gods would not be shunned completely. This persistent presence is what may have provoked Sahagún's following lament in an interpolation found in place of a Spanish translation in chapter 12 of book 11 of the *Historia general*: "We can consider well understood that having preached to them more than fifty years, if today they were left on their own ...I believe that in less than fifty years there would be no trace of what has been preached to them"(also quoted in Klor de Alva, "Sahagún's," 89).

Because the Amerindians would never be left totally on their own the seeds of Christianity did indeed produce some fruit. But in one way or another such seeds would have to share the lands of Anahuac with modes and forms of the pre-Hispanic sacred for all the colonial centuries to come. The pyramid would remain deeply seated under the cross.

PART II | *Nahua Theater of Evangelization in Sixteenth-century Mexico*

2

Introduction to Some Cultural Performance Practices in Medieval Spain and Pre-Hispanic Mexico

One of the most audacious episodes in the Franciscan missionary drama of the sixteenth century was an evangelizing theater. The great twentieth-century scholar and translator of this theater, Fernando de Horcasitas, hints at the overly optimistic expectations the friars had from this theater when he writes that "de la noche a la mañana, los indígenas, que veinte años antes habían adorado a Huitzilopochtli y Tezcatlipoca, deben enterarse y creer en Adán y Eva, en Abraham e Isaac, en la Redención, en la toma de Jerusalén por Santiago" [Overnight, the Indians, who twenty years earlier had been worshipping Huitzilopochtli and Tezcatlipoca, now had to learn about and believe in Adam and Eve, Abraham and Isaac, in the Redemption, in the capture of Jerusalem by James] (Horcasitas, 53). Through this theater and its stories, Horcasitas continues, the Nahuas were expected to learn a new code of morals and to accept new cultural traits or markers.

The reasons why theater was chosen as a means of evangelization were never openly expounded by the indefatigable missionaries. There is evidence, however, that the Franciscans used scriptural plays as part of their evangelical endeavors since the emergence of the order and that they were involved in European vernacular religious drama as early as the thirteenth century (Jeffrey, "Franciscan," 18; Stern, "Reassessing," 130). In their distinctive identification with the human life of Christ, the Friars Minor sought to make scripture more tangible, closer to the daily life of the people in order to heighten their devotion. The friars employed music, lyric, and drama to this end.[1] With such a Franciscan tradition in place, it may be conjectured that the fact that the visual and gestural could greatly supplement verbal communication, particularly in contexts where the latter was threatened by linguistic incompetence, was surely not lost on the resolute Twelve. Possibly sharing a Franciscan traditional "determination to harness popular culture as a medium, and to elevate it as a value" (Jeffrey, "Franciscan," 19), the missionaries must have soon realized the vital role public rituals held in Mexica preconquest society. Hence, they possibly concluded that in order to attract large masses of Nahuas to Christianity "the most effective—indeed, the only—way...was through the use of song, dance, plays, processions, and their accompanying pageantry and paraphernalia" (Burkhart, *Holy,* 43). Moreover, the friars may have felt obliged to transplant some of Spain's own traditions of public religious celebrations in order to fill the terrible void the suppression of the pre-Hispanic rituals had left behind (Garibay, 2:156). In order to situate the theater of evangelization culturally, we need to examine, if only briefly, how it relates to Spain's own specific tradition of religious dramatic forms, as well as to some Nahua performance genres.

It has long been held that medieval religious drama was born in the tenth century with the liturgical tropes *Quem quaeretis?* and the *Visitatio sepulchri.* These were short dialogues in Latin, interpolated in the Easter Mass, in which an angel appeared to the three Marys in order to announce to them Christ's resurrection. Little by little this simple dialogue (of which there are more than three hundred manuscripts in European archives [Hosley, 203]) would grow with the addition of characters and more complex scenes. Interestingly, the scene of the adoration of the Holy Child in the *Comedia de los Reyes* represented in Mexico-Tetzcoco in 1600 was performed inside the church and as part of the mass, harking back to the very origins of Christian religious theater. In Spain, the greatest number of examples of liturgical drama documented is found in the church archives of the eastern provinces of Valencia, Alicante, and Catalonia. Scholars have posited the protracted presence of Islam and the pervasiveness of the Mozarabic rite in Castile and León until 1080 as reasons for the more sparse evidence of a liturgical drama tradition in central and western Spain (Donovan, 21, 69–73;

Stern, *Medieval,* 30). However, from the eleventh century on, the most significant number of Latin plays have been found in Castile in miscellanies other than breviaries and ordinaries.

By the twelfth and thirteenth centuries, vernacular pieces for the Nativity and Easter had emerged in France and other parts of Europe, which, due to their complexity and for reasons of decorum, had to be moved out into the church patio or even the public square. Because they were performed outside the church and written in the vernacular, they were not recorded in the Latin collections or other service books (Stern, *Medieval,* 42). Thus, most of this vernacular theater is believed to have disappeared. Only three twelfth-century religious plays in the vernacular are extant; one of them is the *Auto of the Reyes Magos,* probably written during the second half of the twelfth century and discovered in the cathedral library of Toledo. The complex notational system used in this *auto* has led scholars to think that it was not composed in a theatrical void (Stern, *Medieval,* 50). The auto may attest to an ongoing vernacular theater tradition in which plays, not necessarily linked to particular churches or places, were usually only staged once, hence the difficulty, oversight, and/or lack of motivation in preserving the dramatic scripts. Only as late as the fifteenth century will we again find extant manuscripts of Castilian vernacular religious plays in connection to Christmas and Easter festivities.[2]

Another religious feast aside from Christmas and Easter, and equally significant in the development of a Spanish vernacular religious theater, was the feast of Corpus Christi, which originated in France in 1246 and was extended to the whole of Christianity in 1264. In 1317, Pope John XXII decreed that the consecrated Eucharist was to be taken in procession through the streets. As time went on, the processions grew more and more complex, as did their dramatic possibilities. In Catalonia and Valencia, wooden figures in carts known as *roques* or *rocas,* representing biblical stories and episodes of saints' lives, were paraded around town. Documents show that the floats could be quite elaborate and spectacular: they could carry anything from winged angels with diadems and tinfoil curls to large painted canvases representing dragons. Eventually, the statues would come to be substituted by people; and by 1414 and 1425, some dramatic action was superimposed on the tableaux (Parker, "Notes," 175), though without dialogue or songs. Of interest to this study, there is evidence that Dominicans, Franciscans, and Augustinian friars were involved in the production of the scenes or *entremeses* for the Valencian Corpus procession of 1432 (Shergold, 55). Though the confluence of pageant and play has not been well documented due to the lack of evidence, it is known that by the late fifteenth and early sixteenth centuries, plays representing biblical episodes were represented in Valencia to go with the roques.[3] It is important to point out that in all of these medieval dramatic and spectacular activities, both inside the church and outside in the patio, in the town streets or in the public square, actors and spectators affirmed their identity as Christians congregating together "in the celebration of an act/auto de fe" (Surtz, *Teatro*, 18). Hence, these spectacles were not merely didactic or entertaining: they were strategies intended to suspend or set aside ordinary activities in order to open up the community to a temporality thought to be sacred.

Taking the above historical picture into account, although the number of extant dramatic texts in Spain is not nearly as high in comparison with France, Italy, or England, there are enough references in papal decrees, Latin treatises, penitentials, chronicles, ecclesiastical as well as municipal minutes, and many other source documents to attest to a lively dramatic and spectacular activity, particularly in Catalonia, Aragon, and even Castile.[4] Along the lines of medievalists O. B. Hardison and V. A. Kolve, who in the 1960s dismissed the theory of medieval vernacular theater developing in a continuum from Latin liturgical drama, Hispanist and medieval scholar Charlotte Stern believes that the conception of medieval theater as having originated from a single source (namely, the liturgical tropes) and having evolved from simpler to more complex dramatic forms is too narrow. She contends that such conceptions of theater should be revised so as to reflect its much more encompassing medieval definition "as a place of sights" ("Medieval," 171). Such sights may be argued to include "all the performing arts in their simple and complex forms" (ibid., 174). Thus, by collecting all documented references to street performances, pageants, processions, mimes, roques, representations in the public square, and the like, no matter how apparently marginal, Stern believes that a more accurate image of medieval dramatic activity in Castile (and for that matter, in all Spain) will emerge, in which theater is found to be everywhere ("Medieval," 170–72).

By the time the Twelve arrived in New Spain in 1524, then, it can be posited that there was a tradition of religious drama, processions, and pageantry in Spain to which the Franciscan order must have contributed as it had done in many other European countries, and from which the Twelve would draw for the evangelization of the Nahuas. The famous collection of ninety-six anonymous autos, the *Códice de autos viejos* (now housed in the Biblioteca Nacional in Madrid) linked to Seville, dates from the second half of the sixteenth century and is believed to have been a repertoire of autos for professional troupes (which emerged in the 1540s) to be performed in the Corpus Christi festivities (Pérez Priego, 15–16). It has been speculated that the ninety-six autos as they appear in the *Códice* may have been refundiciones or reworkings of autos of earlier periods and regions (Horcasitas, 65–66; Pérez Priego, 10–15). Horcasitas points out that many of the themes of the plays for the Nahua theater of evangelization appear in the *Códice*. This could serve as further evidence that the Franciscan friars coming to Mexico were familiar with dramatic practices in Spain.

The importance of this brief survey of Spanish dramatic practices in the Middle Ages and in the early Renaissance is that if a wider, more encompassing interpretation of medieval drama is accepted *and its ritual character considered*, we will see that in spite of different cultural universes, the Nahuas from Central Mexico had comparable practices in the pre-contact period. These practices involved an agent or agents, carrying out a set of actions in a more or less spontaneously designed space or frame for a more or less participating audience; the actions activated and recreated meanings of some sort of preexisting text (Schechner, 12; MacAloon, 9–10). Songs accompanied by dance and music, and assumed to have been performed before an audience, were one such practice. The existence of this genre has been deduced from the *Cantares mexicanos*, a large collection of songs compiled during the sixteenth century by Nahua aides to the Franciscans. The *teocuicatl*, for instance, were sacred songs and hymns taught at the *calmecac* or monastery schools (Soustelle, 308)[5] and also sung in celebrations to the gods (León-Portilla, *Literatura*, xxvi). Other songs praised the military deeds of famous Mexica captains and could also be accompanied by music and dance. According to James Lockhart, the internal structure of the songs (possibly the *cuicatl*), their polite language and rhetoric, their complex, florid metaphors and references to preconquest personae of the central Mexican altepetl, or ethnic town, make it logical to assume that it was in fact a survival of a preconquest oral genre (Lockhart, *The Nahuas*, 394). These songs were composed to be performed in public festivities or in more private, aristocratic gatherings known as the *cohuayotl iciniuyotl* (Watts, "Languages," 148). They were usually accompanied by flutes and drums and sometimes even sung or recited by two or more groups who engaged in dialogues among themselves. For Garibay and León-Portilla, this verbal exchange to the sound of music, performed in front of an audience, may be considered a precursor of a very ancient form of representation and dramatic action (León-Portilla, *Literatura*, 119; Garibay, 1:95). This practice was not entirely unlike the court entertainment encouraged by Alfonso X, in which a professional or even high-class performer would entertain knights at their banquets either by reading histories of great deeds or singing *cantares de gesta* (Stern, *Medieval*, 81).

The other form practiced in preconquest times frequently associated with theatrical genres were the calendrical rituals. In these rituals, which León-Portilla insightfully denominates "perpetual Nahua theater" (*Literatura*, 239), individuals usually impersonated a deity and interacted with priests, lords, and/or regular people in designated times and spaces in and around Tenochtitlan. As Davíd Carrasco has described it, "Aztec sacrificial rites were exuberant forms of cosmo-magical rhetoric expressed through imagery about the human body as it moved through, changed and mapped out a ceremonial landscape that was concentrated and dispersed, local and imperial, depending on the particular festival" (121). The individual wore the regalia of the deity honored in the feast, and in his/her interaction with the priest and other specialized personnel, s/he enacted a narrative of the god's mythical deeds and their links to the history of the participant ethnic community. On most occasions, but by no means all, the impersonating individual or *ixiptla* (image) was sacrificed. The role or image force of the god was assumed not only the day that the impersonated deity was sacrificed, but sometimes twenty days or even a year before. During this period, the "ritualized body" was treated and behaved like a god (Bell, *Ritual*, 98–101). Sometimes, on the eve of the sacrifice, the individual had to dance in places singled out for the occasion (González Torres, 202). In this sense, there was clearly an enormous investment of resources among the Nahuas in preparing and arousing attention for the ritual. In the feast of Tezcatlipoca, for instance, the Nahuas sacrificed a young, handsome man, who had been solicitously cared for during a whole year. Throughout this time, he was taught, among other things, how to play the flute. Once he learned, he was free to play anytime, anywhere, all the world becoming a stage. Everyone who ran into him honored and humbled themselves before him. The day of the sacrifice, the image of Tezcatlipoca or ixiptla was taken to a *teocalli*, or temple, a league or so from the city. As he climbed the steps to his death, he broke one by one the flutes he had played in his days of prosperity.[6]

Thus, we can see that Nahua calendrical rituals may indeed be considered religious dramatic performances. The salient point of difference from any form of western reenactments of sacred stories lies in the relationship with the represented object propitiated by the ixiptla and consequently in the borders of liminality. Liminality is a phase or condition in which daily life is suspended for a determined period of time in order to attend to or reflect collectively about social, religious, and/or existential experience. It is "often the scene and time for the emergence of a society's deepest values in the form of sacred dramas and objects—sometimes the reenactment periodically of cosmogonic narratives, or deeds of saintly, godly, or heroic establishers of morality, basic institutions, or ways of approaching transcendent beings or powers" (Turner, "Rokujo's," 102). Hence, though the European medieval religious theater can certainly be thought of as liminal in Turner's sense, the distance between the represented and the representing, between audience and participating congregation, is usually greater than in the Mexica calendrical ritual. For according to Inga Clendinnen, the most approximate meanings of ixiptla are "rendering present by simulation" or "that which enables the god to present aspects of himself" (*Aztecs*, 253). Thus, as Louise Burkhart rightly observes, the individuality of the human ixiptla was overriden and dissolved by the divine presence it had brought forth

(*Holy*, 44). An even more significant difference was, no doubt, the sacrifice of the ixiptla. The boundaries between liminal and quotidian space and time were decisively blurred in the Mexica ritual reenacting the original sacrifices of the deities, because the human individual who had become ixiptla (and who died not as an impersonating individual, but as [the vehicle of] the manifested deity) could never be reinserted into mundane life again. In this sense, liminality spilled over the quotidian and viceversa.[7] In the cases where no human was sacrificed, depending on the intensity and duration of the manifestation of the supernatural forces conjured by the ritualized body of the ixiptla, "sacredness lingered" (Clendinnen, *Aztecs*, 253), and different objects and people remained infused with sacred energy for varying periods of time. This would not be entirely other, however, to the residues of the sacred left by the parading of the consecrated Eucharist in a Corpus Christi procession.

It could be argued that certain aspects of this blurred liminality were carried over to the Nahua evangelization theater. The controversial Thomas Gage, one of the very few Englishmen who traveled to the Spanish Indies in the seventeenth century, mentions that the Indians of Chiapas sought confession before or after representing religious roles:

> The Indians that dance this dance most of them are superstitious for what they do, judging as if it were indeed really acted and performed what only is by way of dance represented. When I lived amongst them it was an ordinary thing for him who in the dance was to act St. Peter or John the Baptist to come first to confession, saying they must be holy and pure like that saint, whom they represent...So likewise he that acted Herod or Herodias, ... would afterwards come to confess of that sin, and desire absolution as from bloodguiltiness." (Gage, 270–71; also quoted in Horcasitas, 87)

Similarly, the actors who played Jesus and other holy characters would go to confession and receive communion before the performance so as to attain a purified state as akin to their characters as possible.[8] This attests to some form of nondifferentiation between the representing individual and the represented character that may have implied some continuity with pre-

Hispanic ritual agency in the colonial context. However, the term the Nahuas would use to denominate the evangelization theater was *neixcuitilli*, or "something that sets an example" (Burkhart, *Holy*, 46). Burkhart concedes that the term was not applied to preconquest performances. It named "a new performance genre, but one possessing continuities with earlier Nahua forms and not quite the equivalent of 'drama' in the European sense" (Burkhart, *Holy*, 46). From the point of view of the friars, the new practice of the neixcuitilli would be closer to the more restricted notion of European theater, in which actors performed a play script in one or more relatively delimited scaffolds, or *loca*, making only occasional incursions in the *platea*, or the audience's non-representational space, and thus blurring the limits between the spheres of actors and spectators.[9] The neixcuitilli would imply, among other things, the emergence of (different) liminal boundaries in the performance. It involved a sharper, clearer differentiation between representing agent and represented entity, a distinction between the world of ordinary existence and that of the sacred, a consequent shifting emphasis from participating congregation to neophyte audience in need of religious instruction.

Now, it should be granted that although written in Nahuatl, the Mexican evangelization theater of the sixteenth century was manifestly Spanish in theme, plot, and religious doctrine. The characters were usually Judeo-Christian, the plots were in general doctrinally satisfactory renderings of the European stories, and the performances were intended by the colonizer to reproduce his culture and show the Nahuas the new Christian deities and behaviors to follow. Nevertheless, this ritual/theater was a cultural form that the Spanish ecclesiastics could not control or possess completely. Scholars have often wondered how much of the dramatic script the Spanish ecclesiastics actually wrote down. An "isolated, unfinished phrase" (Lockhart, *The Nahuas*, 403) in Spanish appearing in a sixteenth-century manuscript of the *Holy Wednesday* playlet has led Lockhart to propose that the Nahua aide did not understand what it meant, but copied it down anyway. He then speculates that the friars might have had the practice of writing something down in Spanish, which the Nahua scribe would then translate into Nahuatl. The unfinished Spanish phrase in the manuscript also indicates for Lockhart that the dramatic script was never supervised by the friar again: "It is as though the directing Spaniard, although in a sense probably deserving to be called the author of the play, never looked at it again once he had given it to a Nahua to translate and realize as he saw fit" (*The Nahuas*, 403).[10] Needless to say, this hypothetical collaborative situation implies at the concretization level of the dramatic script itself (not to say of the theatrical performance) enormous possibilities for appropriating and inflecting the authority of the colonizing discourses by the Nahua/translator/colonized.

Lockhart's hypothesis may be found radical on the grounds of the implausibility that the friars did not supervise more closely the cathecizing dramatic scripts. Nevertheless, the scripts, whether written or oral, whether more or less watched over, by virtue of being translated had already been at least partially severed from the colonizer's conception. Because languages embody different ways of perceiving the world and of organizing experience and cognition, translation is, among other things, an act of appropriation, a recreation, a reconceptualization of the translated text in terms of the cultural universe inscribed in the target language. Translation certainly promotes and augments the circulation of the texts of the source culture, but also erodes the formers' "claim of originality" (de Man, 97), as they are opened up irreversibly to the interventions of a foreign voice.[11]

Moreover, the new cultural universe into which the translated texts of the Nahua evangelization theater were plunged was not only incorporated in the obvious use of Nahuatl, but also in the conspicuous Nahua forms of elevated, polite language, specific oratory structures, social ranks, categories, and conventions. To this we need to add that the script or written text is only one of the components of the total theatrical event. The mise-en-scène and theatrical performance, for which the Nahuas were mostly responsible in the evangelization theater, "are always a stage translation (thanks to the actor and all the elements of the performance) of another cultural totality (text, adaptation, body)" (Pavis, 16). When performed by native actors, whose sign-producing bodies enact intelligibility and meaning out of the (foreign) dramatic text, such text, which is already severed from its origin, is further being inflected according to the receiving or target culture's models. The moment of performance could mean then a second or even third displacement or deferment of the colonizer's authoritative text.

Taking all the above into account and as Max Harris has also proposed,[12] it becomes clearer that the Nahua evangelization theater cannot be adequately theorized only as a colonialist form of cultural domination.[13] For despite the undeniably didactic, edifying, and colonizing intentions of the scripts of this theater of evangelization, it was something more. This theater gave the Nahuas the opportunity of managing public space again, of showing their unrivaled ability to incorporate new meanings, their breathtaking power to deploy highly organized forms of sociality, and the possibility of encoding "hidden transcripts of resistance"[14] for the consumption of the indigenous audience only. Ironically then, the spectacular performances of the narratives of the European colonizer also opened up the possibility for the Nahuas to reactivate, if not reaffirm, their collective memory and to embody many of their cultural categories and values. The theater of evangelization had an ambivalent effect in that it both helped to suppress the pre-Hispanic past as well to establish continuities with it in the colonial present.

On the part of the friars, who according to the Franciscan tradition of affective piety came up with the ingenious plan of converting the Nahua by his own dramatic acts of self-colonization, the Nahua theater of evangelization also shows that the missionaries were sensitive to the need for the complicity and agency of the Nahua subject in the evangelization process. This theater embodied an image of relationships of power in which the subjection of the other was publicly acknowledged as being possible only by his consent and negotiated appropriation (Bell, 207).[15] The participation of the Nahuas in this theater was thus the objectification, the becoming visible of their own agency in the Christianizing affair, which disrupted the illusion, held by some critics even today, that the spiritual colonizer could ever be in full control of the situation.

Very little of this Nahua evangelization theater is available today. Many of the extant manuscripts are usually copies produced in the seventeenth or even eighteenth century. Though there are records of pieces represented and composed during these centuries, the greatest number of references to plays performed date from the sixteenth century. In the following three chapters of this book I will discuss two plays or neixcuitilli scripts and an account of a performance believed to have been produced in the culturally rich environment of sixteenth-century colonial Mexico. These plays and the staging account will give us the opportunity to show how the Nahuas, in embodying and reproducing some of the colonizer's new cultural models, may have also been reaffirming and giving continuity to their own.

Performing the Limits of Colonialist Power: Evangelization, Irony, and Resistance in the *Neixcuitilli Final Judgment*

he first performance of Nahua evangelization theater recorded in chronicles of the period is an *auto* about the Last Judgment, represented in 1531 or 1533 in Tlatelolco. The same play or another with the same title and theme was represented between 1535 and 1550, at the church of San Juan de los Naturales in Tenotchitlan. The U.S. Library of Congress houses a copy of a script entitled *Nexcuitilmachiotl motenehua Juicio Final* until recently believed to be from 1678. Under this assumption, Othón Arróniz has pointed out that the fact that *Juicio Final* appears in Spanish in the title indicates that the Nahua copyist did not know what the term really meant and so left it as it was. Because it is not very likely that copyists would find themselves in this situation almost one hundred and fifty years into the colonization, Arróniz hypothesizes that the text must belong to the sixteenth century (21–22). Marlyn E. Ravicz and Fernando Horcasitas also agree that internal linguistic evidence makes it likely to propose an earlier origin of the play (Ravicz, 141; Horcasitas, 561–67). Though no definite conclusion has yet been drawn, all these scholars contend that the manuscript might be a copy of at least one of the plays with this title recorded by Bartolomé de Las Casas, Chimalpahin, and Gerónimo de Mendieta as having been performed in the 1530s. More recently, however, Barry D. Sell has discovered that contrary to what had been claimed the manuscript of *Final Judgment* at the Library of Congress has no date whatsoever (Sell, "Nahuatl," 6). Given internal linguistic evidence, loanwords, and idiomatic usage, however, Sell hypothesizes that the extant manuscript, most likely a copy of an earlier play, cannot have been produced much earlier than the late seventeenth century (Sell, "Nahuatl," 10).

Closely linked to the possible period of composition, the second polemic around the neixcuitilli *Final Judgment* has to do with its authorship. It is one of the few plays of the evangelization theater to which the chroniclers of the period have attributed an author, in this case the great *nahuatlato* Andrés de Olmos (Arróniz, 37–38; Baudot, *Utopia*, 163–245; Williams, *Teatro*, 50). The polemic hinges on whether the extant manuscript is indeed a copy of the one penned by Olmos, as claimed by John Cornyn and Byron McAfee (Ravicz, 142) in 1932 and more recently by Horcasitas (566–67). In her 1941 study on the play, however, Margarita Mendoza López questions Cornyn and McAfee's position by addressing one salient contradiction in the text, which we will consider later. Uneasy about the possibility that Olmos's script might be ambivalent, she argues that the contradiction might be the result of alterations in subsequent copies of the original (10). What is interesting about the inconsistency pointed out by Mendoza López is that it may have as much to do with the "corruption" of the original at the hands of the copyists through time as with the position carved out by recent scholarship, which holds that "the Nahuas authored, coauthored, or at least edited the scripts" (Burkhart, *Holy*, 47). As discussed above, the latter would mean that the Nahua scribes may have had a much more important mediating and hermeneutic role than has been previously acknowledged, which may account for the hybridities, contradictions, and hidden messages that contemporary critics are uncovering in the texts.

The dramatic text of *Final Judgment* strikes the reader as a gesture of great epistemic violence not only because it dramatizes possibly the most terrifying episode of the Western religious imagination, but also because of its referential intricacies. The play opens with Saint Michael, who, to the sound of wind instruments, warns the spectators about the imminent coming of the fearsome day of reckoning: "O creations of God! Know...that he [God] will finish off, he will destroy the world that his precious and honored father, God, made. He will destroy, he will finish off all that he made, the various birds, the various living creatures, along with you" (Sell and Burkhart, 191).[1] The first disconcerting aspect of the play is that the Nahua

audience is expected to relate to a Christian character of very elusive onto-
logical status. How would the Nahuas interpret who or what Saint Michael
was? Would they know the latter was an archangel, a pure, intellectual creature, incorporeal and incorruptible even though it was represented in full-
fledged human form by a Nahua actor? Would they be able to discern that
the archangels were supposed to occupy the second lowest order in the
angelic hierarchy? Moreover, would they realize that this was the very same
archangel who, along with his army of angels, was supposed to cast down
from heaven the terrible dragon of the Apocalypse? Or would the spectators interpret Saint Michael as some sort of sorcerer, priest, or angry ixiptla
announcing the definite end of the fifth sun,[2] a catastrophe for which a Mexica audience could surely find parallels in the Conquest itself? How were the
spatial and temporal coordinates of this character's harsh admonition to be
construed? Would it ensure a "proper" Western reading of the dramatic
image, in which the audience would be able to differentiate between real and
represented time?

Saint Michael exits, and then enter the allegorical characters of Penance,
Time, the Holy Church, Confession, Sweeping, and Death. They engage
in an anxious dialogue about the dissoluteness of the inhabitants of the
world, namely, the Nahua spectators. These allegorical characters were not
uncommon in medieval morality plays. However, the use of allegory confronted the indigenous audience with one of the most problematic figures
of Western visual and representational culture. In allegory, a concept or
abstract idea is personified but, although speaking and interacting like a person, is not to be thought or interpreted as such but rather as *allos* (other), as
a mode of saying in which something else is always meant. Allegory requires
then a specific relationship of negation vis-à-vis conventions of language
and meaning that should not be assumed will be readily upheld by an audience with little exposure to Western symbolic and dramatic modes of
expression.[3] It may be argued that what was important to the friar conceiving the piece was the enunciation of warnings and admonitions to behave
as "proper" Christian subjects, and that to consider the referential complexities of allegory was superfluous and marginal to such ends. One could,
however, reply that if the depiction of specific doctrinal meanings had been

the only interest of the friars, they could have preached to the Nahuas in the form of the florid huehuetlatolli or "speech of the elders," which the Nahuas knew so well. However, it can and must be assumed that the missionary author (or coauthor) had a specific concern for doctrinal efficacy that he must have felt was best achieved by having recourse to allegory and that the understanding of this figure by the indigenous audience was, if not necessarily central, still an important element in the attainment of desired didactic effects.[4] Perhaps, as part of the program to produce a proper Christian subject from the Nahua, the Franciscans concluded that they had to reeducate the native "idolatrous" gaze in which "la chose représentée et ce qui la représente...tendent à se confondre, à se télescoper davantage dans l'idole que dans l'image (sainte)" [the thing represented and that which represents it...have the tendency to confuse themselves, to merge more in the idol than in the (saintly) image] (Gruzinski, *Guerre*, 80). Fray Andrés del Olmos or the Franciscan playwright may have decided that allegory, a figure that underscored difference and negation between signifier and signified, could be the most appropiate for the task. In any case, the use of allegory is revealing of difficult hermeneutical and perceptual demands made of the Nahua audience to this play, particularly if it was written as early as so many critics have held.[5]

What do these alien allegorical figures talk about among themselves that the missionaries thought the Nahuas should watch and listen to attentively? The figures are all distressed by the fact that the people of the world do not want to abandon their evil doings and because of this their lives will end very soon. Each allegorical figure relates how s/he has supplicated that the people mend their ways before it is too late. Penance cries out that the people will no longer be able to be saved from their sins for they have forgotten their Lord, and life on earth is already over (Sell and Burkhart, 191). Holy Church, however, states that she is the keeper of the seventh sacrament, matrimony, and that she will urge the people once again to receive it (ibid., 193). Scholars of the Nahua evangelization theater have agreed that the didactic and/or "edifying" goal of this play was the erradication of polygamy, which was widely practiced by the indigenous nobility in pre-Hispanic times (Ravicz, 141; Williams, *Teatro*, 53; Gruzinski, *Guerre*, 133).

The scene ends with Death lamenting that Judgment Day will be the next day and then it will be too late for repentance and mercy (Sell and Burkhart, 195).

In the next scene, after the sounds of wind instruments and the exit of Death and Confession, a woman named Lucía decides to confess so that her greatly afflicted soul may be relieved of its sins:

> Oh, O my deity, O my ruler, Jesus Christ! How unfortunate I am! What is happening to me now? It is as if my soul is now oppressed. It is as if it is now entering among the clouds! And what am I going to do now? Let me go, let me confess. Perhaps thus my soul will be a bit calmed. Let me go, let me look for my confessor. Perhaps that will ease my soul a little. I'll go now and look for my confessor. For my face, my heart are really aching! (ibid., 197)

According to Horcasitas, Ravicz, and Sell's respective translations of the neixcuitilli's stage directions, it is not clear whether the morrow of Judgment Day announced by Death in the previous scene has indeed arrived, or whether Lucía has been persuaded by Time, Confession, and the Holy Church to repent and confess. In any case, the priest receives her contrite request gladly: "O my beloved child, what I hear pleases me greatly. Your sins worry you, they oppress you. Let us go into the temple-home of our lord God" (ibid., 197). But while hearing the confession (which, possibly to underscore the secrecy of the sacrament, is not heard by the audience), he stands aback horrified and exclaims that there is nothing he can do to save her: "Why did you never receive the sacrament of marriage? Just to the Devil you sent the seventh holy sacrament…400-times unfortunate are you! …What you will merit will be suffering in the place of the dead. And now what accounting will you give to your deity, your ruler? For in no way can you help yourself now, because it is already time, God's judgment has arrived" (ibid., 199).

Lucía has most probably confessed that she has been living in concubinage or that she is a prostitute. The priest invokes the imminence of Judgment Day as the reason why it is too late for Lucía to help herself for not having observed the sacrament of marriage. He departs scandalized, abandoning the penitent to her fate. Leaving aside the problems of the spectators of a performance as "the final and only guarantors of the culture which reaches them, whether it be foreign or familiar" and how such a reception could split the source culture (Pavis, 19), one could nonetheless observe in the quoted passage how the process of subjecting the other altered the colonizing self. The priest's explanation for his repudiation of Lucía is unacceptable, since he had already agreed to hear her confession, in spite of knowing that the end of the world was at hand. Martín de Azpilcueta's *Manual de confesores y penitentes* was one of the most influential confessional manuals written in the Iberian peninsula in the sixteenth century, having had eighty-two editions in Spanish, Latin, Portuguese, French, and Italian between 1553 and 1620 (Haliczer, *Sexuality*, 9, 43). In this manual, the confessor is admonished first to inquire about and consider any impediments for which he may not be able to absolve the penitent, lest the latter will not complain later saying: "Quesisteis oyr mis pecados y no me quereis absolver" [You agreed to hear my sins but do not want to absolve me] (Azpilcueta, 56).[6] Thus, Azcpilcueta's authoritative position supports the argument that if the priest in the neixcuitilli thought that the imminence of Judgment Day would not allow the penitent to show the fruits of penance with the contrite acts of a new reformed life and that this constituted an impediment for absolution, he should never have accepted listening to Lucía's confession.

The priest's scandalized behavior is also improper. Since the Middle Ages confessors had been frequently admonished never to show horror, revulsion, or contempt at the penitent both for compassion and lest the latter would feel so ashamed, s/he would not dare to confess all sins and the confession would be invalid (Tentler, 94–95). Moreover, if the penitent was repentant, worse sins than concubinage or prostitution (such as incest, murder, rape, bestiality) could be forgiven, although a more severe penance might be imposed or the penitent be sent to an episcopal authority to be absolved unless s/he were close to death. In order to produce proper Christian subjects of the Nahua people, whom the spiritual colonizers had construed as "un poco rudas y un tanto pueriles, no muy capaces de llegar a la virtud desinteresada" [somewhat unpolished and childish, not very capable of attaining disinterested virtue] (Ricard, 314), the relationship between confessor and penitent in the sacrament of confession was unduly rigorous in *Final Judgment*, as Mendoza López convincingly argued in 1941. The Mexican scholar points out that the allegorical figures of Time and the Church in their respctive speeches state that there is still time for people to repent (9–10). In fact, Time goes off to "remind them each hour [so that] they will remember what they will do so that they will not squander and not waste the lifetimes that our lord God entrusted to me" (Sell and Burkhart, 195). Thus, Mendoza López sees as problematic the priest's refusal to absolve Lucía on the grounds that time is up, since the end of the world has not yet arrived. The violence of the rhetoric of repudiation employed in the neixcuitilli to subject the imagined subalterns by triggering in them terror of destruction impinges on the colonialist discourse producing displacements and reversals that estrange such discourse from itself. By having a priest hear a penitent whom he thought beforehand could not be absolved because time was already up, the neixcuitilli falls into the contradiction of portraying the urgings to repentance of the allegorical characters (particularly Time, Sweeping, and Holy Church), Lucía's regret, and the sacrament of penance all as being pointless.

But perhaps there is something here even more disturbing than the impropriety of the confessor's demeanor vis-à-vis the "sinful" other or the futility of repentance and confession. The canon of the cathedral of Salamanca, Pedro Ciruelo, who had written about the Devil's intrigues in America (Pagden, *Fall*, 175), published a confessional manual in 1514. Assuming a clear Thomist position, Ciruelo defines despair in this text as a sin against hope, which is incurred when "por arrimarse mucho el hombre a la justicia de dios:olvidando su misericordia:y negando la condicion necessaria en la virtud dela esperança... Este pecado dela desesperacion es mucho mayor que el dela presuncion:porque niega la misericordia que es muy mas natural propriedad e dios que la justicia" [when man draws too near to God's justice forgetting his mercy: and denying the necessary condition of the virtue of hope... This sin of despair is much greater than that of presumption because it denies mercy, a much more natural property of God than justice] (Ciruelo, A8r). By leaning excessively on God's justice, "a less rather than more natural property of the divinity," one incurs a graver sin than hoping for too much leniency, which is presumption (Aquinas, *Summa,* 2:478–80). And this is precisely what happens with Lucía. After having been denied absolution on the dubious grounds discussed above, she exclaims, "May presumptuousness be despised! What have I done? What did presumptuousness avail me? May the earth and time be despised! Now the world is about to come to an end, about to be finished off. 400-times unfortunate am I! I am a great sinner!"(Sell and Burkhart, 199). In the soliloquy preceding the scene with the confessor, the reasons Lucía gives to herself for desiring to confess do not reveal an unequivocal awareness of the imminent end of time, which would be what would have tarnished such a desire with the hope for too much leniency. The motivating factors stated in that passage are feelings of spiritual malaise and discomfort.[7]

But even if Lucía had been indeed presumptuous in trying to be forgiven for her sins right before time was up, according to Aquinas and Ciruelo's passages, her despair unleashed by the priest's repudiation would be even more sinful than presumption or immoderate hope. Thus, by his scandalized, stern, if not cruel reaction, the priest in the neixcuitilli facilitates rather than obstructs the proliferation of sin in the last moments of the world. By plunging Lucía into total despair by his refusal to absolve her because time was up, he surely forecloses all possibilities of salvation for her. The imperative to chastise, humiliate, and denigrate the other because of her insubordination and (constructed) iniquity does not bring about, then, only the reaffirmation of the colonizer's supremacy and power. In the neixcuitilli *Final Judgment* such an imperative to suppress otherness also ends up cleaving the colonial discourse by having it divert from its own claims to truth and authority and by having it produce the opposite effects of what it intended.

In the next scene, "The living enter. They sit on the ground, along with Lucía.... The Antichrist enters" (ibid., 199). After a short exchange with the Antichrist in which Lucía in her despair falls for his false claims of being the savior, Christ enters followed by Saint Michael and confers with him regarding the end of the world. The living are then called to come forth and the dead are revived. Three living and two dead persons stand before

Christ, and their final judgment begins.[8] Those who admit not having served Christ during their lifetime are irremediably condemned since He twice declares that forgiveness is now no longer possible. Not surprisingly, Lucía forms part of this group and she is pushed offstage by the demons. Christ then asks the third living person what had moved his heart throughout his life: "Come, you who were a living person on earth. What is giving your heart such pains? Is it my sacred word? Did you go about crying out to me when you were sleeping and when you were going about?" (Sell and Burkhart, 205).

The demands are undoubtedly exacting. The judged person is expected to have fulfilled perfectly the commandment of loving God above everything else to the point of having invoked Christ even during sleep. That is, he is required to have had a devout and alert disposition of mind toward his creator even while he was in repose; to have been in possession of himself, even while such self had faded out. And yet, this demand of remembering God at all times is deemed impossible to fulfill by theologian Azpilcueta: "Pero todos [los cuatro evangelistas] se conforman en el sentido y quieren en suma dezir, que manda Dios que lo amemos total, y enteramente: no de tal manera: que a todas las horas, y momentos pensemos en el, y lo amemos: Porque imposible es hazer esto en esta vida mortal, que tiene necesidad de comer, dormir, trabajar, y negociar" [But all of them [the four evangelists] conform to the meaning and want to say that God commands us to love him fully and entirely but not in such a way that at all times, and at all moments we will be thinking about him and loving him. For it is impossible to do such a thing in this mortal life, in which one has the need to eat, sleep, work and conduct business] (*Manual*, 61).

However, perhaps for the Franciscan playwright Christ's onerous demand of the judged person could refer to those monastic ascetic practices in which religious men and women woke up at midnight to pray matins and, in doing so, indeed may be thought as invoking Christ half-asleep. In any case, Christ's demand would also seem to mirror those of the Nahua pre-Hispanic deities who also exacted from humans constant ritual attention. Sahagún himself establishes a similarity between these pre-Hispanic and Christian religious practices when he documents that in the feast for the tlatoque, or gods of the rain, the priests woke up one hour before midnight "y tañían cornetas y caracoles y otros instrumentos, *como tañendo maitines*" [and they blowed trumpets and shells and other instruments, as if they were summoning for matins] (Sahagún, *Historia*, 1:124; the emphasis is mine).[9] At other times, they would go to icy lakes to bathe during the night (ibid.). This was also the time when the people would offer blood from their ears to the gods. In Jacques Soustelle's beautiful words, "The dark hours of the dreaded yet alluring night offered their cover for the most sacred rites...at no time was the dark vault of the sky without its human observer—the anxious watch for a tomorrow that might never come" (162). In this sense, the strategy of representing the terrifying Christ of the Apocalypse demanding attention and devotion at all times ironically may have deployed continuities with the frightening, exacting deities of the pre-Hispanic past still alive in the cultural memory of the audience.

This particular incarnated dead person attests to his pious (and hardly possible) vigilance both in wakefulness and slumber and is rewarded with salvation figured in a necklace of flowers. However, the overall consequences of the apocalyptic Christ's severe demands are truly draconian. Three of the five represented trials in the play end in eternal damnation. That is, more than half the people of the world are represented as not having been able or willing to keep the divine commandments. The demons are then called upon to drag the disobedient down to Mictlan, the Nahua name for the place of the dead, to punish them forever. The irony of this catastrophic situation for the discourse of the colonizer is dramatized in Satan's joyful disposition to obey, at long last, the wrathful Christ. The evil one now promptly runs onstage bringing thorns of red hot metal to whip his new servants: "I am bringing everything right here with which we will tie them up so that no one will flee from our hands. Now we have our drink and our food, there in the depths of the place of the dead. We exerted all our efforts so that our servants fell in our hands" (Sell and Burkhart, 207).

A very ambivalent situation can be seen to arise then in the neixcuitilli *Final Judgment* from the point of view of the discourse of the colonizer. Christ's taxing (and unmet) demands reward the efforts of the devils who had worked incessantly to merit His creatures in order to be fed and served by them in the underworld. The supreme irony of this situation is perhaps best expressed by a lesser demon: "O our lord, we thank you. We are certain that we have just been going about waiting for your coming. We are fortunate! Your precious heart has been very generous. May we merit your creations" (Sell and Burkhart, 205). The devils are flooded with gratitude for having been bequeathed more than half of the Lord's precious creatures to serve their master. Thus, Christ's justice in the neixcuitilli is represented as favoring the interests of evil! In punishing a disobedient (Nahua) humanity so severely, the Savior has become Satan's greatest ally! In the joyful praises of the lesser demons, the play's harsh and terrifying rhetoric, whether wittingly or unwittingly, is subverted.[10] Just as in the case of the repudiating confessor, the colonialist discourse embodied now in the apocalyptic figure of Christ suffers an unexpected reversal; for at the very moment of revealing its frightening power to intimidate, punish, and destroy, the discourse ends up preserving the very same forces it claimed to combat.

Since the friars had assiduously insisted that pre-Hispanic deities were diabolical entities, Satan's remark about having drink and food at his dwelling place could have sparked some connections for the audience.[11] Nahuas had constructed their sacrificial practices in pre-Hispanic times as nourishment owed to their gods by humans (Bernard and Gruzinski, 97–98; López Austin, Human, 1:79–83). Sacrificial eating was what assured the motion of life (Read, 132). It is fairly established that the Mexica believed that the "sun near the earth," or tlalchitonatiuh, needed to be fed human hearts and blood in order to enable it to rise up and move out from the underworld (Krickeberg, 158). But not only was the sun in need of nourishment for its subsistence, "all gods needed food, particularly the gods of water" (González Torres, 84; translation is mine) since in the Mexica ever-changing order of things, for one being to eat and live, another one had to die (Read, 136).

Similarly, the deities of the underworld, Mictlantecuhtli and his wife, Mictecacihuatl, in order to live, ate "the feet and hands of [dead] people. Their stew is made of beetles who live in moist places, their tamales are imbued with gas also passed by beetles, and their atole is made of pus which they drink from a skull"(Read, 136). In spite of their repugnant eating habits, however, the lord and lady of Mictlan were not conceived by the Nahuas to be evil. They were the natural counterpart to the processes of life and generation (Burkhart, *Slippery*, 51). Thus, the gratitude of the devils in the neixcuitilli for having been granted servants who would provide them with food, their eager disposition to obey Christ's commands, and their representation of Christ as their generous Lord and benefactor, not as their enemy, might have been interpreted by the Nahua audience as something quite in line with their old, lingering conception of the cosmos as a balancing act of transformation and exchange between all forces, which now also included those brought into the land by the Christian deities.[12]

In the last scene of the play, a priest comes out to beseech the audience to learn from what they have just seen. "Rouse yourselves, look at yourselves in the mirror, the way it happened to your neighbor. And may it not happen to you in the same way"(Sell and Burkhart, 209). The priest concludes his speech by saying that the end of the world will indeed be very soon for all, and, therefore, the Nahuas should pray to the Virgin Mary that she plead to her Son that they may be saved. This notion of salvation had no counterpart in the indigenous worldview, since for the Nahuas the greatest number of people went to Mictlan regardless of the way they had lived (López Austin, *Human*, 1:328–36 and *Tlalocan*, 261; Burkhart, *Slippery*, 51). The stage directions in the play do not indicate whether this is the priest who refused to absolve Lucía or a second priest. Thus, it is hard to ascertain how the disruption of the dramatic illusion was actually marked in the script and on stage. In any case, from the standpoint of the spiritual colonizer, the passage may be said to be metatextual at least in the sense that the representational quality of the viewed performance is figured as a mirror upon which the public can (and should) project their own images, so as to avoid a similar fate.[13] The deictic representation of time as a here and now, as well as the direct address to the audience also can be said to mark a different referential status and/or context of enunciation.

And yet, the discernment of such referential distinctions is hard to anticipate, predict, or control, particularly in a culturally different audience as were the Nahuas. It is quite possible that they were confused (rather than edified) by the play's referential status, not knowing how or what to make out of the dreadful neixcuitilli. For the mix of allegorical, live, supernatural, and dead-yet-come-back-to-life characters, as well as of the fictive or real priest who preaches to the audience from the stage, makes the figural status of the play a very complex issue. Ironically, then, the *difficulty* of interpreting such mixed forms for the Nahua audience may have perhaps facilitated rather than displaced an "idolatrous" reception where image and referent were not differentiated according to the constraints of a Christian gaze and subjectivity.

To sum up, perhaps most relevant to our analysis of this dramatic text as a partially failed strategy of subjection is the non-oppositional or even harmonious relationship between Christ and the demons in the neixcuitilli. As was discussed above, the representations of the (apocalyptic) inclemency of Christ and the confessor, as well as the doomsday rhetoric of the allegorical characters intended to intimidate the Nahua other into a proper Christian subjectivity, produce a reversal. Not only do they bring out what for us may be the darkest, exclusionary, and almost cruel vectors of that very same subjectivity, but, more significantly, the apocalyptic Christ of the Franciscan colonial evangelization theater is addressed by grateful, devout demons as their great benefactor, not their destroyer.[14] And if the Nahuas had been urged by the diligent friars to associate Satan and his lesser devils with their own pre-Hispanic deities, the audience may have been gratified to see that their own deities' nourishment and survival were secured in the post-conquest world by the new Christian deity itself.[15]

From the perspective of the spiritual colonizer, the forces of good in *Final Judgment* may have been read as excluding, eradicating, and punishing depravity, just as the Christian Spaniards had subjected and destroyed the satanic cults of the innumerable idolatrous people of the Mexican plateau.[16] But as we have seen, this pro-colonial, pro-Christian, self-promoting, quasi-propagandistic meaning cracks under an unexpected displacement of the power deployed and under the consequent conservation of otherness. The colonialist power to crush "malevolent" difference and alterity turns around against itself, for it ends up supporting that which, according to itself, opposes and negates it. Since this rift could not have possibly been part of the didactic intentionality of the evagelization theater, we can propose at least two hypotheses that may account for it. The first is that the "cultural automatisms of the gaze" (Bernard and Gruzinski, 75) of the friar composing the auto (or parts of it) prevented him from considering the heterogeneous and hybrid readings that his own authoritative narratives could produce when addressing the natives. As Homi Bhabha has pointed out, hybridity comes from within the very colonial exercise of power itself "not merely to indicate the impossibility of its identity but to represent the unpredictability of its presence" (*Location*, 114). It is as if at the very moment of fully deploying the power of the colonialist discourse to annihilate the heterogeneity, disobedience, and resistance of the other, the suppressed unexpectedly returned, hybridizing and estranging the images and representations of authority, as the other tried to make sense of the claims of the colonizer through his own indigenous worldview.

The second hypothesis is that, as Miguel León-Portilla, James Lockhart, Max Harris, Louise Burkhart, and Barry Sell have proposed, the friars were not the only agents involved in the production of the dramatic scripts of the Nahua evangelization theater. The disruptive irony of the grateful devils that could correspond to an indigenous conception of the cosmos as a balanced play between forces of creation and destruction might be evidence of interventions of resistance by the Nahuas. According to León-Portilla, they were determined to preserve in the brave new world of colonialism "su milenaria concepción de sí mismos, su tiempo y espacio sagrados, su propia historia, raíz de su identidad" [their millenarian conception of themselves, their sacred time and space, their own history, the root of their identity] ("Insertos," 193). To support his argument, León-Portilla reminds us that as early as 1539 some ecclesiastical authorities had already started to be deeply suspicious of the Nahua evangelization theater, to the extreme of demanding the prohibition of representations during Church holidays ("Insertos," 195). Such suspicions support the hypothesis that the native collaborators, editors, and/or coauthors, in their efforts to preserve their pre-Hispanic identities, may have subtly inscribed their voices in this play of the evangelization theater.

The two hypotheses expounded above may account for the different moments of hybridization that our reading of the neixcuitilli of *Final Judg-*

ment has uncovered. The diversions and reversals of the discourse of colonialist authority may be brought about at different locations in the text both by the colonizer's address to an audience of his imagined subalterns and by the native's subtle appropriation, perversion, and ultimately Nahuatizing of the neixcuitilli's discourse of terror. *Final Judgment* stands, therefore, as a good example of the ambivalence of colonial discursive power and authority. It makes it difficult to think about the colonial evangelization theater only as a reenactment of subjection totally controlled by the colonizer. It resists the dismissal of the capacity of the native culture to accommodate, transform, and preserve itself under the new and dreary colonial circumstances. It belies the power of colonial authority to fully satisfy its desire to impose, repress, and destroy at will. It dramatizes the impossibility of the discourses of domination to remain untainted by and impermeable to the gaze of the other. For even though it presented the triumphal and terrifying image of the capacity of colonialist might to bring about the end of time and the punishment of the people, the neixcuitilli *Final Judgment* may also have been celebrating for the Nahua audience the survival of the gods of Anahuac and their power to adopt new names, shapes, and forms in an ever-changing world.

4

A Judeo-Christian Tlaloc or a Nahua Yahweh? Domination, Hybridity, and Continuity in the Nahua Evangelization Theater [1]

n Motolinía's account of the splendid 1539 Corpus Christi festivities in Tlaxcala, there is a brief mention of a play of the sacrifice of Abraham as one of the four autos performed that year: "Thereupon, the Most Holy Sacrament passing on, there followed another state play. It was the sacrifice of Abraham. It was short, the time already being afternoon. So nothing is said about it, except that it was very well staged" (Motolinía, *History*, 167). A manuscript of a neixcuitilli with this theme has survived; it was entitled *Del naSimiento De iSaac, del Sacrificio q.ᵉ habrahan Su Padre quiso por mandado de Dios hazer* [Of the birth of Isaac and of the sacrifice that his father Abraham wanted to make by order of God]. This text, dated 1760, is believed to be a copy of a 1678 manuscript, as attested by its copyist Bernabé Vázquez in a note at the end of the play. Fernando Horcasitas has hypothesized that the original must have been from the sixteenth century, not the seventeenth, since the rich metaphoric language of the extant copy harks back to a much earlier date than 1678 (191). Because there is no other mention in any chronicle besides Motolinía's of another performance of a neixcuitilli about Abraham's story, Horcasitas proposes that the extant manuscript could be a copy of the dramatic text for the 1538 performance that Motolinía mentions in his *Historia* (191). Barry D. Sell also postulates that the original manuscript of *The Sacrifice of Isaac* could have been composed in the sixteenth century.[2] Moreover, he hypothesizes that *The Sacrifice* was one of a group of dramatic pieces that the Franciscan nahuatlato fray Juan Bautista and his Nahua coauthor Agustín de la Fuente compiled and

reworked in order to publish them in a three-volume collection of come-
dias early in the seventeenth century. The latter never saw the light and the
manuscript containing the collection, if one was ever finalized, is lost (Sell,
"Nahuatl," 15).

An anonymous Spanish auto on this theme appears in the Spanish collection of the *Códice de autos viejos* entitled *El sacrificio de Abraham*.[3] However, even if it was a *refundición,* or reworking, of an earlier play, it is unlikely that *El sacrificio de Abraham* would have been a source text for the
neixcuitilli because of significant differences in the plot. The episode of
Hagar and Ishmael, for instance, is suppressed completely in *the Spanish
auto.* Prefiguring the sprightly *gracioso* or comic figure of the seventeenth-
century Spanish Golden Age theater, the character of the fool in the Spanish
play appears even in the pathos-ridden scene where Abraham travels with
Isaac to Mount Moriah. This character is absent from the neixcuitilli *The
Sacrifice of Isaac,* which is solemn and serious in tone with little relief of
dramatic tension.

Although there are narrative variations and deleted episodes in *The Sacrifice,* it is not in the act of adaptation itself where the ambivalence of the
colonizer's strategies of power becomes most visible in the dramatic text of
this neixcuitilli. In fact, one could argue that the adaptation of the biblical
story is more evident in the non-colonial Spanish auto. The fracture of colonialist power will emerge in this play in the context of representing the
appalling biblical episode of the Akedah (or the binding of Isaac) to the
Nahua spectator, in order to subject him to the universal Christian model.
Marco De Marinis's semiotic concept of the "implied receiver" of a dramatic text is useful in considering this point. De Marinis's "implied receiver,"
which derives from Umberto Eco's Model Reader, entails "a strategy of
interpretive cooperation 'foreseen' by the text's transmission and variously
inscribed within it" (6). The implied receiver in this case, of course, will be
the Nahua spectator. What is interesting and productive about De Marinis's
category is that it allows us to distinguish formally between how the colonizer may have imagined or anticipated the Nahua other as an addressee of
the dramatic text and how this other may have actually received such a text.
In this chapter, I will be dealing mostly with the telling contradictions in

the Spanish colonialist discourse of the sixteenth century as it addresses the Nahua subject as implied receiver of this most problematic Judeo-Christian story.

The Sacrifice of Isaac is divided into two parts. The first deals with the expulsion of Hagar and Ishmael from Abraham's household.[4] Hagar was Sarah's handmaid. Seeing herself barren, Sarah had her maid bear a son to Abraham, who was Ishmael. A few years later, after finally giving birth to Isaac, Sarah urged Abraham to send Hagar and Ishmael away (Gen. 21). Following the biblical episode (and much as in the Spanish auto), the neix-cuitilli represents a feast offered in honor of Isaac. Albeit never stated explicitly in the Mexican play, this feast may be posited to be in celebration of Isaac's weaning, since Sarah refers twice to her breast milk (Sell and Burkhart, 147), and this is the stated motive of the celebration in the biblical episode: "And the child grew and was weaned: and Abraham made a great feast on the day of his weaning" (Gen. 21:8). According to archeological evidence in burial sites in Israel, it has been speculated that because infant mortality rates were high at the time of Abraham, children were not weaned until their third year. The feast was "chiefly to celebrate their surviving the most dangerous period in their lives" (Dennis, 58). Although it is not certain that the Nahuas celebrated publicly the weaning of their children, it also took place during the third year and sometimes even later (Vaillant, 116; Clendinnen, *Aztecs*, 155, 188–92). Thus, it can be argued that the Nahua audience could have related culturally to the importance of the weaning celebration in the play; for them it also marked the induction of children into adult life in their tightly corporate, highly structured society.

Witnessing the arrangements for the feast, both Hagar and Ishmael become jealous, feeling unjustly excluded and ignored. The Devil appears to Ishmael and convinces him to make Isaac humiliate his parents by leaving the banquet in his honor to go out and play. Having been discovered trying to persuade Isaac to disobey, Sarah demands that both Ishmael and his mother be expelled from the household. As has been pointed out by scholars of Nahua studies, the obedience and education of children were chief concerns in Mesoamerican societies, which frequently practiced the public physical humiliation of its members as punishment for social infractions

(Clendinnen, *Aztecs*, 132). The Nahuas would verbally admonish children to obey until the age of eight, after which severe corporal punishment would be inflicted upon the recalcitrant child (Soustelle, 168; Vaillant, 116–17). In many *huehuetlatolli*, or "speech of elders" collected by the Franciscan Bernardino de Sahagún, parents are represented as earnestly exhorting their children to obey and respect their seniors as the only way of securing recognition from others in the future (*Florentine*, 7:87–92). According to this evidence, it may be safely assumed that the Nahua audience would be able to grasp the great shame, evil, and disgrace Ishmael was plotting to bring upon Isaac by inducing him to defy his parents publicly the day of the celebration.

Suppressed in the neixcuitilli is Abraham's regret over his son Ishmael's fate and God's consequent intervention to persuade him to obey Sarah's rigorous demand. Abraham is urged to listen to her in the Nahua play, but by the lords invited to the feast, who tell him that both Hagar and Ishmael have indeed brought dishonor upon God and upon Abraham (Sell and Burkhart, 155). Though the fact that Ishmael is Abraham's son is suggested in passing (ibid., 153), the suppression of Abraham's great sorrow over the exile of mother and son would seem to support the opinion of those critics who argue that the dramatic text wisely avoids the problem of Abraham's extramarital relation (Paso y Troncoso, 4–5; Ricard, 314; Ravicz, 83–4; Williams, *Teatro*, 73).[5] This is not unthinkable in a colonial context where the friars had been struggling with the thorny and delicate issue of polygamy among the indigenous upper classes.[6]

After hearing Abraham's sentence, Hagar weeps bitterly over the great shame she has brought upon herself and her son for not having raised him properly (Sell and Burkhart, 155). By suppressing God's intervention in persuading Abraham, as well as God's subsequent rescue of the banished in the desert, the biblical episode of Hagar and Ishmael (to whom great descent was also promised by God) is contained and translated in the Nahua play into the more culturally akin problems of disobedience, social shame, and exile. Thus, the first part of *The Sacrifice of Isaac* renders no new dramatic examples upon which the audience should model their behavior in order to serve the colonial god. The polished linguistic demeanor of the cast of

Judeo-Christian characters in the play is not represented as other to the sophisticated *pipiltin*, or Nahua nobility. In this sense, the linguistic proto-col codes of Abraham and Sarah do not operate as signs of new models of conduct to be imposed upon the Nahua in order to produce a proper Chris-tian subject out of him. The biblical couple are not only part of an edifying dramatic text "carefully adapted [by the colonizer] to the spiritual and tem-peramental character of the Indians and to their religious situation" (Lopétegui and Zubillaga, 415; translation is mine). Abraham and Sarah's Nahuatized linguistic and social demeanor is also the performance-sign of the appropriation of their story by the indigenous culture. Hybridization occurs, then, already at the material level of the dramatic text, for just by having them speak in Nahuatl, the Judeo-Christian biblical figures are already inserted into the linguistic world and system of the Nahuas. By representing Abraham as a sophisticated, polite, ceremonious Nahua lord of an altepetl,[7] the Nahuas display their cultural paradigms as able to couch and accommodate the foreign models. Hence, rather than put forth the imperative to break away from the pre-Hispanic past altogether, the first part of *The Sacrifice of Isaac* establishes important cultural and social continu-ities with it.

And yet, confining the banishment of Ishmael and Hagar to an episode of social disgrace as well as inserting Abraham and Sarah within indige-nous social conventions that harked back to the pre-Hispanic past are not the most salient moments of hybridity in this neixcuitilli. Much more signifi-cant in this regard will be the tremendous and exacting demand put forth by the Judeo-Christian deity in the second part of the play. Biblical interpreters have grappled for a long time with the patriarch of the Jews, Christians, and Muslims, but Abraham's story has hitherto not received a definite, sat-isfactory interpretation (Arieti, 129).[8] In the colonial context of the Nahua evangelization theater, the already disquieting biblical story will acquire fur-ther unsettling inflections by revealing similarities between the piety of the chosen patriarch of the Judeo-Christian god and that of the subaltern Nahua subject of pre-Hispanic times.

The first scene of the second part of the play opens with the figure of God the Father. After laying his claim to all created beings, he declares that "all the people of the earth" (Sell and Burkhart, 157) will obey his commands and subject themselves to his sovereign will. Abraham then comes onstage, politely but earnestly praying to God concerning Isaac's fate, since he is very worried his son will not obey God as he should. Just like the admonishing fathers in the huehuetlatolli recorded by Sahagún, Abraham's passage conveys a strong fatherly concern for the fulfillment of his son's religious duties. It also indicates that Abraham, the main character of the neixcuitilli, properly remembers his God and treats Him with utmost deference, even fearing the unlikely eventuality that his son might not satisfactorily abide by His will. As an answer to his prayers and devoted concern, however, God the Father calls on Abraham and demands that he sacrifice his beloved Isaac to Him: "If it is true that you can carry out my sacred commands, seize your child named Isaac whom you greatly love and take him to the top of the mountain in the place named Moriah. There you are to kill him. If truly you carry out my sacred command, my heart will be satisfied" (Sell and Burkhart, 157).

The violence of the demand being put forth by the Judeo-Christian god is orthodoxly restrained in the scene in question as a test of obedience for an evidently righteous man. According to Derrida ("Donner la mort," 65) Abraham's instant acquiescence, his readiness to do things that "doivent révolter ceux qui se réclament de la morale en général, de la morale judéo-chrétienne-islamique ou de la religion de l'amour en général" [should horrify all those who profess morality in general, Judeo-Christian-Islamic morality, or the morality of the religion of love in general] is thus represented in the dramatic text as part of the patriarch's exemplary faithful demeanor: "I will carry out your command. I intend to do it for you, the All-powerful, whose words I hear, are eternally worthy of being believed" (Sell and Burkhart, 157). Such a representation is in accordance with the Jewish theology of Abraham as a faithful and honorable man, "deeming that nothing would justify disobedience to God and that in everything he should submit to his will" (Josephus, *Antiquities of the Jews*, 1.225, quoted in Siker, 23). It is also in conformity with the Pauline conception of Abraham as father of all those who have faith in God (Rom. 4:16–19), and who never doubt His promise. However, in the colonial context of sixteenth-century Mexico, Abraham's total obedience acquires unexpected, hybrid meanings. For according to the friars' own ethnographical constructions of Nahua pre-His-panic ritual and sacrificial practices, Abraham's submission to his God would not have been particularly extraordinary to the implied Nahua audi-ence of the dramatic text. Earlier in the first treatise where Motolinía refers to the 1538 Corpus Christi festivities during which *The Sacrifice of Isaac* was performed, he discusses the calendrical feast to the revered Tlaloc, ancient Mesoamerican god of rain and water, to whom the Nahuas sacrificed children:

> Once a year when the corn was a palm high, a feast was held in the towns where the chief lord resided and where his house was called a palace. On the appointed day the Indians sacrificed a boy and a girl about three or four years of age. *These were not slaves, but the children of chiefs, and the sacrifice was performed on a hill* out of reverence to the idol, who, they said, was the god of water and who gave them the rain, and whom they invoked when there was lack of water. (Motolinía, *History,* 118–119; emphasis is mine)

Bernardino de Sahagún records that as the children were paraded on their way to death, the people who came out to watch cried. If the little victims kept shedding tears, this was taken as a good sign that it would rain very soon (*Florentine,* 3:44).

A couple of scenes later, Abraham, as a Nahua pilli, or nobleman, arrives with his beloved Isaac also on a hilltop, where the sacrifice is to take place. Just like the Nahuas had cried for the paraded children to be offered to Tlaloc, the disconsolate lord sheds copious tears as he explains to Isaac that God has asked for his sacrifice in order to prove their obedience to his will (Sell and Burkhart, 159). This depiction of Abraham's immense sor-row (an amplification on the biblical source) surely works within the dramat-ic text as a strategy to underscore his exemplary, pious determination to carry out God's command. However, it also reveals the inordinate suffering the violence of the deity's command provokes in Abraham. In the pain inflicted upon loyal worshippers, the god of the spiritual colonizers does not seem to differ much from the arbitrariness of the god Tezcatlipoca who, according to Sahagún: "Daba riquezas, prosperidades y fama, y fortaleza y ... honras, *y las quitaba cuando se le antojaba.* Por esto le temían y le reverenciaban, porque tenían que en su mano estaba el levantar y abatir" [He gave wealth, prosperity and fame, and valor and...honors, *and took them away at his whim.* This is why they feared and revered him, because they believed it was in his hand to raise or bring down] (Sahagún, *Historia,* 1:38; emphasis is mine). Did the friars expect the audience to relate to Abraham's inordinate suffering at the hilltop without harking back to their own not-so-remote pre-Hispanic sacrificial practices? Did they think Abraham's exemplary obedience to God would produce meaning for the Nahuas without activating a collective memory of the unwavering disposition of their ancestors to feed the pre-Hispanic deities, sometimes with the precious blood of their very own children? What may be most disconcerting here is how the friars' Eurocentrism may have blinded them to the plurality of meanings procured by the perceptible similarities between the sacrifice of the boy Isaac[9] and those manifold, yearly sacrifices to Tlaloc in which only the children of the pipiltin would be offered, and which also took place on mountaintops surrounded by clouds (Brundage, 70–101).

Following closely the biblical story, only when the knife is already descending toward Isaac, only at the very instant when Abraham is about to kill his son, is he released from the imperative to obey the deity's appalling will in the Nahua play. An angel appears and explains that God understands now that Abraham loves him by his willingness to kill his beloved son in order to fulfill the divine precept. The angel then declares Abraham is to sacrifice a lamb instead of his child, but this is never represented dramatically. Horcasitas points out that the restatement of the prohibition of human sacrifice by the Franciscans would explain the dissimulation of the animal sacrifice (189). Jerry Williams and Marilyn E. Ravicz propose that the angel's intervention to stop Isaac's execution served to announce to the Nahua public that still believed in such practices that the Christian god was benevolent since he rejected all human sacrifice (Williams, *Teatro*, 73–4; Ravicz, 97). Though these readings may very well explicate the dramatic text's most immediate didactic intent to its implied receivers, by now it should be apparent that such interpretations do not exhaust the perplexing complexities, similarities, and paradoxes raised by the specific Nahua context of reception. For if the friars wished to ingrain in the minds of the indigenous spectators the Christian prohibition against human sacrifice, they seriously overlooked the fact that in the Akedah episode in the Bible and in the play, it is clearly the Judeo-Christian god himself who demands such a sacrifice from Abraham as proof of his devotion. And not content with Abraham's disposition to perform the sacrifice, it is only at the very moment that the sacrifice is to be consummated that it is finally interrupted. From the moment when Abraham slowly walks to and climbs up Mount Moriah, as he dutifully cuts the firewood and later ties and blindfolds Isaac, to the awful instant in which he draws the knife, in his heart and imagination Abraham had already slaughtered his beloved son not once, but over and over again. This is what Philo of Alexandria clearly saw when he stated that Abraham's sacrifice, "though not followed by the intended ending, was complete and perfect" (*De Abrahamo*, 62–68, quoted in Siker 23). This is what Søren Kierkegaard so poignantly figures when his narrator-character de Silentis writes in his third meditation that from that day on at Mount Moriah "Abraham's eyes were darkened, and he saw joy no more" (12). This is what Eli Wiesel hints at when he writes that, though spared at the very end, the terror of this scene would destroy Isaac's youth forever (quoted in Kuschel, 29), and what Derrida brings to light when he writes that Abraham is only stopped when he had already begun the act (72).

In the Tlaxcalan play, however, far from being shaken by the moral violence of the affair, the character of Abraham is grateful for having been released from the demand of sacrificing his son. As he descends with him from the peak of Mount Moriah, he admonishes Isaac,

> Now may the honored name of the All-powerful, God the Father, whose compassion is very great, be eternally praised everywhere in the world. If all the people on the earth would carry out his precious sacred commands we would greatly please him. And as for you, by beloved child, you have seen how he saved you from death. Now as long as you live, always love him with all your heart and do not take in vain the name of God, and love your neighbors. Such are his orders. (Sell and Burkhart, 161)

In this passage, Abraham celebrates God's mercy in sparing his son on account of the patriarch's commendable obedience to his will. Abraham promises Isaac and the Nahua audience that if they follow his example in obeying God's divine law, they will rejoice and be happy. In the biblical episode, we should recall, Yahweh sends the angel to tell Abraham that he has sworn by himself, that is, by all the power that he would ever wield and muster, that because Abraham had not withheld from him his only son and obeyed his voice: "In thy seed shall all nations of the earth be blessed" (Gen. 22:18). But in the neixcuitilli as well as in the Spanish play this paramount epic dimension of the covenant between the patriarch of the Jews and Yahweh is suppressed.

In the Spanish *Auto del sacrificio de Abraham*, Abraham is also joyous and grateful for having been relieved of his terrible ordeal: "¡Seas, gran Dios, alabado / pues ansí te has satisfecho!" [Be praised, great God / for thus thou hast satisfied thyself!] (22). However, there is no sense of Abraham having accomplished something extraordinary for all the peoples of the world. He is represented as only having fulfilled—albeit exceptionally well—his own special duty to God. The loss of the epic dimension produces the ironic effect of depicting God as a far more terrifying and possessive deity than the unpredictable Yahweh of Genesis. A similar loss can be registered in the Nahua play, except that the context and different positioning of the audience inflect its meaning and effect. At the end of the Spanish auto, the audience is addressed as witnesses of God's mercy: "Ved cuan pequeño servicio / paga [Dios] con tan gran merced" [See what small service / [God] pays back with such great favor] (22). Though this exhortation to bear witness to God's mercy is still extremely violent given the inordinate cruelty of the deity's original demand, the members of the audience are not asked to go as far as to model themselves on Abraham's exceptionally devout behavior. In the Nahua play, however, as the passage in which Abraham exhorts his son Isaac to always comply with God's will shows, Abraham is not depicted as the father of multitudes who, after having passed the supreme test once and for all, will bless all people on earth. Nor is he represented as a unique and exceptional man to whom God has chosen to show his mercy. Rather, in the neixcuitilli, Abraham is represented as an example to follow. Such an exemplariness would seem to be underscored in the dramatic text by the angel's ambiguous closing admonishment to the audience: "All of you who are here have now heard this marvelous thing. And as for you, may you live entirely according to his sacred commands, may you and your children not violate a single one. Take good care that they will not go about playing and wasting time, so that they will serve with goodness our lord, God, and so that they will also merit the kingdom of heaven. May it so be done" (Sell and Burkhart, 163).

The angel defines what the audience has seen as a "marvelous thing," that is, as something extraordinary that causes admiration. However, it is ambiguous what the "marvelous thing" refers to specifically. Is it God's command to sacrifice Isaac that is marvelous and unheard of? Is it Abraham's willingness to carry out such a command, God's sparing of the human victim, or all of the above? The angel then further admonishes the audience that the "marvel" has instructed them to keep God's commandments. By linking the indeterminable "marvelous thing" to the exhortation to keep the divine commandments and to rear children properly, the angel's passage does not give much sense of something irrevocably or even exceptionally accomplished for ages to come by Abraham's absolute obedience. Such a link opens up the possibility of reading that any of the spectators could be required to undertake and readily submit to Abraham's horrific ordeal. The didactic exemplariness of *The Sacrifice* dangerously splits God's unique, tremendous, and perhaps most controversial request in the scriptures into an iterable and duplicable command. Thus, the Christian god that emerges in the dramatic text of this neixcuitilli becomes a hybrid. Unlike in its Judeo-Christian versions, the God of *The Sacrifice* becomes partially Nahuatized, because he so resembles the violent, frightening, demanding pre-Hispanic deities to whom the ancestors of the audience had offered everything at any time and unhesitatingly in order to keep cosmic time alive.

As stated above, many critics of the play have argued that the God of *The Sacrifice* was ultimately posited to the audience as not desiring human sacrifice. This opinion is confirmed by Fray Pedro de Córdoba's *Doctrina Cristiana*, assumed to be among the first ten books printed in Mexico (García Icazbalceta, 68–69). In this widely used *Doctrina*, the Amerindians were taught that the Christian god gives sustenance to all the things of the world:

"Y por todas estas cosas no os pide Dios que le sacrifiqueis los hijos: ni mateis vuestros esclavos, ni otra persona alguna...." [And for all these things God does not ask you to sacrifice to him your children: nor to slay your slaves, nor any other person] (Córdoba, 33). The Christian god is truthful and good precisely because he does not desire human sacrifice: "El Dios verdadero que os predicamos como es bueno quiere bien a los cristianos y a vosotros si quisierdes ser sus amigos; y por esto no quiere que matéis vuestros hijos ni esclavos...ni que derrameis vuestra sangre indebidamente" [The true God that we preach to you because he is good he loves Christians well and you too if you want to be his friends; and for this he does not want you to kill your children nor slaves...nor that you will improperly shed your blood] (Córdoba, 35). Because the *Doctrina* was printed in 1544, it is not unreasonable to assume that the Nahuas would have been introduced to this basic difference between the Christian and pre-Hispanic deities before the *Doctrina* and the 1538 recorded performance of *The Sacrifice of Isaac* by Motolinía.

However, it should be recalled that particularly for Christians, an act does not necessarily need to be fully performed in order to be sinful or to bring blessings. In fact, the possibility that lustful thoughts and yearnings may be already sinful, independently of their sheer materialization, is one of the constitutive aspects of the Christian moral subjectivity that the missionary agents were assiduously trying to implant in the Nahuas. In Córdoba's *Doctrina*, the ninth and tenth commandments are indeed presented to the Indians as sins of desire: "Contra este mandamiento va el hombre que codicia echarse con alguna mujer casada. Y mucho más cuando se echa con ella" [The man who covets to lie with a married woman goes against this commandment. And much more when he actually lies with her] (Córdoba, 97). Though Córdoba specifies that the actual act is even worse than the longing to commit it, the latter is nonetheless already clearly a sin. Such sins of desire evidently reflect Christ's warnings that whosoever looked lasciviously at a woman had already committed adultery with her in his heart (Matt. 5:27–28).

What is relevant to *The Sacrifice of Isaac* about such sinfulness and the interiority that it broaches is that the play indeed shows this new Christian form of subjectivity to the Nahuas while ironically creating strong continuities with their religious past. The neixcuitilli displaces the utter materiality of the external act of human sacrifice, but retains as desirable the thought and internal disposition to perform it. It emphasizes that Abraham was ultimately spared of having to perform the actual immolation of the human body. However, the yoke of having to submit to such a violent command is not lifted, for only by Abraham's unquestionable readiness to surrender to such an atrocious demand, only after he had "renounced every hope" (Derrida, 90) was he rewarded by being freed from acting. Thus, by representing the Judeo-Christian patriarch's excruciating willingness to sacrifice his own son as an example (if not marvel) of obedience, the Franciscan spiritual colonizers failed to show the Nahua audience a new or extraordinary form of religious experience. They only endorsed what was already there. In the specific colonial context of sixteenth-century New Spain, Abraham's seminal act of total surrender to the deity lost its biblical singularity: ordinary men and women in Anahuac had also been capable of showing the will to give up the most precious and beloved to their own gods, believing them to be true.

Ironically, then, when specifically addressed to a Nahua audience, the founding act of the three religions of the book became other, hybridized, something else. It was certainly still an enormous gesture, but no longer a unique one anymore. Human faith and willingness to sacrifice everything to his or her concept of the divine were still not enough to guarantee that God would have mercy and would show the way. The Nahua practice of child sacrifice not only disclosed the easy hand of Satan who, according to the friars, "was forever seeking to imitate his creator, so that... 'the more saintly and devout the things he made men do, the greater was the sin against God'" (Cervantes, 28). The legion of Abrahams in the lands of Anahuac who had sacrificed their beloved sons for the sake of the divinity not once but over and over again may have also revealed to the spiritual colonizer the dreadful silence of his Christian god. He may have felt that because of his God's inscrutable refusal to show himself to all creatures, because of his incomprehensible desire to remain hidden to the multitudes of the Mexican highlands, all the cherished, innocent sacrificed Isaacs, all the human agony offered in earnest on the Mount Moriahs of Anahuac had been cruelly wasted in barbaric signs of a depraved spirituality.

On their part, the attentive Nahua audience may have read in the neixcuitilli of *The Sacrifice of Isaac* that the difference between the Christian god and the pre-Hispanic deities was that, in fact, the *tlacamictiliztli*, or the material final ritual act of giving death, was not necessary to placate the Christian god, feed it, and/or obtain its protection. The alterity of the colonial god lay in the fact that at the very last moment, he would not want to be fed with the human blood of the offered child. Everything else, up to the drawing of the obsidian knife at the *techcatl*, or sacrificial stone, presumably was still expected. In this sense, the dramatic text of *The Sacrifice* would not have presented to the Nahuas the radical difference of the *Doctrina cristiana*'s benevolent, loving Christian deity who abolished and condemned the exacting Nahua practice of human sacrifice. Rather, the text performed a *partial* identification of the Christian god with the pre-Hispanic deities. This was accomplished not only because God spoke Nahuatl in the play, but more importantly because in demanding total, unquestioning surrender of what was most precious from the one whom he addressed, which is the blood of a son, he was not entirely different from Tlaloc or from the capricious and possessive Tezcatlipoca.

In these ways, *The Sacrifice of Isaac* produced unforeseen identities and differences. Hence, in the neixcuitilli about the great biblical story of the colonizer, the Nahua audience may have seen no extraordinary example to follow, no novel, unheard of gods, but rather a mirror of the way they had always related to the sacred. And perhaps in their eagerness to dominate the subaltern native, the spiritual colonizers betrayed the difference of their Christian god by depicting him as demanding from the Nahua audience a total surrender and obedience that in their Judeo-Christian tradition had been reserved only for the supreme test of the human soul. If, however, the degradation of the episode from the unique into the iterative was a result of the intervention of unsupervised Nahua aides, then one could conjecture that there could have been a desire on their part to subvert the authority of the spiritual colonizer by disrupting differences. Contrary to what the prohibition of human sacrifice attested and to what the friars constantly preached in their churches, the Christian god was portrayed in the neix-cuitilli as playing upon the demand for human blood if only as proof of obedience. Or perhaps the many coincidences between Tlaloc and Yahweh are an indication of how the Nahua aides negotiated their understanding of the other as they wrote up the text of the play or amplified the friars' summary indications.

Thus, much as Homi Bhabha has observed about nineteenth-century discourses of colonialism, in the very practice of domination, at the very moment that the discourse of the colonizer displays the plenitude of its powers to suppress the heterogeneity of the other, the "unresolvable problem of cultural difference" unexpectedly reemerges, piercing and splitting, hybridizing and contaminating, undermining and distorting representations of authority, making colonialist discourse other to itself (*Location*, 33). And indeed, *The Sacrifice of Isaac* dramatizes the fact that Spanish colonialism of the early modern period was not a unitary, coherent project but was fractured sometimes by its own internal debates and territorial blindspots, sometimes by the resistance of the other, sometimes by an elusive, indecipherable identity in difference, sometimes by its very will of domination. *The Sacrifice* discloses that the Spanish spiritual colonizer may not have fully mastered the play of meanings of his most sacred narratives when imparting them to the indigenous subjects. The rifts, hybridities, and continuities in this neixcuitilli may thus make manifest that no matter how powerful the colonizer imagined his discourses of authority to be, they may not have been mighty enough to control all the modes and forms of their circulation.

For the Nahuas, on the other hand, *The Sacrifice* showed disruptions with their pre-Hispanic universe by subsituting the animal for the child ixiptla in the mountaintops inhabited by Tlaloc. And even though the Christian deity's behavior in the play was not unlike that of the arbitrary, all-powerful, and feared Tezcatlipoca, who did "that which he thought of, he forthwith made...none might prevent him" (Sahagún, *Florentine*, 4:12), such behavior did alter the regularity of the established pre-Hispanic ritual practices that nourished the cosmic feeding continuum. No longer producing the anticipated forms of calendrical meal equilibrium devised by the *tla-*

matinime, or knowers-of-things, the displacement of the *tlacamictiliztli* in *The Sacrifice* may have confirmed to the audience that they were indeed in a different cycle of uncertainty and chaos in the age of the fifth sun.[10] And yet, the neixcuitilli also instructed that, not totally unlike their ancestors, the Nahua people would always have to keep being ready to sacrifice Isaac, most precious jewel, in order to placate the gods and procure the conservation of the world.

5

Performing Otherness and Identity
in *The Fall of Our First Parents*

s has been mentioned in previous chapters, one important
source for the Nahua evangelization theater is Fray Toribio de Motolinía's
Historia de los indios de la Nueva España (1541). In chapter 15 of the first trea-
tise, the author transcribes a letter by an anonymous friar to his superior Fray
Antonio de Ciudad Rodrigo about the feast the members of the Confraternity of Our Lady of the Incarnation had celebrated in Tlaxcala during the
Easter Octave of the year 1539.[1] In this feast they performed *The Fall of
Our First Parents:* "In the opinion of those who witnessed it, this play was
one of the notable things that had been achieved in New Spain" (157).[2] Fray
Bartolomé de las Casas and Juan de Torquemada will also refer to this performance in their respective *Apologética historia sumaria* and *Monarquía indiana,* but to date no written script has been found. Although there are many
medieval plays and mysteries that treat the subject, the European origins of
the Tlaxcalan auto are still obscure. Hermenegildo Corbató's hypothesis
that the dramatic text of the *Monarquía indiana* may have been based on a
1517 Valencian mystery play ("misterio") has been questioned by Othón
Arróniz (59-61). Neither does it seem to be related to the Castilian *El auto del
pecado de Adán,* which, in addition to Satan, has the allegorical personifica-
tions of Greed and Gluttony as characters (Horcasitas, 175-76).

The previous two chapters have dealt with dramatic texts presumed to
have been composed in the sixteenth century. As was pointed out in the
introduction, the friars would have been most vigilantly involved with the
production of the dramatic texts, though they were never in full control

97

since they depended at least partially on the linguistic skills of their Nahua collaborators.

The friar's account to Fray Antonio de Ciudad Rodrigo offers a description of what we would call the mise-en-scène, which is particularly interesting because, according to the missionary chroniclers, the Nahuas were mostly in charge of this aspect of the production (León-Portilla, "Insertos," 193). In the mise-en-scène, or "the transcoding of the written text into performance" (De Marinis, 15), there are several verbal and non-verbal signifying systems working together and/or competing against one another. In the interaction between these visual, auditive, verbal, and kinetic codes, the mise-en-scène, whether more or less consciously, actualizes a reading of the dramatic text. In this sense, the mise-en-scène may be conceived of as a metatext or "commentary on the text or the stage rewriting it offers of the text" (Pavis, 34). From a more political perspective, James C. Scott proposes in *Domination and the Art of Resistance* that official messages embedded in collective representations of culture can be craftily undercut by the subordinate groups because of the elusive, polysemic dynamics of cultural expression: "By the subtle use of codes one can insinuate into a ritual, a pattern of dress, a song, a story, meanings that are accessible to one intended audience and opaque to another audience the actors wish to exclude" (158). Such displacements are likely to occur because the official dominant cultures usually degrade and demean the dominated groups, which then feel they have to riposte at least among themselves in a more or less concealed way.

Due to the difficulty of localizing hidden layers of meaning, as well as to the perilous attempt of speaking for the other, it might be impossible to prove that the mise-en-scène of the *Fall of Our First Parents* was openly and self-consciously used by the Nahuas in a contestatory way or as an act of organized resistance to the discourses of the colonizer. However, the codified use of space, movement, and time, the tonality, rhythm, and accent with which the dramatic text was enunciated constitute signs of or approximations to the ways the Nahuas imagined, constructed, and/or made meaningful to themselves the culture of the colonial other. The friar's letter in Motolinía's *History*, registering some of these aspects of the performance, offers an important perspective from which to consider and/or hypothesize the process of cultural exchange and appropiation in the Nahua evangelization theater. I am aware, of course, that the friar's account is the colonizer's reconstruction of the other's performance of one of the Europeans' most cherished foundational narratives. This adds still another level of cultural mediation to the analysis of the actual, ephemerous object of knowledge that was the 1539 theatrical event of *The Fall of Our First Parents*. Still, some worthwhile insights can be drawn by considering the friar's testimonial discourse on the auto.

During the Wednesday of the Easter Octave of 1539, the Confraternity of Our Lady of the Incarnation performed *The Fall of Our First Parents*.[3] As expected, the auto opened in paradise. Drawing from their own practices of meticulously setting up forests for spectacles and religious rituals (Horcasitas, 105; Watts, "Languages," 149; Arróniz, 61), the Tlaxcalans constructed their reading of paradisiacal space with great diversity of fruits and flowers, some of them natural, others *contrahechos*, that is, hand-crafted. The tree of knowledge of good and evil stood near the center of paradise, adorned with "many beautiful artificial fruits in gold and feathers" (Motolinía, *History*, 158). The friar remarks that on one of three artificial hills surrounding the stage there was a young man in a lion costume tearing up an actual stag corpse (Motolinía, *History*, 158), a detail not easily conceivable in European medieval religious mise-en-scènes.

This contiguity between live and elaborate artificial creatures underscored the Nahuas' masterful skills to duplicate and/or counterfeit. It is well known that Cortés was dazzled by Motecuhzoma's replica collection of all sorts of indigenous fauna and flora specimens in gold, silver, precious stones, and feathers.[4] Inga Clendinnen speculates that the Mexica passion to represent and copy might have been a way to display cultural capital: that is, a way to showcase Tenochtlan's power to centralize all the wealth and bounty of the lands, by exquisitely reproducing it (*Aztecs*, 27). Not surprisingly, the Nahua's skill to replicate baffled the Spaniards because it stood out as evidence of an extraordinary degree of cultural refinement in people who, to them, had heretofore been isolated from the world. Thus, through this remarkably sophisticated and elaborate mise-en-scène of Judeo-Christian paradise, may the Tlaxcalans not have been representing, presenting before their eyes, as well as before those of the Spanish colonizer, their power to duplicate the European other? By displaying their longstanding skillfulness and precision in handling and "making look natural" the new discourses of the colonizing other (Motolinía, *History*, 158), the Nahuas may have been performing an act of cultural self-legitimation, as Burkhart suggests about the evangelization theater as a whole (*Holy*, 48). *The Fall of Our First Parents* should not be theorized, then, only as a simple, didactic, edifying affair in which a new tale of origins was triumphantly imposed upon the audience, but also as a site to confront the Nahua's bewildering syncretic capacity to mimic and appropriate Western texts. Describing the splendor of the Corpus Christi procession of 1538, Motolinía himself remarks that everywhere "it was a pleasure to rest one's gaze on them and to note how a people, until now regarded as brutes, should know how to arrange such a thing" (*History*, 152). The incongruity between the prodigious artistic skills of the Nahuas and their attributed barbarism by so many Spanish colonizers was indeed dramatized and made manifest in these stagings and mise-en-scènes. The unthought, the repressed and/or the excluded in the constructions of Nahua subalterity returned to be seen in this theater, making the base of the edifice of colonial discourses of discriminatory knowledges, superiorities, and inferiorities sway, at least during the time of the performance.

The prelapsarian space was brimming with small animals, rabbits, and hares. The friar points out that the rabbits and hares "were so numerous that the whole place seemed full of them" (Motolinía, *History*, 157). This is a suggestive detail of the mise-en-scène because rabbits were associated in pre-Hispanic times with *pulque* (Krickeberg, 145), an alcoholic beverage made from maguey, and with drunkenness (Brundage, 158). According to George Vaillant, "Four-hundred rabbits stood for complete drunkenness, while fifteen or twenty suggested mere conviviality" (176). For her part, Louise Burkhart has demonstrated that in many Mesoamerican myths and traditions the rabbit was associated with disobedience, roaming, and the region of "morally suspect women" (*Slippery*, 59). If we take the friar's statement in earnest, the countless rabbits would seem to convey a greater orgiastic abundance of the furry creatures than the twenty of mere cheerful socialization. Thus, for the Spanish audience the countless rabbits might very well have meant the abundance of food, happiness, and high spirits in paradise, but for the Nahua spectators, perhaps the excesses or even drunkenness of an already dubiously moral Eve.

The friar points out in his letter that there were two fierce ocelots tied up in paradisiacal space. He then notes that "once, during the play, Eve was careless and went near one of them, and, as if well trained, the beast went away. This was before the sin; had it occurred after the sin, she would not have been so lucky" (Motolinía, *History*, 158). If this incident was not made up by the friar's spectator's fancy, was the exquisite restraint of the wildcat an uncannily fortunate accident for the actor impersonating Eve, or was it staged?

If Eve's accident was not an intended element of the mise-en-scène, it nonetheless ran most felicitously along the elaborations on the Genesis episode in Pedro de Córdoba's widely circulating *Doctrina cristiana*. In this important catechism, God explains to Adam and Eve their mortal nature, but how he, for love, had decided to suspend death as long as the couple kept his law:

> Debéis saber que vosotros según vuestra naturaleza sois mortales y pasibles.... Y así mismo los animales os pueden hacer mal: y las culebras morder, y empozoñar, y el fuego os puede quemar.... Pero porque yo soy vuestro criador y os amo como a hijos y criaturas mías que sois y os deseo hacer muy grandes bienes... y desde agora os otorgo por gracia especial contra la propiedad de vuestra naturaleza: que ninguna de estas cosas sobredichas os pueda perturbar, ni empecer, ni dañar, ni cosa alguna os pueda venir contra vuestra voluntad que os pueda dañar. (*Doctrina*, 48)

> [You should know that according to your nature you are mortal and vulnerable.... And therefore animals can harm you: and serpents bite you, and poison you, and fire can burn you.... But because I am your creator and I love you as my children and creatures that you are and I wish to do you great good...from now on I grant you by special grace against the property of your nature: that none of the above-said things can disturb you, or hurt you, or damage you, nor any other thing can come to you against your will that can harm you.]

Leaving aside for now the analysis of the figures of Nahua otherness engendered by Córdoba's personal version of the biblical myth, it will suffice to say that at least for the few friars in the audience, the good behavior of the fierce ocelot must have been a most appropriate and satisfactory rendering of the paradisiacal suspension of natural properties posited in the *Doctrina*'s narrative.

If, however, the incident was indeed part of the mise-en-scène, then in order to depict the orderliness of paradise, a dangerously inattentive, absent-minded (perhaps somewhat tipsy?) Eve was shown as having almost stumbled onto the beast. But because this happened in a prelapsarian space the fearful ocelot kept hold of itself and, although grudgingly, got out of her way. So in this possible Tlaxcalan construction of paradise, fierce animals were not absent, but they were urbane and polite.[5] Interestingly, it could be hypothesized that paradise was enacted in the visual semiotic system of the mise-en-scène as a thoroughly socialized, civil space. There, even undomesticated beasts would act properly, but, by the same token, stumbling or tripping over them would be notoriously unsuitable and out of place. As Burkhart has noted, the suddenness of stumbling and falling was considered dangerous by the Nahuas because it could cause the *tonalli*[6] to leave the body, causing illness if not death. Not too unlike the Judeo-Christian tradition, "stumbling and falling were used in Nahuatl rhetoric as metaphors for moral deviance" (Burkhart, *Holy*, 189–90). Thus, although heedless human behavior might not have the same catastrophic effects in paradise as in earthly time (as promised in the *Doctrina cristiana*), it could nonetheless signify turpitude, baseness, and/or tampering with life forces. In this sense, the mise-en-scène could have been subtly appropriating, Nahuatizing, and/or hybridizing the Judeo-Christian myth's original transgression of eating from paradise's tree of knowledge by depicting a prior breach of order in Eve's mindless overstepping the ocelot. The innumerable rabbits on stage associated in indigenous traditions with drunkenness and female reprehensible behavior may be thought of as a dramatic metonymy foregrounding Eve's faltering presence of mind.

The friar then continues with his letter to Fray Antonio by remarking that the auto was very long because Eve went back and forth three or four times from the serpent to Adam before both ate from the apple. Horcasitas has pointed out that since the initial prohibition is missing in Fray Antonio's account, there must have been some way in which the friars made sure it was presupposed by the audience, lest the didactic thrust of the play be lost (178). In any event, it is plausible to propose that the Fransciscans present at the performance may have seen in Eve's long, numerous strolls an embodiment of the concept of free will, since her promenades could be read as perceptive representations of how the decision to eat the apple took hold of her ever more deeply. But according to the *huehuetlatolli*, or "speech of elders," collected by Andrés de Olmos, Bernardino de Sahagún, and Gerónimo de Mendieta, her insistent strolls back and forth could have meant something different for the Nahua audience. Young girls were admonished by their mothers to walk in specific ways in order to avoid the anger, wrath, or impudence of people: "Thou art not to travel in great haste, nor art thou to amble; for [to amble] achieveth pompousness; [haste] meaneth restlessness.... Thou art not to bow thy head, nor art thou to raise thy head in pride; it meaneth ill-breeding. Thou art to go straight forward. Also, thou art not to act shamefully, nor to cover thy mouth" (Sahagún, *Florentine*, 7:100). The female body should always move in a controlled way, so as to signify modesty, honesty, and discretion and not attract negative forces or undesirable interactions.

Although Adam declines and even pushes Eve away "as if indignant," she keeps coming back, pleading and lamenting, throwing herself on his lap,[7] making him angry and uncomfortable, as no self-controlled woman or even wife should. In the semiotic system of the mise-en-scène that activates the collective memory of the audience, Eve's seductive demeanor(s) most likely would not have been read approvingly either by Nahuas or by the Spaniards. Her provocative body language entailed a transgression of sexual codes and boundaries, and particularly for the Nahuas, such a·violation in turn propitiated an imbalance of forces, crystallized in the anger of the husband.[8]

Though in varying degrees, anthropologists and students of Nahua culture generally agree that the boundaries between individual and community in Mesoamerican societies were more permeable than in that of their con-

temporary European counterparts. In order to describe Nahua social relations, Kay Read has recently referred to Richard Shweder and Edmund
Bourne's concept of "concrete-relational" societies in which the behavior of
the individual is "regulated by strict rules of interdependence that are con-
text-specific and particularistic, rules governing exchanges of services, rules
governing behavior to kinsmen, rules governing marriage, etc." (Read, 186).
Ángel Garibay had already pointed out in 1954 that the highest aims of
everything done and worked for were the community, race, religion, and/or
state: "Nunca se pertenecía el hombre a sí mismo" [Never did man belong to
himself] (*Historia*, 1:228). For his part, Alfredo López Austin contends
that for the Nahua, the human being was enmeshed in a turbulent web of
natural and supernatural forces that both guaranteed his survival and threatened to annihilate him. In order to obtain from the gods their life-sustain-
ing benefits and fend off their destructive powers, the Mesoamericans
engaged in complex and elaborate rituals, the most significant of these being
collective activities (*Human*, 1:65–67). By infringing social norms, by not
following the rituals correctly, by doing what one felt like, or because of the
intensity of individual desires, the person liberated ominous forces that
could put himself and his clan at risk (Gruzinski, *Colonización*, 171–72).
The belief in *tlazolmiquiztli* (literally, death by filth or filthy death), or that
one's misconduct could produce harmful emanations that affect innocent
people close to oneself, "gave everybody a stake in the moral behavior of
others" (Burkhart, *Slippery*, 97). It was then as if any strong display of personal inclinations, ignorant behavior, or reckless actions that highlighted
separateness and individuality were feared as breaching proper boundaries.
These breaches in turn produced greater susceptibility to death and destruction and thus were to be avoided as much as possible. In the huehuetlatolli,
which prescribed proper conduct for different age groups and particular
social contexts, even the children of the wealthiest noblemen, or pipiltin,
were constantly admonished to be humble, fearful, and to bend their bodies to the ground, as if they were poor and selfless: "Thou art of noble lineage…thou art a nobleman; [however] thou art to go holding this, raising it,
before thy gaze. Note that the humbling, the bowing, the inclining, the
weeping, the tears, the sighing, the meekness——these same are nobility, the

estimable, the valued; these are honor" (Sahagún, *Florentine*, 7:109).[9] All lively manifestations of individual inclinations were discouraged, or deemed madness in a world of uncertainty and affliction (Sahagún, *Florentine*, 7:105–06), where the deadly power of the deities could be unleashed at any provocation. Taking all the above into consideration, Eve's provocative pleading and Adam's eroding resistance might have been read by the Nahua spectator as signs of the dangerous folly of unrestrained desire, the tradition that the huehuetlatollis had warned against. According to the text enacted by the mise-en-scène, it may be hypothesized that there was something already corrupt in Eve's loose, undisciplined behavior, something displaced and/or off balance before she and Adam actually ate from the apple.

Finally seduced by Eve's insistence, Adam walks over to the forbidden tree. As soon as both eat from its fruit, evil and knowledge of evil are produced: "While they were eating, they immediately recognized the evil they had done" (Motolinía, *History*, 158). According to the friar's statement, his reconstruction of the dramatic script's depiction of original sin entails a particular experience of evil in which the objective violation of an interdiction is not what is focalized as primary.[10] Before eating the apple, Adam and Eve did not know the meaning of evil, only that something was forbidden and that retribution would inevitably come if the prohibition was not respected. But by performing what was prohibited they immediately learned what evil meant (perhaps the awareness of their freedom to degrade themselves in breaking away from God?). Knowledge, therefore, is represented as an essential component in the human experience of evil in the friar's letter: evil was something done and an awareness of wrongdoing. The Fall was both an act as well as (the production of) a change in the state of consciousness that could not be reduced to a fear of vengeance. Evil was not only an external damage perpetrated by an angry, offended deity, but also an awareness of an impoverished self. The latter psychic component is an important element in the Christian discourse of guilt (Ricoeur, *Symbolism*, 100–57). Thus, the dramatic representation of Adam and Eve's evil as depicted by the friar cannot be said to precede the actual eating of the apple, even while Eve conferred with the malicious serpent or as she seductively swayed back and forth trying to convince Adam to transgress.

For the Nahuas, however, the transgression may not have been some-thing produced by Adam and Eve only at the moment of eating the apple. By Eve's risky proximity to the ocelot, by cunningly strolling back and forth and immodestly throwing herself in Adam's lap, she may have been por-trayed as already infringing boundaries and entering in contact with the chaotic, avenging powers of the sacred. By yielding to her "cavernal lust"[11] and walking over to the tree, Adam's heart had already begun to falter and melt: the Nahua Adam and Eve of the mise-en-scène were therefore bring-ing disgrace upon themselves even before eating the forbidden apple! In this sense, the temporal boundaries between innocence and transgression were not as neatly drawn in the staging of the neixcuitilli as in the friar's Christian discourse of guilt and original sin in the letter suggested. There, everything that had happened before the Fall, even though it had brought Adam and Eve ever closer to it, by no means necessarily implied it, since they had always been completely free to act otherwise until the very last moment, and since no real knowledge of wrongdoing was produced until the actual violation of the interdict. For the Nahuas, however, evil was not this type of painful consciousness of wrongdoing or moral suffering for "the internal diminution of the value of the self" (Ricoeur, *Symbolism*, 102), caused by having willfully severed links with the divinity. In fact, no abstract concept of evil existed in Nahuatl (Burkhart, *Slippery*, 38). Rather, the Nahua sense of evil was first and foremost the terrible, objective misfortunes improper conduct could bring upon the perpetrators, whether ignorant or cognizant of their deeds. Evil was the frightening, unprotected contact with the annihilating forces roaming the surface of earth that a chaotic state of emotion could bring about.

Despite the possible different cultural narratives about the onset of evil enacted in *The Fall of Our First Parents* (as construed by the friar's letter), the hapless couple does indeed arouse the terrible wrath of the sacred with its uncontrolled and/or willfully disobedient behavior. Coming down "with great majesty accompanied by many angels" (Motolinía, *History*, 159), a ter-rifying God (not unlike the frightening Tezcatlipoca) curses and expels the couple to a hostile, peripheral space "full of thistles and thorns" (ibid.). The angels teach Adam how to till the earth and give Eve spindles to weave.

This particular gender division of labor was culturally significant to the Nahuas because in many of their own myths of origin they also had a primal couple, Oxomoco and Cipactonal, to whom the gods had commanded the very same duties (López Austin, *Human*, 1:238; Nicholson, 398). The Mexican anthropologist López Austin points out that many elements in the myths about this couple indicated that they were possibly conceived "more as gods or as archetypical beings than as men" (*Human*, 1:238). Oxomoco and Cipactonal were "beings in whom the fundamentals of the sexual division of labor were established and in whom appeared the human characteristic of being mortal" (*Human*, 1:239). Nicholson points out that "from them stemmed the *macehualtin*, the common mass of mankind" (398). Though to have linked Adam and Eve to gods would have been a doctrinal misconstruction, they could have been correctly associated with the category of "archetypical" beings that López Austin described and to the fact that mortality had been introduced through them. Moreover, according to some sources (but by no means all), Cipactonal and Oxomoco had lived in Tamoanchan, sometimes deemed a terrestrial paradise situated in the far west (Krickeberg, 131), in which stood a tree "whose boughs were not supposed to be broken or its flowers plucked" (Brundage, 45–46). According to the *Codex Telleriano Remensis* (and possibly by contamination with Judeo-Christian narratives), Oxomoco had committed a transgression after which she had been transformed into Itzpapálotl, or "Obsidian Knife Butterfly" (López Austin, *Human*, 1:238; Brundage, 46–47). In other versions, however, Tamoanchan was a city where Cipactonal and Oxomoco had been left behind with two other wise men, Tlaltetecui and Xochicauaca. All four entered in consultation and decided to create the *tonalpohualli*, or divination calendar, in order to help the people govern themselves (Sahagún, *Florentine*, 11:191). This was a major cultural achievement because with its aid the counters, or *tonalpouhque*, were able to calculate when the supernatural powers conflated with and manifested themselves in human time (Nicholson, 439–40; Vaillant, 190; López Austin, *Human*, 1:61–68). The tonalpouhque did so not by observing natural phenomena, but by interpreting different sequences of numbers, signs, patron deities, and even the cardinal points (Nicholson, 439–40). The diviners were able to determine the beneficial or malignant character of a day by the conflation of these sets of influences. By knowing the day and hour when a child was born, parents could consult with the tonalpouhque and learn about the conditions, life, and death of the newborn (Sahagún, *Florentine*, 1:61).[12] Taking into consideration particularly the second myth of Oxomoco and Cipactonal, it can be said that rather than exemplifying the principle of free will, the Mesoamerican figures resembling Adam and Eve fostered knowledge of the supernatural forces that restrict the lives of people. In addition, although the divination calendar helped the people to work around these forces in order to produce a more favorable outcome, the very existence of the calendar implied that human beings could never break away completely from the influence of such powers.

It is very difficult to determine whether or not there was a hidden transcript, in the Scottian sense (Scott, *Domination*), attempting to establish or even invent a parallelism between Adam and Eve and the Nahua primordial couple. However, the conspicuous detail of the gendered distribution of labor in the mise-en-scène suggests that such a possibility should not be ruled out. A "hidden message" becomes even more plausible when one considers that producing discreet continuities between Christian and Mesoamerican narratives would enable more of the pre-Hispanic cultural identity to circulate in the colonial reality, if only for the eyes of the indigenous, subordinate group.[13] Miguel León-Portilla has recently pointed out that by accommodating and adapting pre-Hispanic to Christian beliefs in religious feasts, the Mesoamericans have been able to evade Church and state norms in colonial as well as in modern times. In this way, they have preserved a sense of who they were, are, and want to be in a world largely dominated by the Western other ("Insertos," 207).

In terms of the ways the Nahuas participated in the evangelization theater, it has been argued that the members of the native nobility were those most likely to have been involved in the production and performance of the plays as a way of asserting their class privileges and authority (Burkhart, *Holy*, 48). These cultural brokers were educated in the Franciscan boarding or seminar schools built next to the monasteries.[14] Many collegians of these schools became zealous persecutors of the religious practices of their parents. But the great opposition from secular and even religious authorities to the education of the Nahua pipiltin and to institutions such as the Colegio de Tlatelolco should warn us from jumping to the conclusion that a radical repudiation of the pre-Hispanic past would invariably be the case among the young Nahua elite educated by the missionaries. Another happier outcome of this education was that some other students began to write histories and memorials about their pre-Hispanic past (Kobayashi, 232–59). Thus, it may be reasonably assumed that the noble natives involved in the 1539 production and mise-en-scène of *The Fall of Our First Parents*, as students of the missionaries and relatives of people who had held prestigious positions in the pre-Hispanic political and religious order of things, could have possessed enough knowledge of both Christian and Nahua traditions.[15] This in turn would have enabled them to visually invoke, mobilize, and/or perform a strip of the collective memory of the Mesoamerican primordial couple in order to establish a resemblance/hybridization between the ancestors of the pre-Hispanic past and those of the Christian present that would allow the former a place in the new world of colonial reality.

The anonymous friar writes to Fray Antonio that after the angels finished teaching, they departed singing a *villancico*, or carol, in order to console "the two who remained there and showed great sorrow" (Motolinía, *History*, 159). The fact that Adam and Eve remained disconsolate indicates that they were represented as feeling devastated at the prospect of their new earthly dwelling. In the huehuetlatollis the world was also constructed as a place of great affliction, torments, and hardship (Sahagún, *Florentine*, 7:93, 105–06, 176–77), where people became involuntarily indebted to the deities, and where they had to pay "a regular token levy" to them in order to survive (Clendinnen, *Aztecs*, 74–75). Misfortune came easily because that was the nature of things: "the earth is slippery" on the jagged edge that was the world (Burkhart, *Slippery*, 58).

In Christianity, however, the evil and affliction encountered in the world are never to be considered without reference to the history of salvation (Ricoeur, "Original," 286). As St. Paul wrote, "Where sin abounded, grace did much more abound" (Rom. 5:20). And so it is that the angels sing in order to palliate the great sorrow of the first transgressors:

Para que comía
la primer casada,
Para qué comía
La fruta vedada.
La primer casada
Ella y su marido,
A Dios han traído
En pobre posada
Por haber comido
la fruta vedada. (Historia, 67)

Why did she eat,
The first one married,
Why did she eat
The forbidden fruit?
The first one married,
She and her husband,
Have caused God to come
To earth's poor dwelling
By having eaten
The forbidden fruit. (History, 159)

This lovely villancico, considered the first manifestation of Mexican colonial poetry, might be the only surviving part of the lost dramatic script of *The Fall of Our First Parents* (Williams, *Teatro*, 62). The villancico articulates the notion of Christian guilt that the friars wanted to instill in the Nahuas, but greatly mollified by the joyful genre of the carol. The second stanza reproaches the first couple, whose original sin had brought God down to earth (had "made" him incarnate). But such a reproach is not cast in a language of violence or punishment. The villancico displaces the fear of revenge with the bittersweet pangs of guilt, caused by love for the baby Savior born in a miserable manger. For the friars, the conversion of the fear of retribution into such *felix culpa* would be one form of the dispensations of Christian grace to the Nahuas. Nevertheless, it is unlikely that this comforting verbal message got through to the majority of the Nahua audience. Because of its regular line pattern, the villancico must have been sung in Spanish, perhaps by some friars in the chorus (Williams, *Teatro*, 62).[16]

The friar concludes his account of *The Fall of Our First Parents* by pointing out that many in the audience shed copious tears: "This stage play was presented by the Indians in their native language, so that many of them were deeply moved and shed tears, especially when Adam was banished from paradise and placed in the world" (Motolinía, *History,* 159). The friar's causal coupling of representing in the native language and shedding copious tears is no doubt suggestive. We shall never know if those tears shed by the Tlaxcalans in the central square turned theater were the visible signs that the spiritual conquest was triumphantly reshaping their hearts by producing a Christian awakening to sin and guilt. Perhaps, as Othón Arróniz has suggested, those tears could have very well been public mourning for their human world of misery, affliction, and exile (61), so much like Adam and Eve's, particularly since the arrival of the Spaniards.

This chapter included a cultural analysis of the letter to Fray Antonio de Ciudad Rodrigo, describing *The Fall of Our First Parents,* allegedly transcribed by Motolinía in his *History of the Indians of New Spain.* The analysis has shown that when one approaches this neixcuitilli from the point of view of the several semiotic systems that constitute a dramatic representation, more than one cultural narrative may be discerned to be at play. As has been pointed out earlier, in the Nahua theater of evangelization it is the dramatic script that can usually be considered the principal vehicle of the discourse of the colonizer, if only because the friars were able to control and supervise its production more closely. No dramatic text for *The Fall of Our First Parents* has been found to date, however. Nevertheless, the letter to Fray Antonio points to its existence particularly when it describes the Fall both as an act and as consciousness of evil, when it narrates how God curses Adam and Eve, and when it includes the villancico that the angels sing in order to console the couple in distress. Within the Western cultural coordinates of this posited dramatic text, the Fall is represented as the inauguration of an evil moral and physical state in the world. Everything that occurred before the Fall, though bringing Adam and Eve closer to it, did not and could not imply it, even in spite of the presence of the deceitful, malignant serpent. The knowledge of evil produced by the act of eating the forbidden fruit signifies a decisive break with a previous state, a break that operates both at the objective level of the violation of the interdict as well as at the subjective level of consciousness.

The text of the mise-en-scène, which was controlled by the Nahuas, if only during the actual time of the performance, would seem, however, to narrate a history of transgressions. Adam and Eve's infractions were not localized only at the moment of eating the apple. By almost stepping on the scary ocelot, by seductively and pompously promenading back and forth from Adam to the serpent, and by Adam giving in to his carnal desire for Eve, their conduct could have been read by the Nahua audience as signs of a rupture of order and equilibrium, as a degenerating entropy that causes chaos. The Fall of the first parents is not represented only as a localized, wretched exercise of free will with a concomitant painful awareness of wrongdoing. It is also manifested in the deployment of a series of human actions that, insensible and inattentive to the constant presence of the terrible forces of the sacred, motivated by strong inclinations and personal desires, finally brought misfortune to those who perpetrated the actions. In this sense, the mise-en-scene may have not promoted the notion of an unfettered, individual free will, which constitutes the backbone of Christian subjectivity. On the contrary, it may have presented to the indigenous audience something much closer to what they knew: that to act as an individual was dangerous and harmful because it could attract the ominous forces of the sacred and lead to exile. Similarly, the parallels between the Judeo-Christian original couple Adam and Eve and the Mesoamerican Cipactonal and Oxomoco, inventors of the tonalpohualli, or ancient system of divination, may have reaffirmed rather than displaced the Nahua outlook of the world in which human fate depended, at least partially, on a complex set of external forces.

Thus, with the dramatic representation of the biblical story of the Fall, the friars may have thought that their Christian version of origins was being imposed upon the indigenous audience. But the visual, semiotic, and kinetic codes of the mise-en-scène that have been discussed above open up the possibility that the Nahua elite in charge of the staging might have been producing what Jorge Klor de Alva denominates a "counter-narrative of continuity" ("Discurso," 341). In the case of *The Fall of Our First Parents*, the counter-narrative of continuity may be hypothesized as the spectacular positioning of indigenous cultural narratives as precedents, parallels, and/or equivalents of the new colonial narratives, if visible only to the eyes of the Nahua audience. By depicting their plastic capacity to accommodate and hybridize the discourses of the colonialist other, the Nahua elite may have been publicly affirming to the indigenous audience the power of their pre-Hispanic cultural identities to live on in the brave new world of Spanish colonization.

PART III | *Confession, Acculturation, and Resistance in Sixteenth-century Mexico*

6

Confession in the Old and New Worlds

t has been famously observed by Michel Foucault in his *History of Sexuality* that confession, particularly from the Counter-Reformation on, is "the obligatory and exhaustive expression of an individual secret" (61). It is a technology of discipline and knowledge, deftly developed by the Catholic Church for its members. Confession is an imperative to speak one's most recondite acts, thoughts, and desires, sometimes long forgotten, to a mighty other. To confess is both to relinquish and restructure oneself through the production of an onerous discourse of truth. It is to become totally visible to an authority that has the prerogative to interpret, reconcile, or condemn the verity that one has been compelled to tell in very specific ways. Confession, then, has a great deal to do with power, control, and the constitution of subjects.

In this part of the book I will explore two widely circulating confessional manuals written and printed in New Spain during the sixteenth century. The well-known Foucauldian version of confession as a disciplining, controlling, and efficacious act of power is particularly useful for the colonial context. With the colonizer as confessor and the colonized-to-be or subaltern as confessed, the confessional act clearly becomes an agency of acculturation. Confession can be posited, therefore, as an exemplary, visible sign of the production of subjectivity that works also as a colonizing act of subordination and suppression of cultural difference. A discriminated, unknowing subject (the penitent/subaltern) is compelled to come to the authorized subject of knowledge (confessor/colonizer) in order to be (re)constituted and defined by him, under pain of excommunication, isolation, and/or social demotion. Such a restructuring happens, of course, within a discourse that is not part of the displaced culture of the penitent. The subaltern penitent's submission to this extraneous discourse that fixes the boundaries between his interior and exterior, between the permissible and the impermissible, between what one can avoid and what is inevitable, is his accession to the colonized subjectivity. Confession in the contact zone[1] served "effectively as a police device of interrogation, capable of detecting and controlling individual and collective memory, the deep beliefs and the cultural practices of the native, as well as his social and productive activity" (Subirats, *El continente vacío,* 219; translation is mine).[2]

However, such positioning of confession as a perverse agency of domination mobilized by the urge to control the other completely does not account for the whole story. Because the full consent and understanding of the penitent is necessary in order for the sacrament to be efficacious, an act of confession cannot be extracted only by intimidation. In addition, as Foucault has stated, "Pastoral power is not merely a form of power which commands; it must also be ready to sacrifice itself for the life and the salvation of the flock. Therefore, it is different from royal power, which demands a sacrifice from its subjects to save the throne" (Foucault, "Afterword," 214). That is, pastoral power requires readiness to give itself up for the sake of those over whom it is exercised. In an analysis of the role and textual production of pastoral power in the colonization process of New Spain by the mendicant orders, this dimension of self-sacrifice and renunciation, no matter how misconceived it may appear to us, must not be entirely discarded as yet another strategy to secure power. Although still and always a colonizer, at least in principle, the mendicant religious agent had to renounce any personal, economic, and/or political gain for the cause of the salvation of souls, lest he would be falling into the very mortal sin his own discourse claimed to abhor. Such a pastoral imperative to relinquish private, egotistical interests created a specific relationship with the alterity of the colonized-to-be that in the best of cases helps us understand what Homi Bhabha denominates "the significatory boundaries of cultures, where meanings and values are (mis)read or signs are misappropriated" (*Location,* 34). That is, when the pastoral imperative was assumed in earnest, even if never fully carried out, the epistemic barriers and limits involved in the contact became more visible. These barriers were what did and did not allow for certain forms of recognizing and relating to otherness that we deem possible, desirable, or even necessary today.

As the following two chapters will show, in the attempt to exercise his authority as subject of knowledge over the subaltern other, the colonizer first subjected himself to the other's language. In order to Christianize the Nahua, the Franciscan colonizer determined that Nahuatl had first to be fully understood and spoken properly. Later, confronting the reality of the resistance to his designs, acknowledging the failure of his attempts to restructure the other as a reflection of the self, the colonizer split and then sought to reconstitute himself. In this exemplary, almost transparent instance of cultural encompassment that is the confessional act in the colonial context, I wish to show that colonizing institutions both served and obstructed their own expansionist aspirations. The consent of the colonized-to-be was not simply dismissed but sought and fought for, the colonizer's own avowed and disavowed ambivalence as well as the unexpected resilience of the other always kept creeping in: these elements resisted the most grandiose of colonial designs and made them hybrid. Such a hybridity, in turn, was not merely an unconscious process that only we are in the position to recognize from our privileged, postcolonial watchtowers. Though never willing or epistemologically capable of abandoning the colonial enterprise altogether, many sectors of the colonizing "self" would nonetheless acknowledge the untenable contradictions, mixed forms, and regressions to which his extraneous interventions gave rise. These sectors, albeit clearly positioned within the field of the discourses of the colonizer, did not necessarily articulate the narrative figure of a linear, teleological progress, nor did they unfailingly exhibit that "deeply ingrained and unself-conscious bad innocence" so often predicated of colonial discourses at large (Said, 116).

As is well known, yearly private penance was decreed obligatory (under the threat of excommunication) by the Fourth Lateran Council of 1215. Despite controversies about penance, its sacramental, divinely instituted character was agreed to by theologians during the thirteenth century—that is, penance was considered essential for salvation. However, most of these very same theologians thought that the most important aspect of the sacrament was contrition (Tentler, 22). The role of the priest was simply to ratify what God had already done, namely, to forgive the sins of the contrite penitent. It would be the Franciscan John Duns Scotus (d. 1308) who would later try to ground more solidly the church's mandate to confess. He proposed that the grace-producing power of the sacrament was not *ex opere operantis*, that is, a result of the work of the worker (or penitent), but rather *ex opere operato*, by the work of the work, by the almost automatic power of the sacrament itself (Tentler, 26), as long as it was effectuated properly (i.e., willingly by the penitent, in a sober state, etc.). This was the reason why it was necessary to receive absolution from the priest. Perfect contrition as Saint Thomas Aquinas had defined it was very difficult to attain. Most penitents' sorrow was really attrition: an imperfect repentance produced more by the fear of punishment than by regret for having offended God. Duns Scotus held that the sacrament of penance was able to bridge the difference between the two forms of repentance. In other words, because the priest's absolution transformed attrition into contrition, the vast majority of Christians should seek to receive the sacrament. Though the act of confessing and the satisfaction, or penance, were also indispensable components of the sacrament, the emphasis was on the absolution conferred by the priest. The institutionalization of the sacrament was thus much more persuasively theorized, and the mediating power of the church, as well as its role as an agent of social control, more deeply entrenched, at least until questioned by the reformers and Luther.

The sacrament of penance was transplanted into New Spain as early as 1526 (Motolinía, *History*, 192). In their respective *Historias*, both Fray Toribio de Benavente Motolinía and Gerónimo de Mendieta represent the Nahuas as having been illuminated by God to understand the sacrament of confession (Motolinía, *History*, 192; Mendieta, HEI, 282). Mendieta explains that the Nahuas had a similar practice in their pre-Hispanic past, which they performed twice a year or when they were very sick. The emphasis of the act was on repentance, for they considered the body could recover its health by expelling sin from their *ánima*, or soul: "Y esto era tenido por principal medicina: echar el pecado de su ánima para la salud del cuerpo.... Finalmente, tenían entendido que por los pecados les venían todos los trabajos y necesidades" [And this was believed to be an essential medicine: to cast out sin from their souls for the health of the body.... Finally, they understood that because of their sins all their hardships and needs befell them] (Mendieta, HEI, 281). According to Mendieta's words, the Nahuas had established a correct correlation between sin and misfortune: they thought that all hardships and necessities were a result of their sins, a truth, which, the friar remarked, they understood much better after having heard the law of God (HEI, 282). With the passage of time, the Nahuas were able to speak distinctively and exhaustively about their sins (Mendieta, HEI, 282; Motolinía, *History*, 192). That is, they were able to perform an almost perfect confession that, as we will see shortly, implied a particular (and difficult) display of the fullest possible presence of the self to the self, to an authoritative other.

Mendieta rhapsodizes about how sometimes one to two thousand Indians followed the friars through hills and barren lands in order to be confessed, with women giving birth to babies on the road, and very old people who could barely stand dragging themselves behind the masses (HEI, 282). Others, with their wives and children, waited sometimes a month or two in a remote *pueblo* or altepetl for a friar to confess them. The colonizer's sense of the alterity of Nahua fervor surfaces in the text as Mendieta admits that at times the friars would lose their patience with the obdurate crowds who sometimes followed them without having anything to eat (HEI, 283). These crowds, weeping bitterly, would refuse to go back to their homes until they had received the sacrament. Such a vehement feeling about confession during the early decades of the spiritual colonization documented (invented and/or fantasized) in Mendieta's historical narrative was outside the boundaries of Western subjectivity. For the European penitent was never that willing to confess, to weep for his sins, to do penance and/or practice restitution (Tentler, 130–31). In perhaps the most important manual for confessors and penitents in Spain during the sixteenth century, printed in Salamanca in 1553 by the royal printer Andrea de Portonariis, Martín de Azpilcueta deems that shedding tears, sighing, and the like is not necessary because it is not in the penitent's control to feel "sensitive pain."[3] Thus, "basta que mas estime el mal del pecado, y de perder, o tener por perdido a Dios, que otro mal alguno en general. Y que puesto que mas intensamente sienta, y llore por la muerte del padre que por su pecado: Pero mas querria no offender, y no aver offendido a Dios: que la vida de su padre" [it is enough (that the penitent) considers more the evil of sin, of losing or believing that [he] has lost God, than any other evil in general. And since he will feel more intensely and will weep more over the death of his father than over his sin: But he would want more not to offend, and not to have offended God: than the life of his father] (Azpilcueta, 9). In order to be absolved the penitent must correctly consider that losing salvation is much worse than having lost a close relative for whom he may grieve much more. Azpilcueta's explanation acknowledges the difficulty of exciting sensitive pain in the European penitent, which harked back to the Scotian opinion about the saintly exceptionality of the sorrow and devotion required by true contrition. But in Mendieta's invention and/or construction, the (otherly) Nahua masses anxiously and resolutely ran to obtain the sacrament of penance while shedding copious tears. And indeed, Mendieta acknowledges the element of the extraordinary in his representations of the indigenous penitents: "Bastará lo dicho para que se considere la copiosa materia que los hombres cristianos tenian en aquel tiempo para alabar á Dios en la conversion de tan innumerables gentes, que con tanta voluntad y alegria corrian en busca del Señor,...á recibir sus santos sacramentos" [What has been said is enough for considering the abundant cause that Christian men had at that time for praising God for the conversion of innumerable people, who so willingly and happily ran in search of the Lord,...to receive his holy sacraments] (HEI, 286–87).

Such an enthusiastic representation of the new Nahua penitents was not, however, the only description circulating among the Friars Minor during this period. The proto-ethnographer Bernardino de Sahagún did not construct the Nahua subject's confessional act as optimistically as Motolinía or Mendieta. In his great ethnographic monument *Historia general de las cosas de la Nueva España* he pointed out that the Nahuas were persevering in their pre-Hispanic practices when they insisted on receiving from their confessors a *cédula*, or certificate, stating that they had received the sacrament. What they really wanted was to show it to the authorities of their altepetl and thus be protected from any legal action, as was the case in pre-Hispanic times with their once-in-a-lifetime confessed sins: "Este embuste casi ninguno de los religiosos ni clérigos entienden por dónde va, por ignorar la costumbre antigua que tenían" [Hardly any of the religious or clerics understand the tenor of this lie, since they are ignorant of the ancient custom that they (the Nahuas) had] (Sahagún, *Historia,* 1:47). Far from representing the Nahua performance of Christian confession as a cipher of God's favor to the world, Fray Bernardino depicts it as an *embuste*, as a cover-up, for their pre-Hispanic customs, which would legally empower them in their communities.[4] Ignorance about the native past, which his *Historia general* was intended to dispel, had prevented the missionaries from properly identifying idolatrous practices hidden behind a dissimulated Christian demeanor. Motolonía, Mendieta, and Sahagún's distinct positions reflect the tension between the colonizer's claims that Christianity is ecumenical and thus accessible to all peoples of the world, and the more anguishing recognition of the manifold local cultures and practices of the colonized that block submission to such a universal truth.

What was this confessional act, which Fray Mendieta deemed the Nahuas capable of carrying out almost perfectly and which Fray Bernardino considered they were feigning? One of the most important confession manuals for Indians in New Spain was Fray Alonso de Molina's long bilingual *Confessionario mayor*, published in Mexico in 1565 and reprinted in 1569 and 1578. According to Serge Gruzinski, it seems to have been an archetype of confessional manual in New Spain ("Confesión," 185). Other outstanding works of the confessional genre in sixteenth-century New Spain were written by Fray Juan de la Anunciación, a Dominican, and by Fray Juan Bautista, who also authored the *Advertencias para los confesores de los Naturales* (1600).[5] I will argue that the *Confessionario mayor* and the *Advertencias* are documents of incomparable value for studying how the Spanish spiritual colonizer imagined, produced, and tried to implement a new Nahua Christian subjectivity as the sixteenth century unfolded. Such confessional manuals constitute, therefore, very clear pragmatic acts of European imposition upon the other. And yet, the attempts to constitute the new Nahua Christian subject in these manuals will also reveal a crisis in the spiritual colonizer. Never in total mastery of his power, nor of his strategies to wield it, never totally blind to these uncomfortable facts, and yet incapable of renouncing his evangelic endeavor (which, no doubt, placed him in a position of political and cultural preeminence over the Nahua), the spiritual colonizer split as he tried to convert the other into an image of the self.

Molina's *Confessionario mayor*
and the Impossible Nahua Christian Subject

lonso de Molina (b.?–1579) was one of the most prominent figures in Nahuatl studies in the sixteenth century. The son of a Spanish widow from Extremadura, Alonso arrived in Mexico possibly around 1524. He grew up in close contact with indigenous children, thus learning Nahuatl and Spanish almost simultaneously. He was recruited by the Twelve as a child and was their first instructor in the language, as well as their interpreter. According to Mendieta, Alonso shared a cell with the friars, ate with them, and read to them at the table (HEI, 220). As soon as Alonso came of age, he took the Franciscan habit and eventually became a renowned philologist in Nahuatl. As Ascención León-Portilla points out, he was perhaps one of the most fortunate authors of the sixteenth century since he was able to see most of his works published and several of them reprinted (*Tepuztlahcuilolli*, 1:25). His three most important works are the *Vocabulario en Lengua Castellana y Mexicana* (1555, 1571), still consulted as an authority today, *Arte de la Lengua Mexicana y Castellana* (1571, 1576), and the bilingual *Confessionario mayor en la Lengua Mexicana y Castellana* (1565, 1569, 1578), which is the subject of the present chapter. It is relevant to point out that Molina also wrote a bilingual *Confessionario breve en la Lengua Mexicana y Castellana* (1565, 1569, 1577), or shorter confessional manual. The longer and more complex version was destined for the Nahua penitents, literate Nahuas, and preachers and confessors with experience in dealing with their indigenous flock. The shorter confessional was directed to Spanish confessors who were not very proficient in Nahuatl so that they would know how to ask the indispensable questions correctly (Molina, *Confessionario*, 2r–2v, 6v).

Since not all of the Nahua penitents addressed in the *Confessionario mayor* would have been literate, it is thought that the targeted readership was the church-educated Nahuas who assisted priests (Sell, "Molina," 50, 62). These literate Nahuas would have read aloud some parts of Molina's manual to the penitents preparing for confession. In terms of the discursive structure of the *Confessionario mayor*, however, it is clearly the voice of Molina who speaks and addresses the penitents in the prologue.[1] In the second and third parts of the *Confessionario* in which the penitent is admonished to confess correctly, and in which specific questions about the Ten Commandments are asked, the speaker is the figure of an unspecified priest. Thus, the implied relationship in the text is clearly that of the confessor and penitent, even if in actuality the manual may have been used in other ways. And it is this confessor/penitent relationship in the colonial context of sixteenth-century Mexico that we are interested in examining.

In the "Epístola nuncupatoria," or letter in which Alonso de Molina dedicates his work to the second Archbishop of Mexico Alonso de Montúfar in 1564, the author explains that he has been moved to write his two bilingual confession manuals in order to instruct the ministers of the church in the ways of Nahuatl and the natives in important matters pertaining to confession: "Y [para que] los dichos Ministros sepan los propios y naturales vocablos, que se requiere para preguntar y entender en la administracion del Sacramento de la Penitencia...es menester, y se requiere saber el verdadero conocimiento y fuerça del vocablo, e modo de hablar, que tienen [los indígenas](de lo qual muchos [Ministros] carecen) aunque hablan la lengua y sean doctos...[y] materias vtiles y necessarias a los penitentes, para saberse confessar y declarar sus pecados y circunstancias dellos" [And so that the said Ministers know the proper and natural words that are required to ask and understand in the administration of the Sacrament of Penance...it is necessary and required to apprehend the true knowledge and force of the word and the way of speaking that they [the natives] have (which many [Ministers] lack) even though they speak the language and are learned...[and] useful and necessary matters for the penitents, so that they know how to confess and declare their sins and circumstances of them] (Molina, *Confessionario*, 2r–2v).

Full and thorough knowledge of the meaning of the penitent's words was necessary in order to ask the proper questions and understand the answers. For even though many ministers knew Nahuatl in a grammatically correct way, they were ignorant of the moods, the specific contexts, and the inflections of the language the natives used. This prevented confessor and penitent from adequately comprehending each other. On the other hand, the penitent's desire to confess and even to repent his sins needed to be declared in an appropriate way. What produced the necessary cleansing and healing grace was not only the penitent's contrite disposition to state his or her sins, nor was it the confessor's belief that the former merited absolution. In order to trigger the efficacy of the confessional act there was a linguistic and discursive propriety that had to be strictly observed by both penitent and confessor and that lay outside the realms of intent, will, and/or desire. The spiritual colonizer's task was, then, to master Nahuatl completely, to unravel all its secrets, to render its materiality as transparent as possible. In the colonial context of the New World the ministers of penance also had to become linguists, nahuatlatos, very learned in the Nahuatl language.[2] They had to turn philologists in order to reshape the soul.[3] The Nahua penitent, on his part, had to learn how to organize his memory so as to talk about sin, self, and desire and thus produce a Christian subjectivity. Molina's *Confessionario* was intended to help both penitent and confessor attain the specific linguistic and discursive competence required to wield the performative power of the sacrament.

Molina opens his prologue in the first person addressing a beloved son, "quienquiera que tú seas"[whoever you are], who comes to occupy the position of reader or penitent. The pronouns in the text are those that actualize language, and the *quienquiera que tú seas* further underscores the "empty forms" that language provides in order to enable a subject to emerge through the self-referring present of his/her particular exercise of discourse (Benveniste, 224). In other words, the text is not calling upon a particular individual, category, or group: anyone and everyone may fill in the position of interlocutor in the text. This of course implies the universality of address characteristic of Christianity.

According to Émile Benveniste, it is in the reality of discourse where subjectivity, as "the psychic unity that transcends the totality of the actual experiences it assembles and that makes the permanence of consciousness," is objectively founded (224–26). That is, subjectivity is not so much what the individual feels he is or is not,[4] but a position, a location from which he posits himself as a continuity, as an abstract sum of all that he has experienced and felt. Such subjectivity or abstract construct of continuity is produced only at the moment in which an *I* is uttered.

In these senses, confession (both in colonial and non-colonial contexts) can be thought of as a laboratory of subjectivity. It is a linguistic act usually aimed at a *you*. It carefully examines the present in which subjectivity is posited, as it questions those discrete experiences that the subject unwittingly claims to encompass at the very moment of responding as an *I*. Confession, therefore, is a thoroughly self-referential, self-reflexive discourse, which in the great majority of cases exposes the confessing *I* as an absence to itself by producing rigorous knowledge and detailed memory about what constitutes him.

Ever since the time of Saint Thomas Aquinas, confessors were advised to be "dulcis, affabilis, atque suavis, prudens, discretus, mitis, pius atque benignus" [sweet, affable, and pleasant, prudent, discreet, gentle, and also kind] (Delumeau, 25). The confessor should be most careful not to be severe, demanding, or chastising. He should be charitable in his treatment of the penitent, and the latter should be consoled with the promise of forgiveness (Delumeau, 25). Only in this way would the penitent be encouraged to speak. This implies that there was clear recognition of the difficulty of bringing into being, of producing through the confessional speech act that "lucid" (Delumeau, 8), linguistically specific presence of the subject to itself that Catholicism posits as indispensable for salvation.[5] In the colonial context of sixteenth-century Mexico, the confessional linguistic act is further burdened with a specifically nonreciprocal situation, since the colonized will invariably be in the position of the penitent being probed by the *you* of the colonizer and never the other way around. Even so, the confessor/colonizer is not positioned as an "omniscient and all powerful figure" over a helpless colonized *you*, as some critics have argued (Gruzinski, "Individualization," 98; Subirats, 220). In admonishing the penitent to remember that he is a sinner, for instance, the subject of authority or confessor also includes itself in the statement: "Que el justo, cuyas obras son rectas, cae y peca siete vezes al día...[y] *nos es dado a entender por esto a todos que somos pecadores y que erramos y faltamos en muchas cosas*" [That the just [man], whose deeds are righteous, falls and sins seven times a day...[and] *because of this it is made clear to all of us that we are sinners and that we err and blunder in many things*] (Molina, *Confessionario* 3v; emphasis mine).[6] By acknowledging his own sinfulness (albeit in a generic way), the speaker, Molina, establishes a reciprocity and community with the Nahua penitent that will encourage him to speak.

But there is more at stake here than simply a rhetorical gesture of reciprocity destined to persuade Nahua penitents to confess. For one thing, the reflexive and encompassing nature of any universalizing statement about human nature logically means that the speaker must apply the statement to himself. Hence, even at the moment of demanding from the penitent full clarity of mind and knowledge of (sinful) self, the probing subject must be very careful about not slipping into the very forgetfulness that he admonishes the penitent seeking salvation to avoid. In other words, although the confessional discourse of the manual is clearly oriented toward the reconstitution and disciplining of the *you* ("quienquiera que tú seas"), the call to participate in and acknowledge the community of human sinfulness can never be entirely asymmetrical: it requires also the confessor's own avowal at the moment of enunciation. Thus, assertions about the omniscience and absolute power of the European priest over the penitent, even in the markedly unequal context of sixteenth-century colonial New Spain, are not entirely accurate. For even though in the colonial context the spiritual colonizer was obviously imposing his own hegemonic conceptions of (sinful) subjectivity upon the other, the structural logic of such conceptions also compelled him to assume openly such a subjectivity and thus renounce any claim to personal privilege, difference, and/or superiority over the penitent. It is in this sense that the confessional, pastoral relationship is both one of power, of struggling to affect and control the actions of others, and, at the same time, irreducible to the advantages of domination.[7]

In order to emphasize the need for self-knowledge that the confessional linguistic act will fulfill for the Nahua penitent, Molina warns that "aquello que no es tenido por peccado, y la maldad que no es juzgada y tenida por maldad, pone en grandissimo peligro y afliccion a los hombres, que los hace desatinar" [that which is not considered a sin, and evil that is not judged and deemed evil, puts men in great danger and affliction, which makes them go out of their minds] (*Confessionario*, 4v). This disturbing statement posits that evil may in fact be unrecognizable to its perpetrator, that it may have been unintentional. Evil may be incurred unknowingly, inadvertently, unconsciously. Although the problem of the ignorance of evil will be used in the Spanish colonial context as an instrument of cultural encompassment, such ignorance is by no means posited only of the colonial penitent. In European confessional manuals, the penitent is also represented as unaware, "forgetful" of the extent of his sinfulness. As discussed above, one of the most important functions of confession is precisely to disclose this reality in full by meticulously bringing it to memory.[8]

Furthermore, not acknowledging evil is extremely dangerous; because although one may not be aware of its polluting effects, it greatly afflicts the person and alienates him from God. The paradox of this economy of sin is that by being capable and worthy of knowing how profoundly evil one really is, by producing and understanding the truth about oneself, the soul will enable itself to contemplate the majesty of God (Molina, *Confessionario*, 5v). That is, what obstructs salvation and the ultimate vision of divinity is not evil committed, but evil suppressed, evil ignored. By working to overcome the manifold resistances of knowing evil, one makes oneself worthy of knowing the "cosas difficiles y maravillosas y muy gustosas...de Nuestro Señor" [difficult and marvelous and very delightful things...of Our Lord] (5v). Paradoxically then, knowledge of the evil in the self leads the subject to a knowledge of God. The manual will enable the penitent to recognize sin and to discourse about it adequately with the confessor in order that the soul-cleansing event and/or the lifting of the veil of ignorance may take place.

It is not difficult to see how this position enhances the power of penance, of the church, and of the confessor in general, as agencies of colonization in the particular context of sixteenth-century Mexico. Jorge Klor de Alva asserts that in contrast to the Greek dictum's purpose of "knowing thyself" in order to attain personal growth, in the confessional scene the purpose was to repudiate the self ("Contar," 59). In Molina's manual, however, we see that knowing (the misery of) one's self, albeit not directed toward strict personal growth, is oriented toward obtaining the highest Christian goods, which are a difficult yet sophisticated knowledge of the "delightful things of God" (*Confessionario,* 5v) and salvation. That is, the dictum of "knowing thyself" in the confessional colonial context will not result solely in the loss or utter repudiation of the self of the colonized, now revealed as blemished and guilty. This is only an intermediate stage of the process. The onerous labor of self-knowledge will finally achieve other desirable, refined knowledges, as well as the convalescence of the self. These lofty promises in the passage assume as a fait accompli the adoption by the Nahua of a Western, "universal" Christian subjectivity. The exhortation to the Nahua penitent to engage in the process of producing knowledge of the self in order to attain a beatific vision of God implies a spiritual maturity already in place that undoes any clear-cut binary opposition between colonial and non-colonial Christians.

Once the penitent has decided to confess and to engage in the painful labor of self-knowledge, he must work diligently to bring to memory all his sins and bitterly lament having committed them. He must start from childhood up to the present moment, sparing no effort to remember accurately, lest the confession be imperfect, invalid, and thus become itself another sin to confess. The manual both builds a memory and produces the reality of sin by presenting a series of discrete hypothetical situations and circumstantial factors that need to be carefully mapped out: "Tambien traeras a la memoria todos tus malos pensamientos,y malos desseos intenciones y voluntad,con que tuviste aborrecimiento,enojo y malquerencia a tus proximos y con que cobdiciaste a alguna persona,o le desseaste la muerte: desseando mucho tu corazon tomar vengança del que te maltrato,y de las vezes que tuviste envidia a tu proximo" [You will also bring to your memory all your evil thoughts, and evil desires, intentions and will, with which you felt abhorrence, anger, and ill will toward your neighbors and how you did covet someone or desired his or her death: wishing very much in your heart to take revenge upon he who mistreated you, and of the times in which you envied your fellowmen] (*Confessionario*, 10v).

If for the Nahuas of pre-Hispanic times desire and other passions could cause damage, or *tlatlacolli* (Burkhart, *Slippery*, 28–30), this was the case not so much for their corrupting moral effects as for the physical ailments their excesses could bring about. People who desired something or someone vehemently were charged with a negative energy that could harm the desired person, plant, or animal (López Austin, *Human*, 1:267). Indulging in forbidden sexual desire could bring about not only *tlazolmiquiztli*, some sort of death spell caused by lust, but also could afflict the relatives and children of the transgressors' community (Soustelle, 193). Excess of desire as well as other transgressions caused imbalances in the realms of the natural, the social, and the spiritual, which in the Nahua, non-Western society, constituted a single, more continuous, though still heterogeneous realm. The consequences of such imbalances were usually a physical ailment or even loss of life. The purpose of a righteous life for the Nahua was to enable one to be a "member of society [who was] healthy, respectable and accommodated" (Klor de Alva, "Contar," 56), not to strengthen oneself morally or gain eternal happiness in the afterlife. Thus, the Nahua of colonial times could relate culturally to a conceptualization of the dreadful consequences of the excesses of desire. However, the need to confess them in order to avoid "an internal diminution of the value of the self" (Ricoeur, *Symbolism*, 102) caused by disobeying divine commandments, would not have been so evident to him. It is in this sense that the *Confessionario mayor*, both by assuming a universal Christian subjectivity for the Nahua penitent and by uncovering, revealing, and/or producing for him new Western forms and versions of transgressions, functioned as an agency of cultural encompassment.

In Latin and Spanish confessional manuals, sins of idolatry were addressed when dealing with the first commandment of loving God above all else. However, the European authors of these manuals "worked with a smaller range of deviation from an already fundamentally Catholic axis" (Homza, 46). The acculturation function of confession in the colonial context of sixteenth-century Mexico can be observed in the way in which Moli-

na avails himself of this first commandment in order to ask specific questions about vestiges of Nahua religious pre-Hispanic practices deemed idolatrous by the friars:

> Por ventura adoraste o tuviste por dios a alguna criatura suya, assi
> como al sol, a la luna o a las estrellas?...
>
> Llamaste alguna vez a algun hechizero, para que te echase
> suertes, o para sacar algunos hechizos de tu cuerpo...o le llamaste
> para que te descubriese lo que avias perdido, o adevino delante de
> ti en el agua?...
>
> Crees los sueños o porventura tuviste por agueros a la
> lechuza,al buho,a la comadre,al escarauajo pinuiztli,y tlalacatl,al
> epatl que se meo en tu casa...? (Molina, 20r–21r)

[Did you adore by chance or had as god any of his creatures, such
as the sun, the moon, or the stars?...

Did you ever call a sorcerer, to learn about your future...or
did you call him to have him find what you had lost or to practice divination in the water in front of you?...

Do you believe in dreams or by chance did you take as omens
the owl, the weasel, the beetles pinuiztli and tlalacatl, the epatl
(foul-smelling animal) that peed in your house...?]

The first commandment allowed questions about any remaining, obdurate "pagan" practice in specific historical and geographical contexts. It is
then not difficult to see how this type of inquiry transforms the colonial confessional act into a powerful technology of cultural subjugation, as Serge
Gruzinski has observed ("Individualization," 1989), a function it did not
have as prominently in the European context.[9]

In another move for cultural encompassment and subordination, the
Nahua penitent is clearly instructed to assume full responsibility for his sins.
Discussing the necessity to repeat the whole confession if some sin was left
untold for shame, the penitent is admonished not to excuse himself to himself (or the confessor) in the following fashion:

> Y no diras hizome fuerça, o provocome el demonio, a que
> pecasse: ni tampoco diras, era mi amigo o pariente el que me hizo
> cometer el peccado, no lo hize, ni cometi de mi voluntad, sino que
> mi carne me forço a hacerlo, o mi mujer...pues no auía de obede-

cer al que me prouoco a peccar, ni al que me mouio el coraçon a quebrantar el mandamiento de nuestro señor. *Por que aunque muriera yo en sus manos no auia de condescender con el*; y pues es assi que yo hize lo que me mando, yo tengo la culpa de lo que cometí. (Molina, 12v–13r; emphasis mine)

[And you will no say that the Devil forced me or provoked me to sin: and you will not say either, it was my friend or relative who made me commit the sin, and neither will you say, I did not do it, nor did I commit it of my own will, but it was my flesh that forced me to do it, or my wife…for I should not have obeyed he who induced me to sin, nor he who moved my heart to break the commandment of Our Lord. *For even if I were to die by his hands I should not have obeyed* him, and since it is the case that I did what he demanded, I am guilty for what I did.]

Accusing the devil, friends, relatives, wife, or anybody else will not exculpate the sinner. Not even his very flesh, weakness, or lack of virtue are to be blamed for having caused the penitent to sin. Only he himself, *yo mismo*, is responsible. This is a tremendously rigorous injunction that will multiply the instances of sin considerably, imposing upon the Nahua a distinctive Western concept of individual agency and free will.[10] Being strongly corporate and ritualistic, the boundaries between the Nahua individual and his community were more permeable and blurry than the European's. As has already been discussed above, the Nahua lived in a world where people constantly had to establish relationships of equilibrium with forces, spirits, people, plants, animals—everything that shared the violent, precarious earth with them.[11] There were so many circulating forces that the subject had to take into account, so many rituals to be strictly observed in order to influence the gods' behavior and to avoid their retributions, so many social relations affecting his demeanor that the concept of a free and independent will as the sole, internal cause of individual acts in an autonomous person may have been inconceivable to the Nahua Christian neophyte (Gruzinski, *Colonización*, 149–85).[12]

But there is more in this passage than a standard representation of the universal, Christian (read Western) notion of the individual and his/her free will that the Nahuas were expected to have assumed. Molina seems to dismiss the problem of circumstances altogether. This may have been in accordance with the teaching that the penitent should not try to mitigate his guilt by blaming circumstances or other people for his sins in the act of confession. It was commonly accepted that the penitent should only confess *aggravating* circumstances or those circumstances that changed the species and nature of sin from venial to mortal, or from a mortal sin into another even more seriously mortal transgression (Ayala, 18r–18v; Tentler, 116–20). In his influential and learned manual, however, Martín de Azpilcueta declared that the penitent should also confess the mitigating circumstances or those that excuse a mortal sin: "Porque, aunque no la calle, bastantemente se acusa echandose la culpa que tiene, sin quitar, ni poner mas. Y aun es obligado a confessarlas [circunstancias mitigantes]...quando tanto aliuia, que de mortal lo haze que no sea pecado, o no mas de venial, como la circunsstancia de la graue enfermedad aliuia al comer de la carne en quaresma" [For, even if he does say it, he accuses himself sufficiently by assuming the guilt that he has, without taking on or adding anything else. And he is even obliged to confess them (mitigating circumstances)...when it alleviates so much that from a mortal sin, no sin is committed, or no more than a venial one, such as the circumstance of serious illness mitigates eating meat during Lent] (33).

Azpilcueta conceded, then, that the penitent's desire to establish the precise degree of his guilt is legitimate and should not be interpreted by the confessor as an exculpating gesture. What is significant for our discussion is that Molina seemed not to allow the colonized Nahua penitents to do the same even though the latter, due to their many cultural differences and relatively recent conversion to Christianity, clearly should be in need of more tolerance and leniency than any of their European counterparts.

And yet, although the imperative of total agency that Molina espoused in his *Confessionario* is undoubtedly severe, even oppressive, and may be denounced as narrowly Eurocentric, one thing is certain: the Nahua Christian subjectivity posited in this part of the confessional act is not a subaltern, inferior one. Rather, the opposite seems to be the case. The penitent is proposed as a subject of heroic dimensions, with full moral power, capable of resisting the devil himself or any other tempter even though life itself would be at stake, had he only willed it: "Porque aunque muriera yo en sus manos no avia de condescender con el ni obedecerle" [For even if I were to die by his hands I did not have to agree with him nor obey him] (Molina, *Confessionario,* 13r). The possibility of a will stronger than flesh, matter, and fear of death itself is perhaps one of the paradoxical potencies the acknowledgment of sin confers. For the conscientious avowal of having failed to exercise the full capacity of the will (in fending off evil) is one way in which its power (freedom) can be conceived, inaugurated, opened up.[13]

Through the particulars of the construction or "revelation" of evil, therefore, the sacrament of penance produces the possibility of thoroughly controlling the penitent. But by positing the utter autonomy of the subject's will, by declining to invoke any other external agency to minimize the failure of actualizing the full freedom of the subject, Molina was also proposing to the Nahua Christian subject that ultimately he was beyond the colonizer's or anyone's social, political, or even religious control. No pressure, fear, authority, or violent repression was ever powerful enough to force consent. Attributing free will to the Nahua in the context of the sacrament of penance restrained him with the burden of an unmitigated guilt, but it also implied the recognition that he had the agency to withhold his truth from the Spanish confessor's controlling purview or from anyone else he chose.

Confession, then, could expose everything to the priest's surveillance, but could also allow the penitent to imagine the possibilities of his enormous liberty and capacity to transgress. This paradox would be of course the case for all penitents, colonial and non-colonial. But of particular interest in the *Confessionario mayor* is that the reconfiguration of the Nahua as a full-fledged agent both reaffirmed and dismantled the manifold discourses of the Spanish colonial order as a paternalistic agency of amelioration and of the Nahua as a childish, unknowing other in need of guidance and direction. Klor de Alva has pointed out that the missionaries did not properly take into account Nahua difference in the confessional act, but rather interpreted the Nahua subject through Christian categories under the presumption of their universality ("Contar," 53). Within the context of this author's article, such hermeneutics are depicted at best as a conceptual deficiency of the friars, at worst as an "inexcusable instrument of control" ("Contar," 72). I am arguing, however, that Molina's confessional strategies were in and of themselves more ambiguous than this. Clearly, they imposed asymmetrically Western Christian notions of human universality onto the other. In doing so, however, many of the inequalities, discriminations, and exclusions perpetrated by the colonial formations and institutions in sixteenth-century Mexico simply became untenable.[14] By attributing absolute agency, judgment, and accountability to the Nahua subject, what Bhabha denominates as "the visibility of . . . (the) separation which, in denying the colonized capacities of self-government, independence, western modes of civility, lends authority to the official version and mission of the colonial power" ("Other," 171), was seriously put into question, at least in Molina's widely circulating confessional manual.

Now, this formidable Nahua Christian subjectivity posited by the *Confessionario Mayor* is further burdened by the demands of a strict observance of the materiality of Catholic rites and sacraments and with knowledge of all sorts of topics deemed "necessary for salvation" (Molina, *Doctrina*, 30).[15] Under the third commandment, for instance, the penitent was asked if he had observed all Sundays and holidays and heard a complete Mass. He was then asked whether when he was at Mass he gave himself totally ("totalmente") to God and prayed to him with all his heart ("de todo tu coraçon" [Molina, *Confessionario*, 26v]). The penitent should then have wept and sighed for his sins and firmly decided not to offend God again (Molina, *Confessionario*, 26v). After being warned that missing a feast without good reason was a mortal sin (Molina, *Confessionario*, 26v–27r), a list of twelve feasts follows, which the Nahua had to know by heart in order not to skip any. As in the case of the five specific circumstances under which the Christian is obliged to baptize (Molina, *Confessionario*, 22r–25r), the Nahua Christian subject was produced by exacting internal and external imperatives. Perfect interior disposition was not enough, nor flawless liturgical competence. The proper Nahua Christian subject was urged to control his heart and will completely, to be capable of loving God totally, as well as to have a thorough mastery of the mechanics of the rites and of the innumerable details of Christian doctrine.

But perhaps the moment where the "impossible desire for a pure, undifferentiated origin" (Bhabha, "Other," 169) blinding the spiritual colonizer is most manifestly exposed is in the questions asked to the penitent about the potencies of the soul and the three theological virtues. On the theological virtue of charity, Molina admonishes the following to the Nahua penitent: "Porque si...no menospreciases y te aparatares de todo lo malo...por amor y respecto de nstro Señor, sino solamente porque no te acaezca o suceda algun mal o aflicion, o porque no seas castigado por tus pecados, ciertamente no alcançaras cosa alguna celestial, ni te podras salvar (aunque todavia te aprovechara para algun contentamiento temporal, y para disminucion de algunos tormentos, y afflicion del Infierno)" [Because if...you do not scorn and stay away from everything evil...for love and respect for Our Lord, but only so that no evil or affliction befall you, or so that you are not punished for your sins, you will certainly not reach any heavenly thing, nor will you be able to save yourself (although this might help you for some temporal contentment, and for the alleviation of some torments and affliction from hell)] (*Confessionario*, 111r–111v).

What is particularly intriguing about this passage is the exclusionary nature of the two radically opposed poles around which the Christian subjectivity is posited. Molina is instructing the penitent that the only way to obtain every virtue and sanctity is to push sin aside, not for fear of whatever evil consequence could befall therefrom, but for love of God. Otherwise, though staying away from evil for fear of punishment will alleviate the torments of hell, salvation will never be attained, nor sins forgiven. This is clearly an extreme position, which is even more rigorous than the dictates of the Council of Trent. For in a parallel situation of repentance (and following the Scotist position that held that only very spiritually advanced people were able to feel contrition [Tentler, 26]), Trent accepted repentance by attrition:

> As to imperfect contrition, which is called attrition, since it commonly arises either from the considerations of the heinousness of sin or from the fear of hell and punishment, the council declares that if it renounces the desire to sin and hopes for pardon, it not only does not make one a hypocrite and a greater sinner, but is even a gift of God and an impulse of the Holy Ghost, not indeed as already dwelling in the penitent, but only moving him, with which assistance the penitent prepares a way for him-

self unto justice. And though without the sacrament of penance it cannot per se lead the sinner to justification, it does, however, dispose him to obtain the grace of God in the sacrament of penance. (*Canons*, 92)

Molina's severe dismissal of attrition clearly goes against Trent's representation of it as "a gift from God" and as a passport to obtain forgiveness. We are seeing then that he is demanding from the new Nahua Christian subject an inner disposition many theologians in the Old World thought only possible for those who were well rooted in Christian life (Pelikan, 131). In addition, the language of Molina's admonition exemplifies the difficulty of clearly separating, on a psychological level, one type of sorrow from the other. Ironically, by resolutely demanding nothing less than perfect contrition lest punishment in hell would ensue, the *Confessionario mayor* is propitiating the fall of the Nahua penitent into the fear of the loss of salvation and non-forgiveness of sins, which is the very theological definition of attrition.

It must be said, however, that Molina's position is not necessarily representative of the Franciscans. Louise Burkhart points out that in Fray Alonso de Escalona's *Sermones en mexicano* (n.d.) he claims that if the sinners feel sad about their sins and if they obey the commandments, they will indeed gain salvation (*Slippery*, 34). Fray Escalona makes no distinction between the possible types of sadness a penitent could feel for his sins. It is enough that he would feel it and that he would be willing henceforth to obey the commandments. This is more in line with the Council of Trent's pronouncement about attrition than Molina's position in the quoted passage above. Although Burkhart is of the opinion that Franciscan and Dominican friars, while obviously preferring contrition, did not reject attrition necessarily (*Slippery*, 33), this is not Molina's stance in the *Confessionario*.

Why did Molina invent such an exacting Christian subjectivity for the new Nahua converts, one that the average Spaniard would hardly be able to assume? Was the *Confessionario*'s disavowed desire to produce a faltering, guilty Nahua subject, who would always be thwarted by a demand for impossible perfection? Or was the proliferating sinfulness unleashed by this manual's onerous demands also expected to be informed by Paul's dictum in Romans 5:20: "Where sin abounded, grace did much more abound"?

Clearly, the disciplining of the Nahua is definitely one of the objectives of the confessional strategies of the *Confessionario*. Regarding the specific issue of attrition, as we have discussed already, in their pre-Hispanic religion the Nahuas did not confess so much due to remorse as for fear of retribution or for entreating the divine "for material ends and collective well-being in this world" (Taylor, 50). This was carried over into the indigenous practice of Christianity throughout the colonial period: "Indians paid too little attention to the soul's eternal salvation and, therefore, to the scrutiny of personal sin, thought many of their Catholic priests" (Taylor, 50). Molina's stern insistence on contrition and his dismissal of attrition could be explained as an attempt to uproot this particular precolonial disposition to supplication and propitiation of the divine for worldly objectives. However, as part of a broader issue in the *Confessionario mayor*, which is that of carving out a Christian subjectivity for the new Nahua converts that in many instances the average Spaniard would hardly be able to assume, the rejection of attrition points to a more complex problem. Some friars admitted in dismay that the Nahua subject had become more dissolute and corrupted under the colonizer's Christian order than he had ever been in pre-Hispanic times. According to Sahagún, what caused the present vices of the natives were not intrinsic moral flaws but climatological circumstances and/or the position of the constellations (Sahagún, *Florentine*, 1:76). Even the Spaniards, if not extremely careful, only a few years after their arrival to the *tierra de indios* "se hacen otros" (ibid.)—that is, they become "others." Sahagún then laments the inadequacy of the colonizer in adapting himself properly to that alien environment: "But it is to our disgrace that the native Indians, prudent and wise old men, knew how to remedy the harm this land impresses on those who dwell in it, hindering the natural conditions with opposing practices. And we drift with our evil tendencies. And certainly a people, Spanish as well as Indian, is reared which is unbearable to control and very difficult to save" (*Florentine*, 1:77).

Many issues, discourses, and subtexts are being played out in this fascinating passage. But what is most relevant to our discussion of Molina and the rigor of his *Confessionario mayor* is the reference to pre-Hispanic discipline as more appropriate to the particular "climatological circumstances" than the order the Spaniards had come to impose. The order of the colonizer, at least in terms of the morality of the Indians, is constructed by Sahagún as being pernicious, chaotic, undisciplined, and insufficiently or inappropriately structured.[16] Whereas the pre-Hispanic Nahuas had known how to counteract the "harmful inclinations" produced by the environment with "contrarios exercicios," the Spanish colonizers had not been able to contain the tide of these inclinations and thus were being suffocated by their own iniquity.[17] Did Sahagún mean to say that these "contrarios exercicios" were what he and so many other chronicler-ethnographers had perceived as an onerously ritualized order, in which every hour of the day and night had a god, and almost every creature had a religious significance and, according to Mendieta, was even adored as God (HEI, 88)? What had the Nahua wise men understood about the climate and the constellations of this part of the world (which also transformed the Spaniards into "unmanageable others") that they had been determined to counter with a meticulously controlled way of life, and with harsh punishments for any infraction to such order?[18]

Another important reference to the topic of the discipline of the indigenous pre-Hispanic past can be found in the *Códice Franciscano*. The *Códice* was a report about the provinces under Franciscan jurisdiction written by the Friars Minor at the request of the *visitador* (judge) Juan de Ovando in 1570. In the section about Nahua church singers and music players the author, believed to be Gerónimo de Mendieta, states that music, ornaments, and decorations are very beneficial to further Christianity among the Indians:

> Y es muy necesario el ornato y aparato de las iglesias para levantarles el espíritu y moverlos á las cosas de Dios, porque su natural que es tibio y olvidadizo de las cosas interiores ha menester ser ayudado con la apariencia exterior; *y á esta causa los que gobernaban en tiempo de su infidelidad los ocupaban los más del tiempo en edificación de sumptuosos templos, y en adornarlos mucho de rosas y flores, demás del oro y plata que tenían, y en muchos sacrificios y cerimonias, más duras y recias que las de la ley de Moisén*" (*Códice Franciscano*, 58; emphasis mine).

> [And the adornments and ostentation of the churches are very necessary in order to raise their spirit and move them toward the things of God, because their nature, which is tepid and forgetful

of interior things, needs to be helped with external display; and because of this reason those who ruled them at the time of their infidelity kept them busy most of the time by having them build sumptuous temples, adorning them with roses and flowers, besides the gold and silver that they had, and with many sacrifices and ceremonies, more oppressive and rigorous than those of the law of Moses.]

According to the author of the *Códice*, because of their "natural" indifference and forgetfulness about internal things, the Nahuas disciplined and/or busied themselves in pre-Hispanic times with the construction of sumptuous palaces as well as with their rigorous sacrifices and ceremonies, the latter estimated to be even more scrupulous than Judaic rituals.[19]

Taking into account this construction of a severe, yet quite orderly pre-Hispanic society, may the *Confessionario*'s rigor be thought, ironically, as a "contrario exercicio," that is, as a form of disciplining and constituting the new Nahua Christian subject that would counteract that very same "natural tibio y olvidadizo" (tepid and forgetful nature) the pre-Hispanic rulers (according to Mendieta, Sahagún, and many others) had taken upon themselves to combat?

Perhaps. Yet still another different, but not incompatible scenario could be also posited to account for the manual's disconcerting requisitions. In many Franciscan texts of the sixteenth century various aspects of the constructed Nahua difference were favorably compared to the Minorite ascetic practices of utter evangelical poverty. These practices were the spiritual hallmark of the most prestigious sectors of the Observant Friars Minor at the time in Spain. The first wave of Franciscan missionaries, dispatched to combat the forces of evil "in the eleventh hour" of the world,[20] at varying moments in their discursive productions arranged, distributed, and deployed Nahua difference as fulfilling a salient role in their apocalyptic expectations of full spiritual presence. For Motolinía, the (constructed) shyness, meekness, and reserved "nature" of the Indians, rather than evidence of inferiority, made them worthy of the kingdom of God:

Many times they come to be baptized but are afraid to ask for the sacrament or even to speak. Hence there is no need of questioning them with a loud voice.... To Indians so disposed one must not deny what they desire, because to them belongs the kingdom of God, to them who have scarcely a ragged mat on which to sleep or a good blanket with which to cover themselves, while their dwelling is leaky and thrown open to the night watchman of God. The Indians are a simple people, well disposed, neither avaricious nor ambitious. (Motolinía, *History,* 187)

This pious representation of the Nahua within the bounds of the Christian discourse surely should not distract us from the very political fact that that other is placed in a position of clear subservience to the European self. However, we should not forget either that humbleness, meekness, and disposition to obey are virtues that Motolonía's own Franciscan order and Christian doctrine at large posit as essential for salvation. Such virtues hark back to the Sermon on the Mount: "Happy are those who know they are spiritually poor; the Kingdom of heaven belongs to them!" and "Happy are the meek; they will receive what God has promised!" (Matt. 5:3,5).[21]

Taking Motolinía's representation as a possible intertext for the *Confessionario mayor,* could it be plausibly proposed that the latter's inordinate if not incoherent demands for spiritual and ritual perfection may have been modulated by the fantasy of inventing the boundaries for the Nahua Christian subject of the new Indian church in the impending third age of the Holy Spirit?[22] Was the formidable subjectivity posited by Molina destined to constitute the "pure Apostolic Church [which] might be formed again on earth" (Israel, 9), with the Friars Minor, no doubt, at the head?

Possibly an amalgamation of all the scenarios and discursive possibilities expounded above. The onerous expectations of the *Confessionario* may have been conceived as a strategy to eradicate particular pre-Hispanic behaviors that interfered with or even ran counter to a Christian subjectivity. They may have been destined to work as a "contrario exercicio" that would demand total absorption of mind and diligence from people who could be easily distracted, but whose humility, meekness, and obedience, if properly disciplined, could yield the subjectivity of a new, much more spiritually elevated church than that of the Old World. And while all these discourses of boorishness, meekness, and obedience clearly were constructs of alterity that justified colonial rule, they certainly take us beyond the "schema of

Manichean allegory" in which the other was defined in totally negative and derogatory terms by a European colonizer who thought and spoke about himself solely in positive ones (JanMohamed, 2).

And yet, little by little, the anomalous forms to which the confessional strategies of the *Confessionario mayor* gave rise would make it clear that Molina's ritual and spiritual rigor, whatever its intended or unintended aims, was untenable. With a third printing in 1578, and due to the author's great prestige as a nahuatlato, the manual must have continued to circulate widely at least until 1599, when Fray Juan Bautista composed three bilingual confessional manuals, one long and two much shorter, and published them together. Except for a fictional dramatic dialogue in the second manual between a confessor and a Nahua penitent in which the former asks admittedly quite difficult questions about the doctrine of the Eucharist to the latter (who answers very elaborately and correctly) (75–85r), even the most "copious" of Bautista's three confessional manuals is much more simplified, brief, and rudimentary than Molina's *Confessionario mayor*. And never as exacting.[23] One year later Bautista published an admonitions manual for confessors in order to help clear up the most common doubts and reserves about confessing the Nahuas, as well as to console them for the anguishing failure of their efforts.

Bautista's works notwithstanding and as we saw above, it had been none other than Sahagún who had started piercing the millenarian fantasy of the triumphal mass conversions effectuated by the Twelve that prevailed during the first forty years of the enterprise of evangelization (Klor de Alva, "Sahagún," 85). Sahagún claimed that the evangelization endeavor was failing, and that the Twelve, Motolinía in particular, had simply been deluded about the success of the Nahua conversions to Christianity. For outside the public spaces that the missionaries had panoptically reconstructed, the gods of the Mexica and their pre-Hispanic religious practices lived on. In the particular case of confession, whether deliberately resisting (Gruzinski, "Individualization," 104) or not (Lockhart, *The Nahuas*, 203), the colonizer-missionary began to realize that in spite of the alleged Nahua desire to confess and their great disposition to do penance, they were not fully prepared or willing to render a good confession. Neither the Spanish colonizer's evangelizing technologies, nor his sophisticated linguistic awareness achieved through hard, meritorious work, had been able to root penance in the indigenous mind as the spiritual colonizer desired or expected. Perhaps strongly influenced by the Twelve's view of providential conversion, Molina deployed unreasonable expectations from the Nahua neophytes in his *Confessionario*. Maybe his penitential rigor, which was attributed to the Nahuas consummate free will, was an instance of sheer pastoral ineptitude that had intimidated rather than facilitated their accession to Christianity. Or more simply, the cultural differences between colonizer and colonized were much more elusive than the Franciscan philological, ethnographic, and even spiritualist discourses had been able to fathom. In any case, the *Confessionario mayor* did not expedite the historical emergence of the Indian church. Rather, the contrary seems to have been the case. Molina's onerous, pastoral demand for a mighty, perhaps apocalyptic, Christian sameness from the Nahua propitiated a deepening of the gap between the two. As we will see in the next chapter, Bautista's *Advertencias para los confessores de los Naturales* may be read as a remedy for this unexpected outcome of the colonization strategy, which distressed the spiritual colonizer as he confronted the many forms and ways in which alterity lay beyond his reach.

8

Juan Bautista's *Advertencias para los confessores de los Naturales* and the Malaises of Domination

According to John E. Phelan, by the end of the sixteenth century the Franciscan dream of a new Indian church whose spirituality and perfection would belong to the Third Age of the Holy Spirit, bountiful in grace and childlike simplicity, had greatly dissipated. I will argue in this chapter that Fray Juan Bautista's new *Confessionario* (1599) and especially his *Advertencias para los confessores de los Naturales* (1600), as compared to Molina's *Confessionario mayor*, belong to a very different moment in the sixteenth-century evangelical endeavor and in the concomitant production of knowledge and images about the Nahuas by their now somewhat disenchanted and less zealous spiritual colonizers.

The stated objectives of the 1600 *Advertencias* are the consolation of the confessor, the unburdening of his conscience and the urging not to abandon the administration of this sacrament. Many circumstances, both from the part of the colonizer and the subaltern, provided the context for the composition of Fray Juan Bautista's text exhorting the Franciscans not to give up their struggle for the soul of the Nahua. The Third Mexican Council of 1585 was the official, though admittedly belated, adoption of the Tridentine hard line in the New World. The Third Council supported Trent's opposition to the extraordinary powers of the mendicants. Upon its very welcome recommendation, Philip II ordered the submission of the regulars to the diocese as well as the transfer of their parishes to the secular clergy. The argument expounded regarding this most explosive matter was that it was unnecessary for the regulars to keep exercising the extraordinary priestly powers conferred to them by Adrian VI's bull of 1523, the famous Omni-moda, since there were now enough priests adequately trained to take over pastoral and doctrinal duties. The conversion and evangelization of the Nahuas had been an urgent issue during the decades of the 1530s and 1540s. But since the Mexican church had presumably reached a stage of maturity by 1585, it was time to move away from the improvised, more flexible, and creative religious acculturation of the Indians carried out by the mendicants, toward participation in a more stable, centralized, and universal church led by the clergy (Poole, 211–15). With many mendicant parishes in clerical hands by the end of the sixteenth century and a strengthened secular church greatly controlled and administered by its royal patron, the King of Spain, the evangelization activity of the regulars was significantly curtailed and the Indians would eventually end up practicing their own interpretations of Christianity (Burkhart, *Slippery*, 18).

On the part of the natives, Nahua difference proved to be much more recalcitrant to the intrusive, homogenizing powers of Christianity than the friars had anticipated. Such resilience manifested itself in the countless small lineage idols, or *tlapialli*, buried all over the place by too many Nahua Christian subjects; in relics carefully packaged and hidden in corners of the home; in the ardent devotion to the local patron saints, which was a continuation of the cult to their *calpulteotl*, or protector gods (López Austin, *Hombre-Dios*, 76; Lockhart, *The Nahuas*, 238, 243); in the collective intoxications that marked every celebration of the new Christian calendar (Gruzinski, *Colonización*, 154); in the hallucinogenic substances put on the altar of the house oratory (Lockhart, *The Nahuas*, 259); in the magical incantations used for curing diseases or securing influence over others (Lockhart, *The Nahuas*, 258; Gruzinski, *Colonización*, 180–82); and in innumerable other disquieting syncretic forms.[1]

Equally disconcerting and worrisome was what many of the missionaries perceived to be a profound misunderstanding of the practice and meaning of the sacraments. The Nahuas were simply not getting straight the required universals of Christianity, and this greatly demoralized the evangelizing colonizers. For if Christ had died for all humankind, how could a large number of people still be incapable of understanding who they were and what the Creator had done for them, even after having heard the sacred Word in their own language? What could be more distressing for the Christian apostolic missionary than to witness the refractory alterity of the Nahua, which threatened to shake the edifice of the common and the universal upon which the European Christian conception of self was invented? As Homi Bhabha has stated, "The incalculable colonized subject—half acquiescent, half oppositional, always untrustworthy—produces an unresolvable problem of cultural difference for the very address of colonial cultural authority" (*Location*, 33). Fray Juan Bautista's *Advertencias para los confessores de los Naturales* is an interesting and important document precisely because it purports to face squarely the cultural limits and differences of both self and other in order to redefine the pastoral relationship between the two. Undoubtedly, this text can be construed as yet another strategy of colonial expansionism since it is the European and not the Nahua subject who desires to remedy the cultural distance between himself and the other. However, Bautista's text will also acknowledge how the desire to fully control the other by producing in him the Christian presence of the self-to-the-self, which supposedly could transcend nation, race, and culture, had turned around to split the spiritual colonizer. Apart from the ways in which the changing political and religious climate expounded above may have contributed to the evangelization setback, the friars had to face the possibility of an irreducible alterity that might never be in their power to map out completely so that it could be safely and manifestly routed to the Christian god.

What were some of the things that discouraged and caused despair in the confessor, and how did they threaten and impinge on his own sense of self? After decades of preaching and indoctrinating, the confessors were distressed to realize that many Nahuas went to receive the sacrament of penance without showing any feeling of guilt or remorse. This being the case, it made no sense to perform the confession, because it would clearly be invalid. But in order to dissuade the confessors from abandoning their "hardened" penitents, Bautista invokes the authority of Duns Scotus, discussed earlier in these chapters, and his opinion about the ex opere operato (by the work of the work) power of the sacrament to transform attrition into contrition. To receive the fruits of penance, only some pain of remorse was required, a minimal disposition to receive the sacrament properly, and no actual desire to offend Christ: "Las quales palabras son de grande piedad, especialmente para estos naturales...por ser comunmente gente de cortos entendimientos no alcanzan la calidad que ha de tener la contricion" [Which words show great mercy especially to these natives...who are usually people of little understanding and do not grasp the quality that contrition must have] (Bautista, *Advertencias*, 1r–2r).

Duns Scotus's more lenient position shows mercy for all Christians, but is specifically linked in the case of the Nahuas to their deficiency as a people. According to Bautista, in general they lack the necessary disposition to be contrite or to repudiate sin for love of God rather than for fear of punishment. In judging the other so, Bautista reveals his own cultural blindness to the fact that the Christian conception of the person is not universal but bound to Western forms of subjectivity, which the Nahua was not ready or simply unwilling to inhabit. This blindness notwithstanding, or precisely because of it, there is painful insight that Nahua incalculability opens an uncharted territory of difference. In order for the spiritual colonizer to roam such territory, he must probe, rethink, and redefine his own limits. Or put differently, in order to exercise power over the subaltern, the colonizer is constrained by this subaltern to remap his own intellectual and moral boundaries. Such constraint, much like the imperative to the European confessor to learn Nahuatl, is part of the process of "autocolonization or reformation" that Foucault invokes in order to argue that "power is exercised upon the dominant as well as on the dominated" (Dreyfus and Rabinow, 186). Like the master of the Panopticon who two centuries later would admit that his fate was bound with those under his surveillance (Bentham, quoted in Foucault, *Discipline*, 204), Bautista admonishes the Franciscan pastoral agents to engage themselves in the reordering of their subjectivities in the struggle to subject the other, and lead him to salvation.

Another distressing point of difference for the missionary agents was the inability of the Nahua penitents to state clearly the number of times they had committed a mortal sin and, more importantly, the confusion between venial and mortal offenses: "Y no ay que reparar en que preguntados de cosas livianas, diran que las tenian por peccado mortal, porque quando obran o no advierten sino como niños, o ya que advierten que es malo, no hazen juicio de mortal ni venial, y assi queda en su naturaleza de venial, lo que de suyo es" [And one should not pay attention to the fact that when asked about excusable things, they will say that they took them to be mortal sins, because when they act they do not reason but as children, and when they notice that something is evil, they do not judge whether it is mortal or venial, and thus it remains as venial what by nature is such] (Bautista, *Advertencias*, 3r).

This assessment bears witness to some of the obstacles the confessors were faced with in trying to fashion the "universal" Christian subject out of the indigenous other. Some Nahuas were considering mortal offenses those that were only venial. This was a particularly delicate issue because of the intricacies and subtleties of consent. All Christians, Nahuas included, were instructed that a mortal sin was a serious violation of a commandment of God, either by word or by act. And it was called mortal precisely because whosoever committed one such sin could suffer eternal punishment and death of the soul if he or she was not absolved from it (*Códice*, 42). Venial sin was a "small sin" (*Códice*, 40) and thus could be forgiven by attending mass, by receiving communion, or by saying devotedly a Pater Noster, and the like. However, when someone had perpetrated an act of no great moral consequence believing it could be a mortal offense, he had consented to what in his judgment could be a mortal sin.

These confusions between mortal and venial offenses were not specific to the sixteenth-century colonial context of New Spain, however. Such difficulty had been tackled by some medieval theologians. In his *Himmelstrasse*, Stephan Lanzkranna had held that "guilt itself could arise from an erroneous judgment in cooperation with the will" (Tentler, 152). Thus, what was conceived to be a mortal act by the penitent at the moment of executing it was a mortal sin even if not defined as such by the church. The great importance given to these hair-splitting distinctions reveals how will and intentionality were (and still are) major constituents of a Christian Western subjectivity (conveniently constructed from the sixteenth-century until our days as the closest to a universal model) and as a result, how difficult the transculturation and/or transportability of these assumptions were likely to be. In order to ease the conscience of the confessor whose penitents, by ignoring the extent of their evil acts, were actually perverting themselves by their misconceptions, Bautista departs from Lanzkranna's position, positing a suspension of judgment in the Nahua penitent. Bautista proposes a conscience still in the making, like that of a child, that has difficulty discerning between good and evil, as well as determining the mortal or venial degree of sin. The opinions that the Nahua penitent formed of the sins committed were thus not sufficient to alter the objectivity of the venial offense. But if the penitent did not know the number of times he had committed the offense, nor how much time he had been engaged in the sin, if he could not determine whether the offense was mortal or venial, what kind of remorse could he feel? How could the confessor determine the degree of culpability of his Nahua penitent for what he had done? How could the spiritual colonizer ascertain the truth of the Nahua as a Christian subject when he seriously misconstrued the mortal gravity of his acts? [2]

Another distressing point of irreducibility for the confessor was that many Nahua penitents were unable to understand the concept of the invalidity of the confession if some mortal sin had been left out for fear or shame. Sometimes they did not confess a mortal sin for the latter reasons, other times because they mistakenly thought it was venial. In still other cases, they considered what was a virtuous deed a mortal sin (Bautista, *Advertencias*, 4r), and thus did not confess it for shame, making the confession needlessly invalid! Finally, though some were able to fulfill the obligation of repeating the whole confession, most of them would refuse to confess sins again. When this chain of misconceptions had to do with venial mistaken for mortal sins, Bautista advises the confessor just to forget the whole thing; for, as stated above, venial sins would remain such regardless of what the Nahua penitent had thought about them. But when well-known mortal sins were involved, the confessor was obliged to determine whether or not they had been confessed because of shame or "invincible ignorance." If the former seemed to be the case, then the confessor needed to persuade the penitent otherwise by reminding him about the invalidity of the confession. If the second, then the confessor had to explain to the Nahua penitent the concept of the integrity of confession. However, if after doing everything that the confessor could in order to persuade the penitent to repeat the confession, the penitent still did not understand it due to his limited capacity and sincerely thought that he had done what was asked:

> Aunque la confession fue invalida, no ay obligacion de iterarla, porque en este caso la ignorancia invencible le escusa. Y pueden y deuen los tales ministros, no solamente no formar escrupulo en absolverlos, sino tambien quedar consolados, entendiendo su absolucion es fructuosa, particularmente si el penitente por otra parte muestra dolor de haber offendido a Dios.... Pues es cierto que a nadie se le pide hacer diligencia sino conforme a su capacidad, y que el que por no poder mas, o no alcanzar mas, deja de confessar algunos pecados, no hace directa y formalemente contra la integridad y verdad de la confesion, sino sola materialmente, lo cual no estorba el fructo del sacramento. (Bautista, *Advertencias,* 5r–v)

> [Although the confession was invalid, there is no need to reiterate it, because in this case an invincible ignorance excuses him. And the said ministers not only should not hesitate to absolve them, but they should be comforted, understanding that their absolution has borne fruit, particularly if the penitent on the other hand shows sorrow for having offended God.... For it is true that nobody is asked to do more than what his capacity will permit, and if someone does not confess some sins because he cannot do more or discern more, he is not acting directly and formally against the integrity and truth of the confession, but only materially, which does not prevent it from bearing fruit.]

This is a rich passage. It confronts the problem of (sub)alterity in the (nonflattering) figure of "invincible ignorance." Thomas Aquinas had alluded to this term in his *Summa Theologica.* He defined ignorance as invincible when "man...fails to know what he is unable to know. Consequently, ignorance of such things is called invincible, since it cannot be overcome by study. For this reason such ignorance, not being voluntary, since it is not in our power to be rid of it, is not a sin" (2:142).[3] The antithetical mode in which the statements about an invincibly ignorant other are expounded in Bautista's passage bespeaks their engagement with limits. The confession of the recalcitrant Nahua is both valid and invalid at the same time. The allowance made for his "shortness of understanding" implied in the notion of invincible ignorance excuses him from the obligation of having to repeat his sins, for it has proven to be impossible to extract such a repetition from him. Bautista makes it clear, however, that the integrity of the confession is not fully restored, for even if the Nahua did not intend to undercut the sacrament of penance by not disclosing some sins, he nonetheless did it materially. The confession of the Nahua must be accepted, then, as being efficacious ("fructuosa") even though the confessor knows it to be incomplete. The material practice of the sacrament requires a full account of the sins committed to the confessor in order to produce the presence of the self to the self proper to the Christian subjectivity. However, Bautista displaces such a materiality as the real source of the efficacy of the sacrament, since the Nahua penitent was far from being able to achieve it adequately.

Bautista's position on the performance of the sacrament may be argued as revisiting Molina for whom the exact rendition of a sacrament was an integral, inalienable part of its efficacy.[4] Not surprisingly, the problem of impenetrable alterity as an impediment was never addressed in the *Confessionario mayor*. There, the material and procedural demands for the performance of the sacraments implied a universal subject capable of carrying them out undisturbed by place, time, culture, or even language. But in Bautista's consolatory treatise for the confessor (and penitents), Molina's logic of a universal Christian subjectivity has been pierced by the obdurate alterity of the Nahua. For even after more than half a century of preaching the Word of God, the friars still encountered what for them was a deficiency in the other that prevented him from adequately inhabiting the Christian subjectivity that they had labored so hard to present before his eyes.

Bautista goes on to say that the ministers of confession can and should absolve in this case not only without any scruple, but with the understanding that the absolution is efficacious, particularly if the penitent has shown signs of contrition at any other point in the confession. What is interesting here is that the confessor/colonizer himself needs to be comforted and reassured. True, the imperative to produce and meticulously scrutinize the truth of the penitent may be thought of as a religious strategy of control and in the specific context of the lands of Anahuac as a colonialist maneuver. However, such an imperative is also an intersubjective process that affects all the parties involved. Different from a triumphalist conception of the colonial as that which "is extended without being changed" or is "immunized against both any alterity that might transform it and whatever dares to resist it" (De Certeau, 216), the fashioning of a Christian conscience in the Nahua other, though clearly a colonialist imposition, was not carried out without implying the fashioner's own conscience at every point in the process. Bautista's consolatory admonitions are thus the acknowledgment that the confessor/colonizer may be deeply disturbed by the wielding of his missionary power. This may be what Bhabha denominates the revelation of the presence of colonial power as "something other than what its rules of recognition assert" (*Location*, 112). That is, unanticipated forms of resistance and difference are encountered as the colonizer applies his strategies of encompassment upon his others. Although many forms of such resistance and difference are not unexpectedly explained in Bautista's manual in terms of a deficiency of the other ("ignorancia invencible"), they also reveal the unforeseen impotence of the colonizing self to fully subject the other to his discourse of religious universality. In this way the intractable difference of the subaltern turns around and cleaves the colonizer. Ironically then, the *Advertencias* comforts the confessor for his powerlessness in relation to the "deficiency" of the other.

Nevertheless, the consolation of the confessor/colonizer is not the only end pursued in Bautista's manual. Even more importantly, what is at stake here is the redefinition of the relationship between the religious agents and the Nahuas so that the evangelization process may be salvaged as much as possible. And what will be significant in terms of the ambivalence of the discourses of the colonizer is that the irreducible difference of the Nahua (the "invencible ignorancia") will not be represented as the only impediment for the reproduction of such an evangelization process. Analyzing the reasons why so few Nahuas receive the Eucharist, Bautista concludes that the confessors themselves are to blame. He states and then rebuts the four most common arguments given for their refusal to administer the Sacrament to the Nahuas, none of them flattering. The first objection is that the Indians seem to be to these confessors infamous and public sinners (*Advertencias*, 57r). The second is that they consider the Indians incapable of differentiating between the regular and the consecrated bread (*Advertencias*, 57r–58r). Finally, the confessors decline to administer the Eucharist to the Indians claiming they do not know the necessary doctrinal elements to receive it (*Advertencias*, 61v). The third of these arguments is the most relevant to our discussion of the constructions of otherness in the field of Spanish colonial discourses of the sixteenth century. Many religious agents withhold the holy bread because they feel the Nahuas are inferior, boorish, and incapable of reasoning (*Advertencias*, 58r). Dismissing this notion as little more than frivolous, Bautista argues that even the most rustic of the Nahuas is capable of behaving according to the norms of his social status. Like Mendieta, Motolonía, Las Casas, Acosta, Durán, and Sahagún, he alludes to the great political order and civility of the Nahua pre-Hispanic past in order to prove their capacity to reason. And under the colonial order they have shown great skill in all mechanical trades that they have learned from the Spaniards: "De donde claramente se echa de ver que la rudeza que en ellos vemos no es natural, sino falta de instruccion y comunicacion de gente habil y discreta. Y los que han tratado con el villanage de muchas partes de España, dizen que son mas rudos y de mucho menos policia que estos naturales" [From which it is clear that the rudeness that we see in them is not natural, but lack of instruction and communication with talented and discreet people. And those who have dealt with peasantry from many regions in Spain say that they are more rude and much less civil than these natives] (*Advertencias*, 59r).

Although never doing away with the discourses of colonialism, Bautista charges the confessors of the natives with using what we would call today tropes of race in order to account for traits and conduct that cannot even be presumed to be culturally specific (Gates, 5). According to the author, the coarseness or *rudeza* attributed to the Nahuas by these confessors is not natural, essential, but positional, that is, caused by a lack of proper communication and contact with learned people.[5] Furthermore, many who had dealt with both the Nahua and the Spanish peasantry claimed the latter were even more intractable and boorish, and no priest ever denied the Eucharist to them on the grounds of their intellectual inferiority. Such a refusal would have been deemed improper since the understanding required to receive the Sacrament was by faith and not by reason. Thus, "Basta entender aquel rudo labrador que recibe a su Redemptor" [It is enough that that rude peasant understands that he receives his Savior] (*Advertencias,* 59r).

The analogy between the Indians and the European peasantry was recurrent in missionary discourse (Pagden, 161). Bautista's position vis-à-vis the subalterity of the Nahua is a pre-enlightenment notion, within the constraints, of course, of the Catholic Tridentine discourse of the time. But in the passage, the so-called rudeza of the Nahuas has the additional spin of turning out to be a consequence of the spiritual colonizer's own racial misconstructions. It is a reflection of the colonizer's neglect and refusal to consider facts, for the pre-Hispanic past of the Nahuas clearly showed that they were more than capable of learning and rationally obeying laws. If rudeza meant lack of good judgment and reason, then, Bautista would seem to imply, some confessors' hasty and even arbitrary misattribution of rusticity to the Nahuas as natural to them, only revealed their own clumsiness. Bautista's display of the authoritative opinions of Saint Thomas Aquinas (59r–60r) and Saint Anthony of Florence (61r–v) in order to refute denying the Sacrament to the Indians on the grounds of their inability to grasp its meaning denounces such a position as uninformed, undiscerning, and even racist. He then reprimands the missionaries for expecting spiritual perfection from the Indians before administering the Eucharist to them, when Christ himself did not demand this from the Apostles, who were in a state of "spiritual infancy" when the Sacrament was instituted (*Advertencias,* 67r). The discourse of the intellectual inferiority of the other is not employed in these passages as a consolation for the confessor, but rather as his mirror image. In considering the Nahua as naturally inferior to the European self, that self reveals his own inadequacy and/or unwillingness to engage himself effectively with difference, in order to inscribe it in the universality of humankind in Christ. Thus, Bautista's rebuke to the missionaries discloses their blindness to sameness, since rudeza, or inability to discern properly, is a trait the self ironically shares with the other at the very moment of positing the latter's ineptitude to receive the Eucharist.

The *Advertencias para los confessores de los Naturales* seeks, then, to reproduce colonialist pastoral power through diverse strategies. It proposes a hybridization of confessional technologies (such as the relaxation of the observance of the intricacies of consent) as it confronts the spiritual coloniz-er's distress at the recalcitrant (sub)alterity of the colonized. It clearly intends to continue controlling and disciplining the Nahua by exhorting the missionaries not to give up on their evangelization task. At the same time, the *Advertencias* openly declares that the insufficiencies and shortcom-ings that threaten the spiritual colonization endeavor are not only the sub-altern's, but also the colonizer's, for it has been the latter's heedlessness in the constructions of the Nahua flock that has also put the pastoral relationship at risk. Of course, even while proposing the inadequacy of the self in relat-ing appropriately to the other, the spiritual colonizer is clearly unable or unwilling to go beyond the epistemology that posits the superiority and uni-versality of Christianity. However, in urging the despairing confessors not to give up their pastoral power, Bautista is mandating further engagement with the intricacies of difference, as well as the concurrent restructuring of the boundaries of the self that such an involvement implies. This last point in particular supports the position that confession as a regime of control was not a one-sided affair. The confessional act could greatly burden the Nahua penitent who was to be disciplined through this linguistic performance. However, it also put great pressure on the spiritual colonizer who, when faced with the manifold resistance and misappropriations of the penitent other, had to submit to the imperative of his own discourse of trying to over-come them (under pain of mortal sin).

The *Advertencias para los confessores de estos Naturales* shows the enor-mous difficulties, confusions, and failures incurred in the production of the Nahua Christian subject as well as the demands placed upon the spiritual colonizer in order to exact from him the necessary effort to keep up the pro-duction of such a subjectivity. The manual depicts the acknowledgment of the colonizer that the spiritual colonization was very much an onerous process still in the making. Though there was a great asymmetry in the power relationship between the Franciscan confessor and the Nahua peni-tent, Bautista's *Advertencias* reveals that by the end of the century, an afflict-ed, self-conscious colonialist subject had emerged in the contact zone of New Spain. The mirror of the other had precipitated the self into tapping the limits of the authority of his universal Christian culture.

PART IV

*Falling Back
Into History*

9

Historia eclesiástica indiana or Writing the Crisis of Providentialism

In 1572, the minister general of the Franciscan order, Cristóbal de Capitefontium, commissioned Gerónimo de Mendieta to write a chronicle of the Minorite missionary activity in Mexico. The general wanted him to expound on "what the saintly members of our Order have achieved in the past years regarding the conversion of Gentiles and many other things worthy of memory" (Capitefontium, quoted in Solano y Pérez-Lila, "Estudio preliminar," liv; translation is mine). Mendieta, a second-generation missionary, completed the work in 1596, when the prophetic, eschatological colonial fantasies of the Franciscans had definitely been dispelled by an opaque historic materiality, stubbornly resisting to profess the *me fecit Deus* (God is my creator). As a consequence of a policy of the crown, and like so many other important historical and ethnographic works about the New World in the sixteenth century, Mendieta's *Historia eclesiástica indiana* (HEI) was not published until after the demise of Spanish domination in America.[1] In a *cédula* (ordinance) of 22 April 1577, Philip II decreed the confiscation of Bernardino de Sahagún's writings, which treated pre-Hispanic societies, and ordered Viceroy Martín Enríquez to forbid "any person to write things having to do with the superstitions and the ways of life of the natives in any language" (quoted in Baudot, *Utopia,* 500). No justification was given for such a confiscation except that "it seems to be inappropriate for this book to be printed and to circulate in any way in those regions for many important reasons" (quoted in Baudot, *Utopia,* 502). This episode of censorship is revealing of the Spanish Crown's typically hypersensitive policies and attitudes toward literature about the New World.[2] Ever since 1527, for instance, no foreigner could access works on the subject without special permission. Because the crown wanted to keep track of what was being written about America and by whom, from 1556 on any book treating the topic had to be officially approved by the Council of Indies or be confiscated (Baudot, *Utopia*, 516–17). Surely enough, the crown's apprehensions about the political volatility of historical and ethnographic representations of the New World were not totally misguided. Many of them, such as Las Casas's *Historia de Indias* and the HEI, were incisively critical about the way the colonization enterprise was being carried out. Others, like Motolinía's *Memoriales* and particularly Sahagún's *Historia general de las cosas de la Nueva España*, while claiming to be contributing to the extirpation and erasure of idolatry, seemed to be doing the opposite. For by offering relatively realistic, credible and even integral representations of pre-Hispanic life "in the very process of exposing them in order to bring them to an end, he [Sahagún] helped to propagate the beliefs described" (Klor de Alva, "Sahagún," 45).[3] The crown mistrusted this predicament and not only because of its ironic edge. The empathy and even admiration that Franciscans expressed in ethnographic works such as Motolinía's and Sahagún's for many nonreligious aspects of pre-Hispanic life could indeed foster the millenarian aspirations the Minorites were rumored to have of a separate Indian Republic of Christ (Phelan, 93–95; Lafaye, 32–33; Kobayashi, 195; Baudot, *Utopia*, 520; Klor de Alva, "Sahagún," 37; Todorov, 238; Rabasa, *Inventing*, 164; Bakewell, 303).

Marginalized by the very imperialistic and hegemonic powers they were supposed to reproduce and discursively promote, these censored chronicles of Indies occupy a precarious position in the field of colonialist discourses. Such a silenced textual body must be thoroughly examined and brought into postcolonial dialogue if we are to understand adequately the great ambivalence, doubleness, and reversability lurking in the colonialist discursive production in the specific context of sixteenth-century New Spain. My choice of the HEI is motivated, among other things, by the piercing clarity with which a crisis of the colonizer is represented in the text. Mendieta's HEI exposes the fracturing of the newly constituted Western self, which had to posit its superior difference in order to engage in a historically unparalleled colonialist endeavor that would ultimately reveal, also in an unprecedented way, the uncleanness and misery of that self. At a more immediate level, disabled by his epistemic horizons to renounce the colonialist Christianizing enterprise of freeing the other from the grip of the devil, Gerónimo de Mendieta is compelled by that very same enterprise to historicize, denounce, and lament what he sees as its demonic corruption by the Spaniards in Mexico.

The HEI, then, will help us to acknowledge that one of the positions occupied by the colonialist subject in Spanish America was the open recognition of the inadequacy and impotence of the colonizer to command legitimate authority over the discriminated other. By acknowledging this, and as Rolena Adorno has urged us, we will be moving beyond the reductive stereotypical view that relations between Spaniards and Indians were strictly oppositional in character, motivated only by the expansionist interests of Spain ("Colonial," 346–47). In this sense, it may be not only postcolonial interventionist readings that are in the position to uncover the contradictions and splits undercutting the colonizer's discourse. The figure of the denunciatory colonizer offers evidence of what many postcolonial critics have been arguing during the last decade about the questionable prefix "post" and the suspect hyphen: namely, that the colonial contact on many occasions engenders a discourse of oppositionality both from the colonizer and the colonized that does not materialize after the fact of colonialism, but is contemporary to it. By the same token, such coexistence between the colonial and its contestation also suggests that few postcolonial, postindependence spatio-temporalities are ever fully free from and fully after the colonial.[4]

A disciple of Motolinía, Gerónimo de Mendieta writes his HEI at the close of the sixteenth century from the waning spiritualist perspectives traversing the construction of the early evangelization enterprise in Mexico. Although there is an ongoing debate about the actual impact of Joachimite discourses among the Twelve,[5] the Franciscan missionary zeal in the New

World during the sixteenth century cannot be fully understood without reference to the Calabrian abbot's provocative historical schema and prophecies. Joachim de Fiore (1145?–1202) divided history in three states or eras, each presided over by one of the three persons of the Trinity. God the Father was the predominant agent in history from the expulsion from Eden until the birth of Christ. In this state, humankind was under the law, had received the gift of knowledge, but was burdened by the fears of chastisement and old age. It was the era of the Twelve Patriarchs and tribes of Israel, and was lived in the bondage of the slave (Reeves, 14; Douie, 23–24). The second state ran from the birth of Christ until a very near expected future. In this second age, wisdom, or *sapientia*, prevailed: it was a time of action, of faith, of young men; a time of spring, grace, and of the joyful servitude of sons to their fathers. But the third state was to be the culmination of history. It would be an era of freedom, of love, of childlike simplicity, when the Holy Spirit would confer *plenitudo intellectis* (full understanding) (Reeves, 14), with which humankind would be able to see truth without mediations or substitutions. Joachim de Fiore prophesied that in order to lead the church into the fullness of this third status, two new orders of spiritual men would appear. Great tribulations would ensue in which the temporal, hierarchical church, or "new Babylon," would be severely chastised. Only then would God come to the faithful in consummate simplicity of presence, and the millennium of the third and last status of history would finally begin (Reeves, 1–29; McGinn, 161–203; Baudot, *Utopia*, 71–91).

It is not hard to see why Joachim de Fiore's teachings were extremely controversial. They implied an indictment of the institutionalized church, as well as a rebuttal of St. Augustine, who held that the plenitude of history had already been achieved with the Redemption and death of Christ. Although the Fourth Lateran Council in 1215 condemned Fiore's doctrines, renewed interest in them arose with the foundation of the Franciscan and Dominican mendicant orders in the early thirteenth century. In 1255, the generals of the two orders issued an encyclical in which they proclaimed to fulfill a prophetic role very much along the lines of Joachim's prohibited teachings. But the Dominicans finally sided with Thomas Aquinas's rejection of the Calabrian abbot's ideas. It was the Franciscans, and among them the branch of the Spirituals,[6] who enthusiastically embraced the idea that their order alone would produce the *viri spirituales* (spiritual men) that would lead the world into the third status (Reeves, 31–32).

The Joachimite currents and eschatological legends were current in Spain from the end of the thirteenth century until the fifteenth, mainly through Catalonian Franciscans, who were strongly influenced by the Spirituals. One remarkable work expounding Joachimite teachings, which circulated in Spain, was *Vade mecum in tribulatione*, written by friar Jean de Rouqueitallade in 1356. In this book, Rouqueitallade urges his readers to hasten the conversion of Jews and Mongols, for that would bring about the defeat of Islam. The end of history would then be at hand, since all the people of the world would finally submit to the power of Christ and the church. According to Georges Baudot, with the Mongols on the fringes of the West converting to Islam rather than to Christianity and the consequent loss of all land routes to the Far East, the millenarian anticipation of Rouqueitallade was discredited and his followers were disappointed (*Pugna*, 18). What is significant here is the evidence of apocalyptic expectations in Spain during the fourteenth century among the Franciscans, because these would, alas, flare up once again in the encounter with the New World. According to Margarita Zamora, the spiritual and material Columbian goals of spreading the faith in the Orient and returning with gold, spices, and gems that would enable Christianity to recover Jerusalem "appear to respond to the Christian millenarian yearning for the end of the world and the concomitant restoration of humanity's prelapsarian integrity" (*Reading*, 137). We should recall that in 1485 Columbus spent three months in the Franciscan monastery at La Rábida and was greatly encouraged to appear at the court of Ferdinand and Isabella by the learned astronomer and cosmographer Fray Antonio Pérez de Marchena. Let us not forget either that in his letter to the Catholic Kings about the third voyage, Columbus writes that he believes that he has been near paradise,[7] which was thought to have a concrete geographical location at the end of the world (Flint; Zamora, *Reading*, 140–51).

During the last decades of the fifteenth century, the Franciscan houses in Spain underwent reform, bringing them under the control of the Observantine branch. This branch, founded in 1368, was heir to the Spirituals, who had been ultimately disbanded for practicing a vow of utter poverty and declaring that Christ and his disciples had held no worldly possessions at all, either individually or in common. Two key figures in the Observantine reform in Spain were Franciscan Cardinal Jiménez de Cisneros, who encouraged the return to a primitive Christianity beyond the walls of the monasteries,[8] and Fray Juan de Guadalupe, who obtained from Pope Alexander VI in 1496 a bull authorizing him to found a hermitage in Granada where he and other willing brothers could live according to the first rule laid out by Saint Francis. As had happened repeatedly in the past with the Spirituals, there was opposition and turmoil about this desire to live in utter poverty. However, by 1500 five monasteries had been established, four missions in Extremadura, and one house in Villaviciosa, Portugal (Baudot, *Pugna*, 21). By 1505, the reformed houses achieved a more official status, becoming the custody of the Santo Evangelio of Extremadura, and finally the Province of San Gabriel in 1519.

As a result of the efforts of both Fray Francisco de los Ángeles[9] and the emperor's former confessor Fray Juan Clapión, and due as well to Hernán Cortés's request for missionaries of the reformed Franciscan order, the province of San Gabriel was granted vast ecclesiastical powers by Leo X to start at once the formidable evangelization enterprise in Mexico. Having been chosen as minister general of the Friars Minors in the chapter general of Toulouse in 1523, Fray Francisco was unable to preside over the first missionary contingent to Mexico. He was allowed to choose its members, however, and selected those friars in the Province of San Gabriel who had proven beyond doubt their adherence to the Guadalupan ideals of the Observancy. These were the renowned first twelve missionaries to the New World.[10]

The contingent of the Twelve started their long journey on 15 January 1524, sailing from San Lúcar de Barrameda. The task of converting great masses of people, heretofore unknown to the rest of the world by the inscrutable designs of God, was construed as apocalyptic, in the literal sense of things pertaining to the end of the world. How vibrantly the Twelve lived these eschatological discourses is of course impossible to assess except through the texts that wove the great narratives of the missionary enterprises in the New World. One such text is the HEI.

The HEI is composed of five books. Book 1 deals with Spanish colonization in the Antilles, where the role of the Franciscans was marginal. The second book is an ethnographic study of the Mexica pre-Hispanic past. The
story of the Indian church in the Valley of Mexico during the sixteenth
century under the auspices of the Franciscan Order is the subject of the
third and fourth books. The fifth and last is an eulogistic collection of short
narratives on the lives of the Franciscan missionaries in Mexico. Although
all these books contain material that is of great ethnographic, cultural, biog-
raphical, and political interest, the constraints of time and space do not allow
us to examine the five in detail. The chapter will focus on the third and
fourth books, which deal specifically with the Franciscan evangelization in
Mexico during the sixteenth century, the topic of this study.

Because of their general concern with the expansion of Christendom
in the world, particularly books 3 and 4 of the HEI are strongly informed by
the medieval genre of the universal history of the church. As part of such a
history, actors and events not only meant their own specific, immediate
materiality, they were also the signs of a larger, providential force that fused
past and present into the future of redemption. The medieval universal
history of the church was, therefore, strongly moralistic and eschatological:
all relevant temporal events, including wars, persecutions, and other evils,
had to be ordered and interpreted so as to show how they were the tools with
which God fashioned the edifices of his city the church, which little by little would extend all over the world. And indeed, although political unity
would be staunchly resisted throughout the Middle Ages by local forces, the
church succeeded in maintaining its institutional continuity and, thus, its
claim to be at the center of the history of the salvation of the world.

In the sixteenth century, however, the notion of the universal history of
the church was decisively challenged in Europe by the Protestant schism.
The Catholic Church had based its authority to be the legitimate heiress of
"the Apostles as heralds of Christ" on the irrefutable evidence of its long-
standing visibility, unity, and continuity, in spite of the ups and downs of

political history (Pelikan, *Reformation,* 110). But the Protestants would challenge many if not all the administrative innovations that the Catholic Church had introduced throughout the centuries, showing that they were not fully warranted by the scriptures (Dubois, 32–33). To make things worse, some of the church's centuries-old claims to authority based on documents were eroded by the philological practices of the Italian humanists.[11]

With the traditional universal church historiography in crisis, the humanists turned to the more political and city-centered Greek and Roman models of making history that their classical learning had made available. A less universally invested focus emerged in humanist historiography, moving away from a providential explanation of historical events to the secondary causes of human motives such as individual passions, virtues, and reason. This did not mean, however, that the Christian universal history model was supplanted by a new one. The humanist historians were still Christians and in this sense they accepted the basic biblical tenets of the Creation, the Incarnation, and the Last Judgment (Breisach, 160). Nevertheless, they thought that the designs of God were too unfathomable to be deciphered, and thus turned their attention to less fundamental issues that could be more accessible to educated, secular human beings.

Spain, however, would take a different historiographical route than England, France, Italy, and Germany. With the 1493 *Inter Caetera* bulls of Alexander VI granting the Catholic Kings the newly discovered lands so that they would christianize them and with Charles I of Spain acceding to the throne of the Holy Roman Empire in 1519 (with the title Charles V), it is not surprising that Spanish historiography would be greatly informed by medieval notions of Christian universal history. Charles V's son Philip II was hailed as the holy monarch who would once again unify Christendom under one sword: "Ya se acerca, señor, o es ya llegada / la edad gloriosa en que promete el cielo / una grey y un pastor solo en el suelo / por suerte a vuestros tiempos reservada" [The time is near, O Lord, or it is already at hand, / the glorious age in which Heaven promises / one flock and only one shepherd in the land / luckily reserved for your time] (Acuña, quoted in Rivers, 108; translation is mine). Just like Rome and Charlemagne's

France in the past, Spain was now the country chosen by God to propagate Christianity around the globe through its military and political prowess.

Mendieta, the historical narrator, will speak in the HEI from within this Spanish universal, imperialist, and medieval historiographical scheme, whose cornerstone is a providential agency. Thus, a great deal of the authority of the historical narrator in this text will stem from his ability to make seen and known the ways of Providence in the expansion of the church in Mexico. In addition, being a chronicler of the Franciscan Order, Mendieta writes the HEI to commemorate the deeds of the Friars Minor in the lands of Anahuac and to exalt "his own province of the Holy Gospel [Santo Evangelio] as the 'head and leader of this [Indian] Church'" (Brading, 111). Added to these motives we must also consider the possibility of a Joachimite millenarian perspective in the HEI, as has been proposed by John Phelan and Georges Baudot, among many other critics and historians.

By the end of the sixteenth century, however, the obdurate worldly interests of colonial power, imperial expansion, and settler personal wealth had all but put the Franciscan millenarian vision to rest. Thus, the fin-de-siècle HEI will also be a chronicle of bitter *desengaño*, or disillusionment. Unpublished until 1870, Mendieta's text may be posited as one of the silenced origins of the discourse of Baroque disillusionment that overtook Spain in the seventeenth century. This somber Baroque mood may have come about because of the blows that the Spanish imperial destiny had received from the rival European powers and/or by the growing "sociopolitical despair—compounded by constant warfare, crop failure, plague... [that] disrupted trans-Atlantic trade, and bankruptcy" (Graziano, 33).[12] Baroque gloom may have also been a result of rumors that the ways of the Lord had (again) become inscrutable in the chaos of the overseas provinces of the messianic monarchy of Spain. The country that had been chosen to unravel the divine plan of salvation on Earth in modern times had sunk history into untrodden forms of iniquity. The long-awaited second culmination of history[13] had again been aborted by the dark forces of a meaningless present.

The third book of the HEI opens with the pivotal discourse of providential intervention. The narrator sees the veiled signature of God in the coincidence that Cortés and Luther were born in the same year and that the Spanish captain had started preaching the Gospel in the Mexican highlands the very same year Luther began to "corrupt" it.[14] For the great damage that Luther inflicted on the Catholic Church, robbing her of innumerable souls, was to be neutralized by the converts gained in Mexico: "De suerte que lo que por una parte se perdia, se cobrase por otra" [So that what was lost in one place, was recovered in another] (Mendieta, HEI, 174).[15] And yet, in spite of the totalitarian universality (Dubois, 23) and fullness of meaning proper to the discourse and representation of divine intervention, the providential agency in Mendieta's ecclesiastical history is rarely articulated in terms of unequivocal abundance, victory, or cessation of pain. Written from the perspective of its (woeful) dispersion at the end of the century, providential agency in the HEI is usually employed as an austere counterbalance against the forces of evil, a counterbalance always already pierced at the origin by the absences and gaps of history.

Thus, souls are talked about in terms of quantity, as if a massive loss of them could be mended by an equally massive gain. Moreover, Mendieta claims that the divine choice of Cortés as rescuer of the church was further confirmed by the fact that he was born in 1485, the year that eighty thousand people were sacrificed to the gods of the Templo Mayor of Tenochtitlan, according to Nahua records. The clamor of so many souls and wantonly spilled blood would finally have moved God to put an end to such horror and to send someone in his name, namely Cortés, to remedy the situation (175).

This providential interpretation of the birth of the one who would open the way for the emergence of the Indian church yields modest if not ambivalent results. For such a divine intervention supposedly succeeded in putting a check on evil later on, but did not defray the high costs of human pain and damnation perpetrated at the Templo Mayor. A dismal amount of injury and injustice appears to have been necessary before God decided to do something, as if such horror had occurred without his consent, or as if he had been surprised, bewildered, and then infuriated by such cruelty, or as if only after seeing so much pain and affliction, his patience had finally run out. And considering that Cortés arrived in Mexico in 1519, thirty-four more years would still go by and thousands of souls would be lost before the situation took a turn toward the better (according to the Spanish point of view). It may be argued, then, that these founding instances in the HEI already exemplify a construction of an abstruse providential economy enveloping the first century of Spanish colonial history. God seems to act in a reactionary, improvised manner, intervening only to control the damage perpetrated by his ancestral foe, the devil. Consequently, loss and gain, good and evil are not decisively set apart. They will be elusively multifaceted forces, crisscrossing and ever changing into their opposite throughout the HEI.

In order to provide more evidence on the preordained character of the colonization of the Mexican Valley and on the dramatic beginning of the new times it was supposed to entail, Mendieta borrows the account of eight prodigious omens that had appeared to the Mexicans announcing the destruction of their world from Sahagún's twelfth book of the *Historia general de las cosas de la Nueva España*.[16] For omens that the narrator classifies as "natural, albeit unusual events" (HEI, 178), he gives the exact year in which they had occurred, thus seemingly accepting their objective historical reality. For other omens of less admissible morphology for the Christian mindset, Mendieta cautiously uses "the impersonal passive of the 'legetai' 'it is said that'" (Hartog, 271) or the "dizen que." One omen represented as *legetai* was a strange, grayish-brown bird with a round diadem in its head. In this diadem, which was like a mirror, one could see reflected the stars and the sky, even during daytime. The people took the bird to Montezuma's specialized magic room, where his sorcerers gathered to produce knowledge about the disconcerting signs of nature. When an understandably dismayed Montezuma looked into the diadem, he saw odd creatures in formation, half men, half deer (i.e., the Spaniards on their horses), and as the necromancers began to discern what the bird was forecasting, it disappeared (HEI, 179). According to Mendieta in book 2 of the HEI, the indigenous people of the Mexican highlands had been made avid and superstitious readers of omens by the devil (107–11). But at this point in the narration in which such omens would seem to announce a "cataclysmic punctuation" (Graziano, 14) underscoring the providential commencement of a new age, the Franciscan does not deny the Mexican world of divination or denounce it as nonsensical, even when inhabited by bizarre creatures that became invisible in front of necromancers' eyes.

Moreover, the narrator declares that the legetai of the Indians claiming that during four generations their elders had been announcing the arrival of the Spaniards and what would happen to them because of it is worthy of consideration (HEI, 181). According to the author, the devil, who cannot foretell the future but only conjectures about it, could not have possibly known the events that would happen so far in advance, unless by having read the scriptures or by having told the truth by chance, thinking he was lying (HEI, 181). Mendieta offers as another alternative that the Indians may have miscounted the years, taking thirty for three hundred, thus moving back the devil's prophecies by generations. Finally, without arriving at any conclusion, he ponders that it may have been God himself who revealed to the Nahuas the coming of the Spaniards so that they would start preparing themselves with good deeds for this event (HEI, 181).

Mendieta's vacillation between the godly, human, and/or demonic origins of the Mexican prophecies further suggests that in his ecclesiastical narrative, the mode of God and the devil's interventions in history are not always easily discerned. This vacillation is particularly significant in the Spanish American colonial context because it places the spiritual colonizer in the position of being unable to dismiss pre-Hispanic knowledge as outright idolatrous. Mendieta's account of the Nahuas' power to produce the truth about their own future and about the advent of Christianity hybridizes the colonizer's privileged providential perspective by making the Nahuas much more knowledgeable and informed about the encounter with the other than the Christians themselves. Even the chosen Cortés, who is represented as having been divinely inspired to take fearful risks in the conquest, is never deemed to have had knowledge of the future (HEI, 175–77).[17] Through their anticipation of what would happen, then, the Nahuas and their pre-Hispanic past are incorporated into the divine unfolding of events.

And thus, the location of the preconquest Nahuas in the HEI becomes unfixed: they were definitely not inside but neither completely outside the

Christian community. They had been blinded by the devil into sacrificing the thousands of people that finally moved God to put an end to Satan's idolatrous reign of evil. But they had also been illuminated by God in expecting the arrival of the Spaniards for four generations; decades before the Europeans had even started entertaining the idea of reaching the East by sailing west. And just as the location of the preconquest Nahuas in relation to the Christian community was ambivalent, so the borders between the Spanish Christian as the emissary and agent of truth and the Nahua as the bewildered, misguided practitioner of idolatry would also be blurred. For the Indians, who according to the missionaries had been ruled by God's malevolent other during most of their pre-Hispanic past, soon manifested a strong inclination to Christianity when they were preached the Word. Concurrently, however, contact with the Nahuas had the nefarious effect of blinding the Spaniards with greed, arrogance, and selfishness, so as to become as contemptuous of God and of Christian values as the most barbaric of the pagan natives of the New World. As will be seen throughout this chapter, this confusion of boundaries and roles, the difficulty in separating good from evil, self from other, faithful from heathen, are important elements in what will produce a breakdown in Mendieta's providential account.

Because the HEI is also a chronicle of the deeds of the Franciscans in Mexico, a significant part of the third and fourth books is devoted to recounting their exemplary efforts in producing Christian subjects out of the Nahuas. Making veiled, strategic allusions to a Joachimite millenarian framework, Mendieta will ingeniously couple the discourse of providence with the eulogy of the Franciscan Order. Thus, the author relates how a very small group of Minorite friars engaged in the formidable task of converting multitudes of heathens and the astounding success with which God usually rewarded their efforts. First and foremost among these was language acquisition. For in spite of divine intervention in the discovery and conquest of the New World, the diligent friars soon became aware that in order for the God-willed Nahua Christian subjectivity to come forth, the arduous, very mundane task of learning the language of the natives was essential. Regardless of the incontestable truth and irresistible power of the Word, it had to be preached in Nahuatl in order to bring about its redemptive effects. Thus, the brightest among the children of the tlatoque and the pipiltin were recruited to help the missionaries learn and perfect their Nahuatl and to translate the first catechisms and sermons into this Mexican language. These advanced pupils even put some Christian doctrine into song, which greatly pleased other schoolchildren:

> Fue tanto lo que se aficionaron a ella [Christian doctrine], y la priesa que se daban por saberla, que estaban hechos montoncillos como rebaños de corderos tres y cuatro horas cantando en sus ermitas y barrios y casas: que por doquiera que iba de dia y de noche no decian ni se oia otra cosa sino el canto de las oraciones, artículos y mandamientos de Dios: que era para darle á ese mismo Señor que lo obraba infinitas gracias, con que se despertó entre los indios gran fuego de devocion. (HEI, 225)

> [They became so fond of Christian doctrine, and wanted to learn it so quickly, that they used to gather like flocks of little lambs for three and four hours in a row singing in their hermitages, neighborhoods, and houses: everywhere they went day or night they did not say or one would not hear anything other than the recitation of prayers, articles, and commandments of God: so that one had to be thankful to the very same Lord who had made it possible that so great a devotional fire was ignited in the Indians.]

Mendieta compares the groups of Indian children singing catechism songs for hours with flocks of lambs so as to illustrate their great obedience and devotion to the teachings of the friars. But even though they were clearly learning what the Franciscans and their collaborators had taught them, the text allows a reading of alterity in the demeanor of the children. For the passage also gives a sense of uncanny docility, of immoderate imitation by the constant repetition day and night that situates the children beyond the friars' control. Difference is also articulated in the use of an antithetical figurative language in the passage, since there is an incompatibility between the meekness, passivity, and timidity of the lambs and the fire of devotion instilled in the Nahua children for which Mendieta claims God should be praised. There is something unfathomable to the Western self about the excessive, unquestioning subordination of this other and his inordinate desire to reproduce the new religious discourses of authority. There is a force that seems to move the children that is neither their own individual, willful initiative nor what the friars had demanded. However, since the children's elusive demeanor does not go against the friars' teachings, it is finally translated into the more familiar and comforting alterity of God's providence.

Fearing that they were not sufficiently fluent in the language, Mendieta narrates how the friars started preaching by proxy. They would listen attentively to see if their Nahua aides and students said something improper when preaching to their countrymen, but they could find no fault: "Sino que eran muy fieles y verdaderos, y en extremos hábiles: que no solamente decian lo que los frailes les mandaban, mas aun añadian mucho mas, confutando con vivas razones que habian deprendido, reprehendiendo, y reprobando los errores, ritos y idolatrías de sus padres, declarándoles la fe de un solo Dios. . . ." [But that they were very faithful and truthful, and skillful in extreme: for they not only said what the friars told them, but added much more, confuting with lively reasons what they had learned, rebuking and reproving the errors, rites, and idolatries of their parents, declaring to them the faith in only one God] (HEI, 225–26).

The young cultural brokers were very faithful and true to what the friars had ordered them to say, but they were no mere imitators. In the process of imparting Christian doctrine to their fellow countrymen, they made it not quite the same. And this was so not only by virtue of the obvious act of linguistic translation into Nahuatl demanded by the indigenous context of enunciation but, perhaps more interestingly, by the coterminous gestures of exorbitance that supplemented the translation. The Nahua aides wittingly or unwittingly subverted the Franciscan spiritual authority by manifesting too fervent a desire for and comprehension of things Christian. By going beyond what the friars demanded, by supplementing their teachings with eloquent reasoning and passion, by zealously reprimanding their audiences for their sins and blindness, the Nahua pupils showed themselves repeating Christianity with a difference of extreme facility and desire. Many were skeptical if not outright opposed to this (hybridizing) dangerous practice of preaching to the Nahuas by the friars' bicultural aides. But Mendieta attributes this excess of skillfulness and fervor not to a cultural misunderstanding of Christianity, or to what Inga Clendinnen denominates as continuing "habits of conceiving the sacred...while various practices and beliefs changed" ("Franciscan Missionaries," 241), but rather to providential design (HEI, 226). He further defends this Franciscan evangelizing strategy from its critics by invoking the biblical example of Saint Paul and his disciples who also had started preaching soon after their conversion.

As the two passages above exemplify, the pious Christianizing agency of the Minorites is depicted as encountering such avid receptivity and predisposition among the Nahuas that its efficacy becomes hardly distinguishable from the corporate will of the latter. That is, the text works in such a way that when the relationship of the Nahuas to Christianity is represented, it will repeatedly allow other readings to emerge different from the providential, panegyric ones. In what will be a recurrent pattern in the third and fourth books of the HEI, the narrator, wittingly or unwittingly, would seem to be attempting to contain and/or appropriate the anxiety-producing cultural difference of the other that he registers in his text. His interventions usually dissolve this difference by attributing it to the more familiar alterity of divine providence and/or by linking it to the heroic, holy agency of the Friars Minor. Neverthess, what such attempts at containment disclose is not so much the bright, homogenizing power of a world-expanding, universal Christianity and the Franciscans as its chosen vehicle. Rather, what they show is a rudimentary fabrication of providential causality, an inadequate construct of the teleology of the church that can no longer control the ambivalence of colonialism "split between its appearance as original and authoritative, and its articulation as repetition and difference" (Bhabha, *Location,* 150).

Starting with the disconcertingly positive reception of baptism, Mendieta recounts the Minorites' divinely inspired strategies in imparting this sacrament. The first to be baptized were the students of the friars, but smaller boys and girls were also baptized provided that they would become Christians when they reached the appropriate age of discretion (seven years old). The historian clarifies that this was almost a given since "la ley evangélica estaba generalmente promulgada en las cabezas, que eran los señores y principales, y por ellos en nombre de todos sus vasallos admitida sin contradicción alguna, porque sin dificultad fueron convencidos del error de la idolatría y servicios de ella" [evangelical law was generally promulgated to the leaders, who were the lords and most prominent people, and by them in the name of all their vassals, accepted without contradiction, because without difficulty they were convinced of the error of idolatry and of its services] (HEI, 257). This clarification is significant, because it acknowledges the fact that the friars actively engaged pre-Hispanic social and political structures in the production of a Nahua Christian subjectivity. These structures and their concomitant functions were kept in place long after the conquest, particularly in the ranks of the upper classes (Lockhart, *The Nahuas*, 204; Gibson, 154–56).

But as is well documented and could not have passed unnoticed by Mendieta as late as the end of the sixteenth century, religion had been an inextricable part of the Nahua pre-Hispanic sociopolitical world. High-ranking priests and political officers had been usually recruited from the same noble families, and many principales of the towns, or altepetl, had important religious duties.[18] The tutelary gods, inventors of professions and of work technologies, were thought to have had selected the pipiltin, or noblemen, to administer and carry out different governmental functions (López Austin, *Human*, 1:388–89). The privileged position of the tlatoani, or rulers, was reinforced by certain ceremonial practices that endowed him with magical, sacred force and by a specialized education (López Austin, *Human*, 1:396–400). This special knowledge, transmitted in utmost secrecy in the *calmecac*, or specialized religious schools, was thought to be essential in "conferring to the cosmos a norm, a measure, a stability" (Gruzinski, *Colonización*, 17, translation is mine). And so it was, that due to his semidivine status as mediator between the gods and men, the authority of the tlatoani was only in very rare cases challenged by the people.[19] Thus, when Mendieta states that in the early bright years of the missionary endeavor, once the evangelical law had been accepted by the *cabezas*, or rulers and noblemen, that all their subjects would invariably also become Christians, the unquestionable, collective obedience that he is presupposing is, at best, a hybrid. It is based as much on a pre-Hispanic sociopolitical, magico-religious conception of the power of the rulers alien to Christianity, as on the prestige won by the saintly and austere lives of the seraphic brothers in the Mexican highlands.

Another phenomenon that the narrator attributes unconvincingly to a direct intervention of God or to the saintly agency of the Minorites is the wondrous native reception of the sacrament of penitence. The administration of the sacrament had already begun in 1526. Soon afterwards, the Nahuas came to confess thoroughly and distinctly their sins. Mendieta acknowledges that they had had a form of vocal confession during pre-Hispanic times, which they performed twice a year: "Apartandose cada uno en un rincon de su casa, ó en el templo, ó se iban á los montes, ... cada uno donde mas devocion tenía y allí hacían muestras de grandisima *contricion*. ... Y los dias que duraban en este ejercicio nunca se reian, ni admitian placer alguno, sino que todo era mostrar tristeza, pesar y amargura" [Withdrawing each in a corner of their house, or in the temple, or they went to the mountains, ... where each one felt more devotion and there they made signs of a very deep *contrition*. ... And the days in which they were engaged in this exercise they never laughed, nor accepted any pleasure, everything was supposed to show their sadness, sorrow, and regret] (HEI, 281; emphasis is mine).

Although attributed to false gods (under the nefarious influence of the devil), the respect and devotion with which the Nahuas practiced their confession had more than a few points in common with the solemn disposition due to the sacrament of penance in Christianity. Furthermore, it is noteworthy that the author uses the term "contrition" to characterize the feelings of repentance the Nahuas felt in their preconquest past, because by the time Mendieta writes the HEI, priests and regulars administering the sacrament of confession already had complained about the very literal notion with which the natives approached it (Durán, 1:40; Sahagún, *Historia*, 1:46–47). Priests and missionaries claimed that the Nahuas were much more concerned with the direct relationship between sin and physical illness than with sin as a sickness of the soul. They seemed to conceive of confession more as a way of appeasing the anger of the offended deity and of obtaining material goods and well-being in this life than as a means to save their souls from damnation in the next (Taylor, 50). This concept harked back to the pre-Hispanic concept of sin as defilement. As we stated earlier, the Nahuas considered sin or immorality to be the actual cause of bodily ailments and disgrace (Burkhart, *Slippery*, 170–83). Epidemics, disease, deformities, and any form of physical suffering were deemed to be the consequence of infringements on the established natural order and balance of forces. When the Nahuas confessed their sins in pre-Hispanic times, what they were look-ing for was not so much for a cleansing of the soul, but rather for the expul-sion of "the immoral deeds that have disturbed one's inner equilibrium" (Burkhart, *Slippery*, 172).[20] Thus, the contrition or remorse for having sinned that Mendieta attributes to the Nahuas even in pre-Hispanic times was not warranted by earlier testimonies and opinions of other friar-ethno-graphers like Sahagún and Durán, nor by later views such as Fray Juan de Bautista's in his *Advertencias para los confessores de los Naturales*, studied in the previous chapter.

What is significant about this discrepancy is the ambivalence of Mendi-eta's more favorable representation within the economy of the narration. Although represented in other parts of the HEI as agents of the devil, the sorcerers and magicians to whom the Nahuas confessed believed that the most efficient cure for the body was to eject sin from their ánimas (HEI, 281).[21] They ordered as penance sexual abstention, regulation of the diet, periods of solitude in a cave, and the like. In short, both the pre-Hispanic conceptualization and acts of cleansing as represented by Mendieta were not incompatible with or repugnant to Christian practice. Thus, the text opens up the possibility of reading that the magistrates of the devil had not hope-lessly blinded the Indians to all Christian values during preconquest times. In the case of confession, they had helped to establish points in common that would greatly facilitate the reception of the sacrament in the future (as dispensed by the chosen agents of God's will, the Franciscan missionaries). And so it was that many Nahuas willingly confessed their sins not only once a year, but also during holidays and Christmas time. And since there were but a few confessors during the first decades after the contact, the friars were followed by one or two thousand Indians, determined to be confessed even if they had to abandon their homes and estates for a month or two. Pregnant women and very old people sometimes walked many miles trying to find confessors. The sick and the handicapped would be taken to the roads where the friars were expected to pass by. Seeing that it would be impossible to confess the multitudes of Indians following them or coming to the monasteries to receive the sacrament, the friars would scold, threaten, and admonish them to go back home, to no avail (HEI, 282–83).

However, in spite of his acknowledgment of a pre-Hispanic practice similar to Christian penitence and of the role of healers in preparing the ground for an appreciation of the curative virtues of the sacrament, the narrator insists on a providential biblical explication for the overwhelming reception of confession among the Nahuas. Citing a line in Psalm 58, he states that God had revealed in Spain to Fray Martín de Valencia, the provincial of the Twelve, that the as yet unknown Indians "convertirse han á la tarde, y padecerán hambre como perros hambrientos y andarán cercando la ciudad" [They shall return at evening and shall suffer hunger like dogs and shall go round about the city] (HEI, 287).[22] According to Mendieta's allegorical and anagogical exegesis of the psalm, the conversion in the evening referred to the conversion to Christianity of the Indians in the last age of the world.[23] The prowling dogs were those very same Indians, and the canine hunger, their hunger for the sacraments and for the bread of the Word of God (HEI, 287).

Revealingly enough, however, Psalm 58 is a prayer in which King David invokes God's help and protection in order to be delivered from wicked enemies. The latter are compared to hungry dogs *returning* in the evening to roam the city.[24] The speaker asks God, his protector, to scatter them and bring these prowling dogs down because of their pride. Mendieta's spiritualist interpretation is then off the mark because it runs opposite to the literal meaning of the text. It is, therefore, as if the Franciscan historian dramatized in his (mis)reading of the psalm the insufficiency of a prophetic providential discourse to master the otherness and hybridity of colonial dynamics in sixteenth-century Mexico. There are many hints in the text that suggest that the natives might have been establishing connections between their pre-Hispanic and the Christian confession practices and that this may have been why they sought confession so vehemently. Furthermore, Mendieta disregards the opinions of his contemporaries about the literal way in which the Nahuas approached the sacrament. He sticks to a prophetic reading of the phenomenon, founding it on an interpretation of a psalm that goes totally against the grain. The providential discourse is thus pierced both by an elusive alterity that cannot be entirely fixed in an external, alien location to Christianity and also by too ardent a desire for divine intervention that leads to a questionable production of meaning.

Another significant force puncturing the discourse of the divine unfolding of events in the New World will be the power struggles among the mendicant orders depicted in the text. Skirting issues of individual conscience and free will implied by the collective obedience to the cabezas and principales that was described above, Mendieta recounts with delight that when the ministers arrived in a town, they would be received with great pomp, and all the people would already be gathered to receive the sacrament of baptism. The author says that sometimes there were so many people to be baptized that the friars could no longer raise their arms to pour the water (HEI, 266). In Xochimilco, two friars baptized in one day more than fifteen thousand adults and children (HEI, 266). Mendieta posits the fervor of the Nahuas seeking baptism as the fulfillment of the parable of the great banquet (Luke 14:15–24).

This overly optimistic representation of the biblical desire of the Nahua masses to become part of the ecumenical Christian community harks back to Motolinía's 1541 *Historia de los indios de la Nueva España*, which concludes by claiming that the Indians "have forgotten the idols completely as if a hundred years had elapsed since they abandoned them" (337).[25] But this view had already been seriously questioned by the Franciscan Sahagún in his own *Historia general de las cosas de la Nueva España* twenty years before the composition of the HEI.[26] And although Sahagún's *Historia* remained unpublished during the colonial centuries, his ideas if not papers must surely have circulated privately among the members of his Franciscan order in central Mexico. The fact that Mendieta does not even acknowledge Sahagún's challenge has an important strategic and political function in the narrative.

According to the narrator, the real and disturbing resistance to the fervent march of the Nahuas into the Christian community and into the history of salvation did not come from the Indians, but from the Christian ministers themselves. As soon as the Dominicans and Augustinians arrived in Mexico to evangelize, dissent and bitter differences of opinion cropped up about the way baptism was being administered by the Franciscans. The Minorites were accused of having sinned by simplifying the sacrament to an unacceptable degree and by dispensing it much more often than the traditionally appointed days by the Church. Mendieta contends that those who defended the purity of the administration of baptism had hardly interacted with the natives, because they despised their poverty and nakedness (HEI, 268). Nor had they even tried to learn indigenous languages. But what is perhaps more significant is that Mendieta construes this resistance from the camp of the Christians as a ploy from the devil (HEI, 267). According to the historian, the excessive scrupulousness of the new ministers caused many children and adults to die without having received baptism, and some others simply gave up trying to receive the sacrament because of constant delays in its administration (HEI, 268). The seriousness of Mendieta's accusations reinforces previous patterns of reversals between self and other, good and evil, God and Satan. For now the obstacles to the spread of Christianity were produced not by those outside the church, but by those within its core. The cunning of the devil to prevent the emergence of truth in the Mexican highlands was exercised not on the natives over whom he had supposedly reigned for centuries, but on the very Christian ministers who had come to the new lands to unseat him. Thus, while providential intervention had ignited the ardent desire of the Nahua other to become a Christian self, the unremitting agency of Satan split the self by moving him to obstruct that desire. The representation of this confusing turn of events is intended to defend the exemplary, apostolic role of the Seraphic Order, but at the expense of scattering the providential force that had preordained the expansion of Christianity in the Mexican highlands.

The third book of the HEI ends with the account of another power struggle regarding the mendicant orders, but now carried out by the Indian towns in a *doctrina*.[27] The struggle was to have *frailes de asiento*, or resident friars in the town, who would be of no other order but the Seraphic. According to Mendieta the devotion of the Nahuas to the Friars Minor was so extreme that when there were not enough Franciscans to take care of all the doctrinas to their charge,[28] the towns that could not have frailes de asiento asked to be granted at least a habit of San Francisco: "Y los domingos y fiestas ponerlo hemos en un palo, que nosotros confiamos que le dará Dios lengua para que nos predique, y con él estaremos consolados" [And on Sundays and feast days we shall put it on a pole, for we trust that God will give it a tongue to preach to us, and with it we will be comforted] (HEI, 331). In 1554, at the request of the ministers from another order (which Mendieta does not identify in order to maintain decorum) the Franciscan provincial granted them the parish of the town of Guatinchan. Due to the shortage of Minorites, this town, a cabecera in pre-Hispanic times, had been reduced to a visita, subject to the town of Tepeaca. Claiming that they had been introduced to Christianity by the Franciscans and that like children with some exercise of reason they would never abandon the mother that had fed and cared for them, the whole town of Guatinchan refused to receive the new apostolic ministers. In an attempt to persuade the natives to change their minds, the spurned friars reminded the people that Tepeaca had received city status and had been greatly ennobled because they had resident clerics in their church. They pointed out that not having friars de asiento in Guatinchan was a great affront to the community, since newer and lesser towns already had them (HEI, 336). After vehemently expounding the argument of altepetl status, the friars spoke about the need to have resident clerics in order to receive the sacraments regularly and lead fuller Christian lives. But the Indians remained unconvinced and threatened to abandon the town if forced to receive friars other than the Franciscans. After many failed attempts to persuade the people, and even after the principales were jailed for their steadfast loyalty to the Franciscan order, the community finally remained a visita of the Minorites until they were allotted resident friars sometime later. Mendieta gives several additional examples of unswerving native loyalty to the Friars Minor. Reprimands, threats, whipping, and incarceration had been useless in trying to dissuade the people from their resolve to have only Franciscan friars in their churches. The hardships of mass exile were suffered without hesitation, sometimes for as long as an entire year. Sixty adults and twenty children from San Juan of Teotihuacan had died without having received confession and baptism respectively as the whole community during a stormy night fled from Spanish authorities who came to force the town to receive the unwanted friars (HEI, 351–52).

The great weight put on the issue of prestige by the aspiring friars' speech in Guantichan may raise suspicions that altepetl politics, and not only providence, may have been involved in a community's strong preference for one order over the others. The Franciscans may have been perceived to be the most powerful of the mendicants since they were the first to arrive in the Valley of Mexico. This might explain the tenacity with which their presence was defended in some towns, for, according to Lockhart, there are as yet no known pre-Hispanic precedents to explain the differences the Nahuas saw between the orders (*The Nahuas*, 207–08). José Rabasa explores how a *tlacuilo* (painter) of the *Codex Telleriano Remensis* identified the Dominicans with the sacrament of baptism, while the Franciscans were depicted as the ministers of confession. Rabasa writes, "Clearly, from our historical vantage point preference for one of these sacraments amounts to different forms of evangelization. For the Indians, however, they meant multiple understandings of Christianity" ("Franciscans," 19). If both Rabasa and Lockhart are right, the Nahuas may have been perceiving a heterogeneity between the orders alien to the way the Europeans organized and understood their differences. Due to their cultural habit of conceiving "the coexistence of a plurality of equally valid worlds" (Rabasa, "Franciscans," 33), the Nahuas could have interpreted the orders as different Christian religions worshipping diverse tutelar deities. Desire to identify with one powerful religion or the other could have been why they fought so hard to retain Franciscans, Dominicans, and/or Augustinians (for in some cases the fight was to keep friars from the latter orders [Gibson, *Aztecs*, 110–11; Lockhart, *The Nahuas*, 207–08]).

In any case, what is important to point out is that the tenacious loyalty of the people for the Franciscans represented by Mendieta did not always necessarily further the emergence of the church in the lands of Anahuac. Requesting a Franciscan habit when no resident friar was available and trusting that God would confer it the power to speak was imagining the garment not totally unlike the regalia of the pre-Hispanic gods. For the Nahuas, these regalia had had a "transforming power" (Clendinnen, *Aztecs*, 257) because they "represented the god via a metonymic substitution" (Burkhart, *Holy*, 44). The person dressed up with a god's feature garments would be imbued with its power, thus becoming an ixiptla, or a "god-presenter," as Clendinnen defines the term (*Aztecs,* 253). But ixiptla could be vegetable too, and there is wide testimony of objects being dressed up with regalia and consequently becoming sacred.[29] Thus, what Mendieta deems as the pious insistence of some communities on acquiring a Franciscan garment may have harked back to pre-Hispanic notions of attributing to costumes the synecdochal powers of conjuring the supernatural presence of the gods.

Furthermore, the desire to have only Friars Minor to impart Christian doctrine could have spurred an undue fetishistic attachment to a form, a procedure, a rule. It could have procured superstitious confusion between what was accidental and what was substantial, according to the Christian worldview. Needless to say, many Dominicans and Augustinians must have had the capacity to preach the Word and administer the sacraments as effectively as any Friar Minor. Ironically then, the staunch loyalty to the Seraphic order at times incited the refusal of the Word of God in favor of a particular way of enunciating it, as if the protocol, dress, and custom of preaching procured a different form of power, a different meaning, a different protection from evil. And in a conflict in San Juan Teotihuacan, not only had the image of Saint Augustine been defaced and the church sacked in order to prevent the entry of the unwanted Augustinians (Gibson, *Aztecs,* 111), but precious souls had also been lost when the aforementioned eighty people died without receiving the necessary sacraments for salvation (HEI, 351–52).

Hence, Mendieta's detailed representation of the Indians' bitter struggle for resident Franciscans as sign and evidence of native devotion toward the Minorites kindled by their saintly behavior may not be contrary to the providential, eschatological discourse of "the New World as the End of the world" (Phelan, 104). But neither is it identical to it. The eschatological discourse speaks about the conversion of the Nahuas to the universal Christian Church at the very end of history and about the embodiment of "the City of God in the Indian commonwealth" (Phelan, 73). However, the episodes of native resistance to the non-Franciscan friars speak nonapologetically about the power and prestige of the Minorites in central Mexico, sometimes to the detriment of the spread of the Word or even at the cost of salvation, if only of a few.

Taking the above into account, it becomes clear that the providential discourse framing the eschatological discovery of the New World and the emergence of the Indian church is insufficient to account for all the events narrated in the third book of the HEI, and for the production of the text itself. This providential discourse, central to the genre of the universal history of the Church to which the HEI first and foremost belongs, is hybridized by the presence of pre-Hispanic religious practices in the Nahua reception of Christianity, by the power struggle among the mendicants for control over the evangelization process, and by the politics of representation of the third book itself, all of which the text wittingly or unwittingly evinces. To recapitulate: the fervent reception of baptism and confession in the Mexican highlands may have been procured not only by the holy, providential labor of the indefatigable Franciscans, but also by similar Nahua practices belonging to their preconquest past. The greatest resistance for the pre-ordained emergence of the Indian church as posited in book 3 did not come from the Nahuas, but rather from the camp of the very apostolic emissaries, at times struggling more for territory, power, and ideological domination than for impressing the truths of Christianity upon the Indians. And finally, the very textual act of constructing the Franciscans as the most privileged, most beloved, best, if not only fit apostolic agents in the New World bespeaks of a desire for prestige and recognition that, while not reproachful in itself, still belongs to the all too worldly city of Man of the second era of history, when the illuminated subjectivity of the Holy Spirit could not as yet become full.

The engraving preceding the fourth book is a powerful visual metaphor for the processes of inversion and hybridity between self and other that have been depicted in the third book of the HEI. The caption, which is a quote from Paul's first letter to the Corinthians, gives us the key to read into the engraving at least two levels of representation. It reads in English: "For I judged not myself to know anything among you, but Jesus Christ, and him crucified" (1 Cor. 2:2). The speaker in the quote is Paul, apostle and preacher to the Gentiles. He says that his teaching is based in no other knowledge but that of the power and immensity of the crucified Christ. In the fore-ground of the engraving we see a Franciscan friar in a position parallel to that of Paul's, since he is also preaching about Christ to the Gentiles, in this case the Nahua Amerindians. The smaller size of the Indian figures in comparison to that of the friar-preacher signifies the hierarchical father-child spiritual relationship between the two. In the central plane, there is a crucified Christ, and to his right a group of cavalrymen in military formation, seemingly ready to prey on his dead body. What will be particularly suggestive of inversion and hybridity in the engraving is the fusion between the two planes of representation. The friar is clearly teaching to the attentive and pious Nahua masses about the crucified Redeemer, who is represented in the engraving not as an image, but as the very person itself. It is as if the friar were pointing out to the Indians something that was actually happening right behind them. This is connoted by the fact that although the relative position and size of the figures in the frontal plane of the engraving are allegorical, the ground on which all the figures stand is depicted in realist perspective. The spatial continuity works, then, as a metonymy of temporal simultaneity. Moreover, the Roman soldier who opens Christ's breast with a spear, is dressed "muy al modo como podrían estarlo los conquistadores europeos del Anahuac" [much like the European conquerors of Anahuac would have been attired] (Solano y Pérez-Lila, "Estudio Preliminar," lxxxi). Similarly, the cavalrymen approaching the cross from the right side of the engraving also seem to be Spanish. It is, therefore, as if the Romans/Spaniards were represented as the executioners of Christ on the Cross, while the Indians look on, adoring the Redeemer, as instructed by the friar. This will be the moral gist of the fourth book. The painful split of the European self in its colonial endeavor will be represented more dramatically than in the previous book due to a progressively more intricate jumble between the forces of good and evil and a more radical inversion of locations with the other.

Book 4 tries to cover a lot of ground, following no definite or well-structured plan. It sketches very briefly the origins of the missionary activity of the Dominicans and Augustinians because "á cada una de las órdenes

Franciscan friar teaching the Nahuas about the Crucifixion of Christ.
Drawing in Gerónimo de Mendieta's book 4 of the *Historia eclesiástica indiana*.
(Courtesy of the Benson Library at the University of Texas at Austin.)

incumbe el cuidado de dar entera y larga relacion de lo que á su parte tocare"
[it is incumbent upon each order to give a full and detailed account of what
is pertinent to it] (HEI, 461). These accounts, although short, will give a different idea about the activity of the other mendicant orders than what was
depicted in book 3, albeit without ever making direct, concrete allusions.
The mendicant orders will now be shown to be allies supporting the Indian
church, rather than obstacles to it. Similarly, Mendieta will give just a brief
account of the Franciscan missionary activity in the provinces of Michoa-
can, Guatemala, and Yucatan "remitiendome en todo su progreso y suceso
a los que los historiadores de cada povincia escribieren" [abiding by what has
been written by the historians of each province regarding all their progress
and outcome] (HEI, 461). The summary account he gives of Fray Diego de
Landa's troubles in Yucatan is clearly partisan, since Mendieta merely glosses over the passionate and divisive controversy over Landa's idolatry extirpation practices that went on almost for ten years in the peninsula.[30]

But as both the engraving and the preface of book 4 anticipate, one of
the main focuses of this part of the HEI will be the progress of the Nahuas
in all things Christian, especially under the auspices of the Friars Minor.
After recounting in several chapters the great diligence shown by the Indians in constructing and adorning churches as well as in supporting their
ministers, Mendieta resorts to the discourse of the Christian marvelous in
order to portray the great aptitude of the Indians for Christianity. He relates
that many Indians had had direct contact with God through visions, revelations, miraculous cures, apparitions, and resurrections. Some had seen a
small child when the priest was raising the consecrated host in the Mass,
others had seen a globe of flames hovering around the chalice, and still others a beautiful golden crown floating over the head of the preacher (HEI,
451). Many had resurrected in order to confess themselves fully; others had
had visions of their imminent death so that they would put their souls in
order. There was even a case when a consecrated host had flown from the
priest's hand right into the mouth of an Indian woman waiting her turn to
receive communion (HEI, 458–59). Young children had also been granted
gifts of prophecy in order to persuade their relatives and acquaintances to
repent and to remake their lives.

Nevertheless, in spite of the three long chapters in the HEI enumerating marvelous visions and revelations and the divine satisfaction toward the Nahuas that such intimate gifts manifested, this was not enough to provide them with access to positions of authority in the church. Their difference squarely stood in the way to the latter's institutional hierarchy.[31] For although God had sent his signs of approval to the Nahuas, and albeit their otherness articulated by Mendieta in recognizably Christian terms of obedience, simplicity, and docility, their alterity nonetheless overflowed the limits deemed acceptable by the Western self. True, the Indian was biblically humble, patient, and simple but, Mendieta intimates, to an inordinate extent. He was constantly being assaulted by all non-Indian sectors, races, and classes of colonial society. Never did he say no to anything he was ordered to do. Never did he utter a word of reproach, or worse still, did he ever give signs of making any distinction between what was fair or unfair, right or wrong "como si fuese obligado á todo" [as if he were obliged to everything] (HEI, 441). He was used and deceived by all. Ironically, then, because of this difference in humbleness, patience, and simplicity that made the Nahuas the best-equipped people in the world to become Christians, priesthood was more emphatically denied to them by the church than to other descendants of the Gentiles. Mendieta claims that their "extraño natural" [their strange nature] was so given to submission and conformity that it made them unusually unfit for governing (HEI, 448). They would become unduly vain and infatuated if they found themselves in high positions of authority: "Y así quiero decir, que no son para maestros sino para discípulos, ni para prelados sino para súbditos, y para esto los mejores del mundo" [And so I want to say that they are not fit to be teachers, but disciples, not prelates, but subjects, and for this they are the best in the world] (HEI, 448).

But the narrator's reasoning about Nahua incapacity to rule in order to support barring them from church positions and priesthood is particularly inconsistent with his own ethnographic work in book 2. For one thing, it was clear that during preconquest times the Nahuas had governed themselves with a propriety that many a friar had admired, Sahagún and Mendieta included.[32] The hypothetical self-conceit that would overtake those Nahuas acceding to positions of authority within the church is contradicted by

Mendieta's own account that during pre-Hispanic times, the legitimate son of
an ailing tlatoani could be barred from the throne if he showed any sign of
arrogance or ambition: "No querian ver que el mayorazgo dende mochacho
ó mozo fuese muy entremetido y mandoncillo...sino que fuese humilde y
de virtuosa inclinacion" [They did not want to see that the heir was too med-
dlesome and haughty from a young age...but that he was humble and of virtuous inclination] (HEI, 154). Just like Sahagún in his monumental *Historia
general*, Mendieta represents the ritual exhortations to justice, self-control,
and self-deprecation to the new tlatoani in his investiture ceremony. Sahagún
also collects several huehuetlatolli for this occasion in which the tlatoani is
reminded of the brevity of life and of the constant dangers and risks that face
the human being, tlatoani included, on the slippery slope that is the earth.[33]
Similarly, the year-long ritual penitence preceding the investiture ceremony
of the *tecuhtli*, or high functionaries, of the Aztec republic guaranteed that
only meritorious people would accede to the position. In sharp contrast,
among the Spaniards the ways and means to attain high-ranking positions
were by "sobornos, favores y dádivas, y pluguiese á Dios que muchas veces no
interviniese simonía" [bribery, favors and gifts, and may God have willed that
in many occasions simony was not involved] (HEI, 161).

Mendieta's incongruent if not contradictory locations of Nahua subjectivity disclose an inadequacy in coming to terms with the difference of the
other. Although glorifying God for his direct, unmediated communication
with the Indians that signaled that he had taken pleasure in their devotion,
the narrator nonetheless supports barring the Nahuas from the power structure of the church. Because they were "la gente mas dispuesta y aparejada
para salvar sus ánimas [en el mundo]" [the people (in the world) most disposed and prepared to save their souls] (HEI, 437) on account of their meekness and forbearance, they were reduced to a state of perpetual infancy by
virtue of those very same qualities. And even though they were to be excluded from the ecclesiastical hierarchy of the church because presumably they
did not know how to rule, it was common opinion among the friar-ethnographers, including Mendieta himself, that the Indian republics in the pre-
Hispanic past had been much more orderly, rational, and virtuous than in
the colonial present, when governed by the Spaniards. These inconsistencies,

along with the discordant representations of the other mendicant orders in book 3 and at the beginning of book 4, disclose a lack of control over the text, a dispersion of events not recovered by the historian's narrative weaving, a coherence assaulted by ambivalence and hesitation. Moreover, the "estilo desordenado" [disorderly style] (Solano y Pérez-Lila, lxxv) of the text, the way it jumps from one topic to the next without a clear plan images and reproduces its own narrative object: an increasingly monstrous colonial dynamic in which a teleological providential meaning was ever more difficult to discern.

But the breakdown of the providential signification reaches its critical point in the HEI with the construction of the great rift inside, the deep wound inflicted on European subjectivity by the infamous abuse perpetrated on the natives of the New World, that not even the sacrosanct, military power of the Spanish universal monarchy had been able to control. Clearly aware of the political implications of historizicing the failure of the Spanish state to nourish and conserve properly the new Indian church under its care, Mendieta makes sure to deploy first a "parapeto documental" (Cesareo, 106–07, 114–15, 117), a paper shield of the many ordinances issued by the Catholic Kings, the emperor, and Philip II. He declares that he includes texts of such ordinances in their integral form "para que se vea el ferviente celo y cuidado que estos muy católicos príncipes tenian cerca de la defensa y amparo y buen tratamiento de los indios" [so that the fervent zeal and care that these very Catholic princes had regarding the defense, protection, and good treatment of the Indians should be seen] (HEI, 476). The king, as the God-designated depository of the general rule of natural law, was assumed to be always embarked on the quest of redeeming his kingdom from evil. Due to the enormous scale of the Spanish empire, writing and bureaucracy played a pivotal role in this quest.[34] The Spanish king embodied his power in the letter, in order to be able to manifest and extend his will throughout his vast domains, for their well-being and preservation.[35]

Mendieta assumes this theocratic, patrimonial concept of the monarchy in his narrative.[36] Thus, according to the historian, the emperor had always been very involved and interested in the care of his Indian subjects. Fearful of his conscience, he had issued numerous ordinances mandating

that all Spaniards treat the natives justly and fairly. Charles V had moderat-
ed the excessive tributes paid by the Indians; he had prohibited the rendering of personal services to the Spaniards by the indigenous people and their
use as carriers, or *tamemes* (HEI, 484). Mendieta narrates how the friars
made themselves vehicles of the royal will by proclaiming the ordinances
from the pulpit, so that the Indians would be able to stand up for the justice to which the monarch entitled them. Much like his father, as God's
representative to rule over the body politic, Philip II had shown his good will
toward his Nahua subjects and their progress as Christians. In order to represent the monarch's strong commitment to the wellness and preservation of
the Indian church, Mendieta includes in his text five ordinances issued by
Philip II. Not by chance, all of them have as their main tenor the king's
desire to favor the three mendicant orders and to preserve their ecclesiastical privileges by decreeing "que no haya novedad, ni se ponga impedimen-
to alguno á los religiosos en la administración de los sacramentos" [that there
be no novelty nor any obstruction imposed upon the religious in the administration of the sacraments] (HEI, 487).

But from the 1560s on, Philip II had done precisely the opposite. Backed
up by the Council of Trent's decision to subordinate the religious orders to
episcopal authority, little by little the king stripped the mendicants of their
extraordinary powers, converting their churches into secular parishes that he
could control more readily in his capacity as royal patron (Bakewell, "Conquest," 302; Phelan, 40). The period 1564–96, to which three of the five
quoted ordinances belong, was deemed by Mendieta to be that of the decline
of the Indian church (Phelan, 77). King Philip II, who "constantly equated
his own interests, and those of the lands he ruled, with those of God" (Parker, "David," 259), was persuaded by anti-mendicant factions in the Council of the Indies and by Archbishop Pedro de Moya that the friars, particularly the Franciscans, had too much authority over the Indians.[37] Such an
excess was attributed, among other things, to their knowledge of indigenous
languages and to their insistence on keeping the Indians separate from the
Spaniards. Philip II's policy of hispanizing the former was inspired to counteract this trend (Phelan, 82–83). Characteristically distrustful, perhaps he
began to harbor suspicions that with their millenarian reveries, the friars

wanted a separate republic of Indians, with themselves and not the king of Spain at the head (Baudot, *Utopia,* 516–24).

Skillfully armed with a misrepresentation of the prevalent historical trends that shielded both the integrity of Philip II and the by then less-empowered Franciscans from further accusations of unruliness, Mendieta ironically enunciates as one of the main causes of the downfall of the Indian church the very same manipulation of information that we see enacted in his own historical narrative. According to the historian, geographical distance had finally taken a toll on the breathtaking power of the monarch's word. Its sacred, fearsome potency had shown its vulnerability in a space co-opted by the satanic, temporal interests of undeserving subjects, who constantly deceived and misinformed the king. Even the Franciscans were to blame for this sorry situation, since they had succumbed to reprobate intrigues that sought to break the powerful alliance between the mendicant orders in their staunch defense of the Indians (HEI, 492). The Minorites had been made fearful of appearing to betray their vow of apostolic poverty by constantly siding with the Augustinians and Dominicans who, albeit mendicants, had many more temporal interests, possessions, and concerns than the Friars Minor (HEI, 493). Falling prey to this political temptation split the spiritual colonizers, allowing their enemies, the impious Spanish settlers and crown officials, to deceive and misinform their king and bring down the Indian church pre-ordained by God.

The last twelve chapters of book 4 are a lamentation for the plunder and tyrannical oppression brought about by the Spaniards in the New World. All the conflicts, factions, and divisions among the colonizers that ravaged New Spain during the sixteenth century are invoked in one way or another in these chapters. The inversion of the positions between self and other vis-à-vis the universal church will be all but complete: almost all sectors of Spanish colonial society will be portrayed as serious if not insurmountable impediments toward the growth and conservation of the new Indian church. Even the denomination "Christian" acquired a satanic spin in the Valley of Mexico, because the Spanish settlers referred to themselves as such in order to enact an unholy exclusion of the natives from the community of the church. The *alcaldes mayores* and *corregidores*[38] appointed to impart justice shamelessly teamed up with notaries and interpreters in order to extract from the Indians double and triple amounts of tribute and then sell back the surplus to the despoiled, needy natives at outrageous prices (HEI, 511). Secular priests, who were increasingly occupying mendicant parishes in New Spain, were noxious examples of intemperate drinking and eating, of inordinate desire for luxuries, and even of sexual misconduct (HEI, 512).

Many people of high rank and prestige such as the second viceroy of New Spain, Luis de Velasco I, and the diligent historian and auditor Alonso de Zorita supported the friars in denouncing the excesses of the secular clergy, their constant demand for services, their ignorance of the native languages, and their despotic condescension toward their indigenous flock.[39] The seculars, led by the second archbishop Fray Alonso de Montúfar, assumed too readily that the spiritual colonization had already been completed: "Por cuanto esta nueva Iglesia en esta provincia es adulta, y ha dejado de ser renaciente... es ya tiempo de ordenar en ella las cosas canónicamente..." [For since this new Church in this province is of age and is no longer renascent, it is time for ordering things in it in a canonical way...] (Audiencia de México 1555, quoted in Baudot, *Pugna*, 65). Thus, at best the secular clergy were deluded in expecting a fully Christianized flock that could be subject to the same duties and rendered the same services as their Spanish counterparts, without significant amounts of extra work beyond their allotted share in Europe. The friars, for their part, had been willing to undertake the baffling challenges presented by the very different flock of the Nahua Christian faithful.

However, Mendieta glosses over the fact that the friars were also accused of the very worldly demeanor of clinging to their enormous power over the Indians. They were charged with continuing to administer sacraments without permission of the bishops[40] and of constructing monasteries on the best and most populated lands. The mendicants were accused of leaving their brethren spiritually unattended when there were not enough available friars rather than allowing seculars or even brothers from other orders to take over empty parishes in their territories (Ricard, 364). The friars were also imputed with having abused their ecclesiastical authority by sentencing, incarcerating, and physically punishing delinquent natives, "muchas veces tan cruelmente que no parecen serles padres como publican que les son, sino enemigos sin caridad ni piedad, muchas veces por cosas levísimas" [sometimes so cruelly that they do not seem to be to them the fathers that they claim to them that they are, but enemies without charity or mercy, often for the slightest things] (Anguis, 252). The third archbishop of Mexico, Pedro de Moya y Contreras, charged that the friars lived outside the rule of their orders, that they did not respect their votes of obedience and poverty, and that they defied the authority of the king (Poole, 236).

Making a tacit reference to Motolinía's portrayal of eight plagues that had devastated the Valley of Mexico after the conquest in *Historia de los indios de la Nueva España*, Mendieta struggles to discern in the shocking *cocoliztli*, or catastrophic epidemics, of the sixteenth century in which more than half of the native population had perished, the disconcerting yet merciful design of God.[41] Firmly against explaining the terrifying pestilence as divine punishment of the Nahuas for their sins past and present, as many Spaniards had claimed, Mendieta reads the cocoliztli as providential gestures toward them. For by taking the Nahuas away soon after their conversion, Mendieta construes, God had prevented their sacrilegious repudiation of the Christian faith, which would have been more than justified because of the intolerable demands made upon them by the rapacious Spaniards (HEI, 518). In addition, God had also punished the latter by taking away from them those whom they were remorselessly willing to work to death in order to enrich themselves.

If the three cocoliztli were part of God's inscrutable designs, the "mayor y más dañosa pestilencia" [the greatest and most harmful pestilence] (HEI, 519) in the lands of Anahuac had been brought about by an institution ordained by the Spanish monarchs: the *repartimiento*. The repartimiento was a temporary, forced labor mechanism that provided Spaniards with a small percentage of the male Indian population for tasks with a demonstrated need for manpower. Slightly different from the encomienda, the Indian workers in theory had to be remunerated for their services, food, and transportation. According to Charles Gibson, the repartimiento came as a solution to the drastic labor shortage produced by the awful 1545–48 cocoliztli and to the impossibility of the encomienda system to supply an adequate workforce to new landowners and other non-encomendero entrepreneurs (224). Although controlled both by Spanish corregidores and Indian governors rather than by the traditional tlatoani rulership, the repartimiento was based on pre-Hispanic compulsory patterns of rotation. Established during the tenure of Viceroy Luis de Velasco I (1550–64), who, ironically, was a strong supporter of the regulars, the repartimiento was greatly developed during the rule of Viceroy Martín Enríquez (1568–80). It became the only major mechanism for the exaction of indigenous labor in the Valley of Mexico (Israel, 16). Due to the further labor shortages caused by the 1570 cocoliztli, the repartimiento had become even more coercive and onerous, since ever-increasing Spanish need for labor had to be satisfied with a catastrophically diminished number of workers (Gibson, *Aztec,* 230–33).

In order to indict the abuses and humiliations of the repartimiento, Mendieta exploits the colonialist assumption of the universal Western Christian subject as a rhetorical strategy. Through the powerful fiction of an outraged, looted other who thinks, feels, and speaks just like the Spanish self, the historian bitingly exposes the split of the Spanish colonial enterprise in the New World, torn between its spiritual, ecumenical task to win the great masses of Indians for the Catholic Church and its temporal imperial ambitions to expand, dominate, and endure (Lynch, 217). Mendieta attempts to demolish the legal foundation of the colonial presence in New Spain by having his fictional Nahua character eloquently question the justice of a law that allows strangers to steal the land of peaceful natives and to punish their unresisting acceptance of the foreign ways with forced labor. The fictional universal Nahua subject decries the legitimacy of a law that mandates that those who had formerly been sovereign princes in their lands should now take as lords foreigners who in their own country would be considered the lowliest of peasants. He goes on to represent the impossibility of rationalizing the demands made upon the natives, who had to abandon their own sick wives and children in order to go and tend the fields of the invader; the truth of a law that permits institutionalized pillaging of the only means of sustenance of the dispossessed: their labor. He derides the checks and balances in place to prevent the sacking of Indian toil by claiming that the appointed judges of the repartimiento were the first to become accomplices

in the exploitation that it was their job to curtail. The indignant imaginary
Nahua closes his incisive questioning with a blasphemous syllogism: no
law based on universal reason would allow such things to happen; Christian law allows them; hence, Christian law is the worst law of the world and
should be rightly loathed by all (HEI, 519–23).

From Mendieta's indictment of the repartimiento through his fictive
character's litany of objections, the reader cannot but infer that this institutionalized labor system mandated by the Spanish crown was just a meager
disguise for sheer, brutal exploitation, and, thus, abominable and offensive
to all nations with any sense of civility. Moreover, Mendieta embarrasses the
monarchy further by depicting the word of the king not only as blinded by
misinformation, but also as crippled and scorned. For even though Charles
V had issued ordinances prohibiting certain types of very high-risk labor in
the mines, "darles ordenanzas á nuestros españoles de Indias, es como poner
puertas al campo" [to issue ordinances to our Spaniards in the Indies is like
putting doors in open fields] (HEI, 527). That is, the king was unable to reg-
ulate, ordain, and control his faraway dominions in the New World. His
sacrosanct word had been reduced to an empty, sorry signifier of royal good-
will by his Spanish subjects who scoffed at the feebleness of its paper materiality. Mendieta's depiction of some of the abuses committed in the repartimiento and prohibited by royal cédula construed them not only as acts
against Christianity, but also as acts of lese majesty. These suggestions that
the law of the Spanish crown was not founded on universal principles of justice that could stand the scrutiny of reason and that decried the impotence
of the word of the king may be thought of as performative. That is, they not
only reflect or give knowledge about a supposedly extra-linguistic reality,
they *produce and make happen* at the level of the utterance the very reality
they depict. These words affronted the Spanish monarchy by the act of
chronicling to the world and to posterity the spectacle of an emasculated
Spanish rule. By writing that the king's conscience was stained on the issue
of the repartimiento, Mendieta was not only giving knowledge about the
monarch's unhappy state of being, but he was also already producing a
blemish on the king's honor and reputation by the mere linguistic act that
proclaimed the lesion.[42]

Thus, it can be said that the great persuasive power of book 4 hinges on the dangerous performativity of a rhetoric of scandal.[43] The pathos of this rhetoric consists in the great risks for tarnishing his legitimacy and authority that the historical narrator takes by trying to persuade his readers through a shocking representation of the infamous. This can be seen in his attacks on the seculars and the crown officials and in the portrayal of the discredited word of the king. Because of the constant possibility of slipping into slander by making known to the world the abjection of another, such an act of denunciation always implicates the ethics of the speaker. Mendieta's charges against most colonial sectors are so scathing and conclusive that the reader is both shaken by his accusations and by his boldness in positing debauchery. And even if such charges were only unintentionally partial representations of a complex colonial reality, the mere act of the historical utterance itself would be promoting, creating, and performing the very depravity it so bitterly represents. For whether wittingly or unwittingly, falsely defiling the conscience, reputation, and demeanor of Spanish subjects, clerics, government officials, and the crown itself could be as destructive an act as the hypocrisy and perfidy they were accused of. Much like Bartolomé de Las Casas's extremely controversial *Brevísima relación de la destrucción de Indias*, whether historically true, false, or just half-true, the HEI guarantees the scandal of Christianity in the New World, if only as a defamatory piece of writing produced by a highly visible and respected friar.

Book 4 concludes with a powerful lamentation for the fall of the Indian church. The narrator decries that he cannot close his history glorifying the Lord for the great number of souls reaped in the New World, which could have balanced out the awful evils of pain, death, and destruction inflicted in the lands of Anahuac by the Spanish conquest. Rather, he has to end it with a long litany of miseries, so piercing, pitiful, and vociferous that it cannot but wring a sign from heaven. Mendieta compares the sorry situation of the Indian church to the account of the destruction of Jerusalem in Psalm 79. According to the historian, although it could not be held that the Indians had seen God face to face as did the Israelites, it had to be acknowledged that the natives had responded with resolve to his Word, preached by his apostolic ministers. Consequently, the universal church had indeed extended its roots and manifested its visibility in the New World for the greater glory of God. But now the Judeo-Christian God had once again abandoned His Indian children; He had withdrawn His merciful agency from the spiritual colonization endeavor, allowing everything to collapse into despair, chaos, and abomination.

In the very midst of this apocalyptic lamentation, Mendieta indicts the *diezmo*, or tithe, introduced by *Visitador*[44] Valderrama in 1564 as the other great cause for the fall of the Indian church. According to the historian, the tithe, along with all other tributes owed by the Indians,[45] unleashed a frenzy of greed and despoliation that caused havoc in New Spain and the extinction of its indigenous population. The divinely ordained Indian church had been ruined by the vain temporal interests of those ecclesiastical officials who, charged with cherishing and protecting it, were much more concerned about the benefices they were entitled to as dignitaries of the church.

Indeed, this tithe was the main target of the bitter, political struggle between the secular clergy and the friars over jurisdiction, power, and control of the Indians since 1544. Supporters of the tithe like Cervantes de Salazar claimed that since all Christians were obliged "de derecho natural y de derecho divino" [by natural and divine right] to pay a tenth of their earnings to the church, so were the Indians (Salazar, quoted in Baudot, *Pugna*, 84). Destined to support the transfer of the Indian church from the mendicant orders into the hands of the episcopacy, some contemporary historians believe that the regulars may have loathed the tithe not only because of the additional economic burden it represented for the Indians, but also because the diezmo would provide the fiscal means to displace the friars from their doctrinas and territories (Ricard, 376; Baudot, *Pugna*, 71; Poole, 70–71). Other historians consider it ironic that Valderrama would raise against the friars the very same reproach that was usually made of the secular settlers: namely, that "de España venía lo peor de cada casa" [from Spain came the worst of every house] (Iglesia, "Invitación," 171).[46] Hence, if in fact Mendieta's construction of the tithe as the great enemy of Christianity and of the conservation of Indians was itself not entirely free of the less spiritual motives of mendicant prestige, territoriality and desire for power, then the text itself as a linguistic act would be irremediably enmeshed in the turmoil of temporal interests and passions that it documents. The HEI would be performing the same bickering and manipulation of facts in defense of self-interest that it claimed had subverted the providential emergence of the Nahua Christian subject.

The text comes to a close giving a sense that the Christian god had again become a *deus absconditus*[47] in the lands of Anahuac, much like in pre-Hispanic times. The scourge of Spanish greed had so utterly destroyed the lands formerly ruled by the devil, that no man, including the sacrosanct king of Spain, "lord of everything in the East and West" (Parker, "David," 253) was powerful enough to eradicate it. Finding no possible human agency capable of delivering the colonial edifice from the clutches of evil, unable to discern signs of divine will, agency, and intervention, the historian of one hundred years of colonial depravation resorts to one last option. Invoking the misery of utter defilement and "á imitacion...del afligido pueblo israelítico" [in imitation of the afflicted Israeli people] (HEI, 562), Mendieta implores Providence to manifest itself. Because the Indian church had been ruined by the evil of Spain, the failure of colonial history in the New World, and the wretchedness it had brought upon humankind could only give unceasing hope that God would finally be moved to compassion for his debased children and show himself once more to make them clean. While not acknowledging the possibility of his own narrative act as part of the perversion of the history recounted, Mendieta nonetheless includes himself among the fallen supplicants to whom the scandalous misery of the Indian church had given no other choice but to wait for a redeeming sign from God:

> Abrasada está la viña, y poco le falta para ser á remate perdida; mas como tú vuelvas tu rostro en nuestro favor, y contra la bestia causadora de tanto mal, luego perecerán sus fuerzas y nosotros cobraremos aliento.... Esto esperamos, Señor, de tu mano, con entera confianza, sin apartarnos de ti, ni buscar otro socorro, y hasta lo alcanzar, no cesaremos de invocar tu santísimo nombre. Por tanto, Señor Dios de las celestiales virtudes, conviértenos a ti, muéstranos tu serenísimo rostro, y seremos salvos. Amen. (HEI, 563)[48]

> [The vineyard is burning, and there is little left before it will be totally lost; but if only thou wilt turn thy face to our favor, and

against the beast, perpetrator of so much evil, its powers will perish and we will be encouraged to go on.... We hope for this, Lord, from thy hand, with full trust, without ever parting from thy company or without seeking other succor, and until we attain it, we will not cease from calling thy holy name. Thus, our Lord of heavenly virtues, convert us to thee, show us thy most serene and beloved face, and we shall be saved. Amen.]

The Pyramid under the Cross

The attempt to produce Nahua Christian subjects during the sixteenth century in central Mexico was an extremely complex story that yielded mixed and unexpected results. Not only today, but already in its time, this story was not told as an unqualified triumph of Christianity and consequent liberation of indigenous nations from the clutches of idolatry and evil. Focusing on texts concerning the Franciscan missionary endeavor in central Mexico during the sixteenth century, this book examines the epic project of Christianization, the limits the Spanish spiritual colonizers faced in achieving it, and their awareness and unawareness thereof. Bordering those limits, the book also imagines voices of the Nahuas. The pitch of these voices is not high. Sometimes it is a soft, polite voice of riposte (Burkhart, *Holy*, 5), one that would not be fully convinced of the need to forsake deities that until the arrival of the Christian god had provided in abundance to those who had served them well. Sometimes, it is a voice weaving continuities between old indigenous practices and the new. Still at other times, it is a voice that may have not fully grasped the cultural intricacies of Christianity.

The first part of the book dealt with the reconstruction of the origin of the evangelization endeavor in Mexico, featuring the renowned twelve Franciscans. This reconstruction is the bilingual *Colloquios y doctrina cristiana*, penned by Bernardino de Sahagún and his four learned Nahua collaborators from the Colegio de Tlatelolco, Antonio Valeriano, Alonso Vegerano, Martín Jacobita, and Andrés Leonardo. I argue that whether intended in the *Colloquios* or not, we can discern a paradigm of the Franciscan spiritual colonization and of an emerging Nahua Christian subject during the six-teenth century. First and foremost, the narrative genre used in the text to depict the evangelization endeavor is that of dialogue, a conversation between two parties holding different views. This is significant because in the genre of the coloquio, although there is usually one privileged prevail-ing voice, winning over the opposing party is not accomplished by force, but through a clear, civil exposition of ideas. What is sought through dialogue is not merely an imposed acceptance from the opposite camp, but a free con-sent to demonstrated truth. This humanist aspiration, constituent of the genre, is recast as providential in the prologue to the *Colloquios* when Sahagún declares that the Twelve's civil, orderly, and efficient way of addressing the native lords and priests was inspired by the Holy Spirit. Such an attribution was considered in our reading of the text as a possible allusion to Joachim de Fiore's historical schema, argued to have been an important influence in the missionary mindset of the twelve Franciscans; for it was precisely the third person of the Trinity who was supposed to rule the last and most perfect age of history. Literary critics and historians of the Spanish American colonial period think that the Twelve believed the Indian church would be part and parcel of this culminating era of freedom, love, and childlike simplicity.

Nevertheless, in Sahagún and his Nahua collaborators' reconstructed origin of the providential conversion of the Amerindian masses to Chris-tianity, many elements of the all-too-historical Franciscan evangelization and hybrid Nahua Christian subjectivity can be discerned. In examining the founding arguments of the Twelve, one can locate a gap between their attrib-uted divine inspiration and their depicted articulation. Although always elo-quently and politely expressed, some arguments could sound contrived, inaccurate, circular, or simply deceptive even to a sixteenth-century Span-ish reader. It would seem that the epistemic violence implicated in the Twelve's pious objective to persuade the Nahua lords and priests that their deities had to be repudiated split the rhetorical power of the friars' posited universal truths. Or perhaps, knowingly or unknowingly, the insufficiency of some of the Twelve's represented arguments in the *Colloquios* hinted to the worldly, cultural limits of the Christian truth, as it strove to become equally manifest to all. In any case, without ever rejecting the new god, the Nahua lords and priests are represented as remaining unconvinced by the expositions of the friars. Finally, in the extant chapter summary of the *Colloquios*, the tlatoque and tlamacazque submit to a proposition that appeared to have properly matched pre-Hispanic beliefs, namely, that their deities had been unable to help them defeat their conquerors, because the latter served a more powerful god. After this, the tlatoque and the tlamacazque handed over their idols and brought before the friars their women and children. According to the extant summary of the *Colloquios*, then, after long conversations, refutations, and demonstrations, the friars finally conquered the hearts and minds of their elite Nahua audience. The door was open for the Word of Christ to reign supreme in the lands of Anahuac. Or so the Twelve may have believed. However, at the time that Sahagún was preparing the text of the *Colloquios*, his own field research had produced evidence that the cult to the pre-Hispanic deities lived on along with the worship of the Christian god. Much like their ancestors had done, the Nahuas adopted the gods of the victors, but they did not fully give up their ways of understanding and relating to the supernatural forces that roamed the earth.

The Nahuatl theater of evangelization, the subject of the second part of this book, was a new colonial cultural practice not entirely controlled either by the colonizer or by the Nahua people. It was indeed a "didactic" spectacle, in which the religious narratives of the colonizer were presented before the eyes of the Nahuas in order to be recognized as new truths and to set examples to follow. But it may also have been a site in which the Nahuas displayed the uncanny power of their culture to interact with, placate, and/or, perhaps, ultimately incorporate alterity. It is unlikely that the friars would have conceived this practice in such culturally affirmative terms. But when considering Motolinía and other friars' performance accounts, it is not the case either that this theater was constructed as indiscriminate dramatic reproductions of the new hegemonic narratives by passive, dominated, colonized subjects.[1] Rather, the neixcuitilli were depicted as appropriations by consenting agents, who in turn negotiated a sense of empowerment and prestige among themselves through their representation. There are clearly many interests at stake in representing the Nahuas as willing participants in the theater of evangelization, particularly deflecting the epistemic violence of colonial rule. But there is also an implied recognition of the limits of the colonizer's power to impose such didactic theater without the acquiescence, desire, and industry of the other. If only because of the conspicuous participation of the Nahuas, the evangelization theater cannot be properly accounted for solely as an instrument of indoctrination and control, devised for "underdeveloped intelligences" (Lopetegui and Zubillaga, 1:415), even from the point of view of the colonizer.

And yet, our readings of the three neixcuitilli show that they could be more disconcerting, split, and problematic than what the friars may have foreseen, even while depicting this theater as great collective enterprises offering admirable renditions of Christian stories and teachings. In the case of *The Final Judgment*, an unexpected hybridization effect occurs with the presence of the implied Nahua other to whom the dramatic text is addressed. This other is constructed in the text as needing to be terrorized into accepting the Christian ethical world. Such terror is produced by the (not unorthodox) representation of Christ as an implacable judge, but ultimately results in the ironical conservation of the pre-Hispanic deities who now posed as demons in the colonial world. By condemning all those who had not submitted to his will to a woeful eternity in Mictlan, ironically the Christian god also guaranteed the preservation of his demonic, pre-Hispanic foes, who had always tried to steer away humankind from him. In this sense, the discourse of the spiritual colonizer, as it is negotiated into a neixcuitilli, ends up producing figures of its own failure to fully suppress otherness.

We saw in *The Sacrifice of Isaac* an attempt to emphasize the eradication of the limit pre-Hispanic cultural practice of human sacrifice. However, the violence of total acquiescence to a capricious, terrifying deity was not superseded in the neixcuitilli by the new Christian colonialist discourse since the internal disposition to perform a human sacrifice was upheld by the example of Abraham. A hybridization effect occurs in the similarity between the (shockingly) pious consent of the great patriarch of Judaism, Christianity (and Islam), and that of the Nahua lords when they had offered their children to Tlaloc in pre-Hispanic times. The intent of the religious discourse of the colonizer was thus undermined by this confusion, because it reaffirmed rather than discouraged the other in his way of relating to the sacred.

In *The Fall of Our First Parents* it was proposed that the mise-en-scène reconstructed by the anonymous friar and produced by the Nahua elite may be read as a commentary, appropriation, or even Nahuatization of the story of the primordial couple. It was shown how the visual, kinetic, and semiotic codes of the staging may have been an interpretation of the Fall not as a free (moral) act of disobedience, but as unrestrained individual behavior. Thus, rather than ingraining in the Nahua audience the pivotal Christian notions of guilt and personal responsibility promoted by the dramatic text (if ever there was one), the mise-en-scène of the neixcuitilli may have been performing an act of cultural continuity by presenting before the eyes of the indigenous audience the need to abrogate strong manifestations of individuality and separateness. Finally, the suggested reference to the Nahua primordial couple Cipactonal and Oxomoco through the regalia brought to Adam and Eve by the angels might have been another gesture of cultural self-affirmation. By associating Adam and Eve with the creators of the tonalpohualli, the divination calendar that would help humanity preserve itself by discerning the cycles and influences of the supernatural forces, the staging of the Fall in *The Fall of Our First Parents* might have been a performance of resistance as continuity with the pre-Hispanic past, only visible to the Nahua audience.

The three neixcuitilli examined thus support the position held by León-Portilla, Harris, Burkhart, and others that the Nahua evangelization theater was an ambivalent, shifting, unstable discourse. It displaced, resisted, and sometimes may have even reversed the colonizer's hegemonizing intent while disseminating his narratives among the Nahuas. Rather than a triumphal spectacle and statement of Christian sameness, this colonial cultural form engages doubleness and difference, becoming a site where the power of colonial narratives was publicly displayed, negotiated, and reterritorialized. From our postcolonial and historical locations we can see that, ultimately, the fissures and ironies in this theater, as well as its collaborative nature, may have been prefiguring that the spiritual conquest as the suppression of otherness and a radical break with the religious pre-Hispanic past would never be fully played out.

Alonso de Molina's *Confessionario mayor* (1565, 1568, 1579) and Juan de Bautista's *Advertencias para los confessores de los Naturales* (1600) embody what according to Tzvetan Todorov are "the two great figures of the relation to the other that delimit the other's inevitable space" (146). These two figures are "difference ... corrupted into inequality, equality into identity" (146). Molina's *Confessionario* articulates the Christian belief in the equality of all humanity in its call to salvation by God and in its redemption by Christ. But equality became an onerous burden of identity for the other. The Nahua had to assume the universal Christian subjectivity imagined by the Spanish colonizer, sometimes even beyond what was demanded from European Christians, and he had to do so unaffected by cultural specificity and memory. The disconcerting freedom and full agency attributed to the Nahua penitent in the *Confessionario* are a clear case in point of the oppressive application of this universal cultural equality upon the other. And yet, this application also opened several possibilities of resistance to colonial power, if only because such full agency and freedom negated the spiritual infancy of the Nahua, an attribute frequently invoked in the colonizer's discourses in order to justify his presence.

And resistance indeed there was, although in a soft, nonconfrontational mode. Witting or unwitting resistance to Molina's heroic, colonialist universal Christian subjectivity gave rise to Bautista's *Advertencias*, in which freedom, agency, and equality were transformed or "corrupted" into the inequalities of subalterity and "ignorancia invencible." But this transformation was not merely an objectification of the other that enabled the self to protect itself from a threatening difference. In other words, the posited recalcitrant alterity of the Nahua by Bautista was not only an easy recourse to racism. It did not simply consolidate and legitimize the colonizer's position of power to himself. Such a "corruption into inequality" exacted a price from the spiritual colonizer because it also hinted at the limits of his power and authority, and this produced anxiety in him. The resistance or the posited cultural unpreparedness of the Nahuas to accede "properly" to a Christian subjectivity demanded from the colonizer the labor of relocating the truth of his religious universality and of reinventing himself in his relationship with alterity.

Thus, the *Confessionario* and the *Advertencias* indeed deploy a narrative of the "master" figures of the places carved out for the colonized by the colonizer at different periods in sixteenth-century Mexico. And yet, while these texts certainly tried to "foster the institutions of Empire" (Jara and Spadaccini, 15), they demand a critical approach that goes beyond a focalization of colonial discursive possibilities only as instruments of domination over clearly inferior others. For however unequal and asymmetrical the power relations in the (exemplary) discursive colonialist context of the confessional practice in sixteenth-century Mexico, the production of a "proper," universal Nahua penitent implied the recognition of the most delicate issue of a consent that could not be forced, dismissed, ignored, or trampled upon, but only reckoned with. However, because cultural difference proved to make such consent ever more elusive, the mass of common Nahua Christian subjects was acknowledged to be beyond the full grasp of the spiritual colonizer at the turn of the century.

The closing text of the book, the *Historia eclesiástica indiana*, narrates the demise of the Franciscan eschatological imagination in the New World. This eschatological imagination is wedded in the HEI to the genre of the universal history of the church and its central role in the grand plan of salvation. For the Indian church was fancied by many as the first of the last great churches that would emerge in the twilight of history, as Christianity providentially extended itself throughout the globe.

However, from the vantage point of one century after the divinely ordained discovery of the end of the world, the HEI narrates how the plan of salvation had become inscrutable again. The providential agency shaping the history of the church in the Valley of Mexico had worn down to brief, flickering moments of intervention that quickly became unreadable by turning into their opposite. For even more than a chronicle about the emergence of the Nahua Christian church and about the exemplary missionary deeds of the Franciscans in the New World, the HEI is a testimony of the deep rift within the Western colonizing self, caused by its dealings with the other. The violence of the New World encounters of early modernity consisted not only in the destruction inflicted upon Amerindian societies, but also, as Michel de Certeau believed, in the "transformative violence of the meeting with the Other" (Giard, 317) that befell the European self. And, according to the HEI, what the transformative violence of the encounter with alterity did to the European self was to unleash in him a scandalous form of barbarism. Thus, while, according to Mendieta, the otherness of the Nahuas had been dissolved in the ecumenism of the Christian Church, a frightening alterity appeared within the European self in the form of a predation that mangled and stained the signs of Providence. The demolition of the European self as a moral being and his miserable incapacity to relate to others in noncoercive ways made it impossible to envision unity and direction in history any longer. The text itself, in its enraged, partisan engagement with the newly revealed alterity of the European self in the Valley of Mexico, also shows evidence of this transformative violence within.

In this book I have examined important yet relatively unstudied texts, belonging to a wide variety of genres, produced as part of the Franciscan evangelization enterprise in sixteenth-century Mexico. From the *Colloquios*, which reconstructs the origin of such an enterprise, to Mendieta's HEI, which depicts the frustration of the millenarian dream, I have shown many of the great complexities, unexpected hybridities, reversals, and internal splits that were involved in the epic emergence of a Nahua Christian subject in sixteenth-century Mexico.

Needless to say, other texts, time frames, and historical agents could have been studied in order to map this hybrid Nahua subject, the spiritual colonizers' failure to fully encompass his soul, and the impact that all of this had in early modern Spanish and Mexican identity, imagination, and sense of history. After the demographic catastrophes of the sixteenth century, the consequent changes in Nahua social structures, the gradual takeover of mendicant parishes by the centralized secular church, and more decades of a hegemonic Christianity discourse piling up, the Nahua Christian subjects of the seventeenth and eighteenth centuries produced other cultural responses and registers of hybridity whose study is far from being exhausted. The specific agents and historical period of this book were chosen by the fact that the Franciscans laid the foundation for the propagation of Christianity in the lands of Anahuac. They went far and deep in engaging Amerindian alterity in order to insert it into their imagined universal Christian community that so much mirrored their European Christian selves. Hence, the Friars Minor in the sixteenth century provide a solid point of departure to explore the "limit-text of culture" (Bhahba, *Location*, 34), or the boundaries at which cultural difference became disruptive of identities in the Mexican colonial environment. These boundaries would change throughout the colonial centuries, but there is a core limit-text that would linger and whose configuration is discernible in the works that we have examined.

And indeed, in the texts studied in this book we have seen those disruptive forces of difference at work. The friars' onerous labor to translate their religious system so that it could be apprehended by the Nahua others certainly helped to propagate Christianity. But this translation also produced partial presences, contradictory and unexpected locations of alterity, ambiguous meanings, disquieting intersections, failed or ironical receptions. Thus, Molina's beautifully written and widely circulating bilingual *Confessionario* addressed a titanic, ultra-developed Nahua Christian subject that possibly was never in place. The overwhelming power of the colonizer's god to punish in *The Final Judgment* ironically provided the nourishment of his pre-Hispanic god/demon foes for all time to come. The missionary triumph of the Twelve as represented in the *Colloquios* was countered by the survival of the cults to the pre-Hispanic gods uncovered by the fieldwork of the very editor of the work, Sahagún. The imperative to translate the other into an image of the self revealed the cultural opacity of the authoritative discourses of the colonizer as in the *Advertencias* of Bautista, who nonetheless willed to change, adapt, and split his hegemonic discourses when confronted by the disruptive difference of the "ignorancia invencible" of the indigenous other. Last but not least, the translation strategies of using cultural similarities between Christians and Nahuas in order to displace the latter's notions of the supernatural ended up guaranteeing that the presence of the Mesoamerican gods would not be shunned completely. Hence, Tezcatlipoca would live on in the lands of Anahuac sometimes as Lucifer and sometimes as God the Father, the One by Whom All Live. And perhaps this God of the Smoking-Mirror, who without reason sometimes bestowed riches to mankind and sometimes anguish and affliction, also reflected a likeness to Mendieta's silent Providence, inexplicably tolerating the millennial Mexican church to fall prey to the worldly evils of self-interest and greed.

For the Nahuas, a polytheistic people, accepting and serving the new victorious Christian god was not felt to be in contradiction with the worship of their deities. As Serge Gruzinski has pointed out, "the plasticity of the native cultures" or "the indigenous aptitude for syncretism were possibly the most difficult cultural obstacles that the friars had to face in their evangelization endeavor" (*De la idolatría*, 104; translation is mine). Thus, the greatest resistance put up by the Nahuas during the sixteenth century was that of transforming similarities into identities, translating many of their multifaceted pre-Hispanic gods and religious practices into a Christian guise (and not without the help from the friars [Burkhart, *Slippery*, 191]). Such translations may have sometimes been conscious interventions of bicultural Nahuas, as could have been the mise-en-scène of *The Fall of Our Parents*. At other times, transformations may have been unwitting acts of interpretation conditioned by indigenous cultural habits: thus, the possible transformation of Tlaloc into the God of Abraham, of confession as a way to shield the people from illness and bad luck, or of the unpredictable and amoral pre-Hispanic deities into the Christian god of the *Colloquios*, who allowed the devils to wreak havoc on Earth.

So it was that the pyramid remained embedded in the lands of Anahuac long after the arrival of the powerful Christian god. True, it would henceforth have to bear the cross; consequently, its pre-Hispanic meaning, shape, glory, and visibility would be forever displaced, as all three colonial centuries would attest, each in its own way. But the weight of the cross did not bury into oblivion the pyramid, which had been summoning the presence of the Mesoamerican sacred well beyond a thousand years.

Notes

Introduction | Franciscans, Nahuas, and Colonialism

1. All translations into English in brackets are mine unless otherwise stated.

2. Throughout the book I will refer to Mendieta's most important work, the *Historia eclesiástica indiana*, as HEI.

3. The *adventus* was the triumphal, carefully choreographed entry of a leader or conqueror into a city in late antiquity. The ostentatious triumphal entries of monarchs and princes in the Renaissance and the Baroque were supposed both to evoke and to exceed in greatness the Roman model and tradition. See Jacques Jacquot, *Les Fêtes de la Renaissance*. What Watts is proposing is that the friars inverted the Roman ceremony in the sense of making a public display not of their glory and power, but rather of their humility, poverty, and lowliness.

4. The term "Nahua" is a linguistic-ethnographic category referring to the Nahuatl-speaking people of Central Mexico at the time the Spaniards arrived. Seldom did the people so denominated by this category refer to themselves as such. However, this is a category that is frequently used today in Mexico, as an alternative to Aztecs (Lockhart, *The Nahuas*, 1). The latter is a political, pre-conquest denomination, which refers to the short-lived triple alliance between Tenochtitlan, Tetzcoco, and Tlacopan or Tacuba.

5. In order to avoid awkwardness and cumbersome repetitions, I will subject myself, under protest, to the Western Judeo-Christian patriarchal privileging of the male gender as synecdoche of humanity. Thus, anytime I use "he/him/himself" to refer to indigenous men and women, I very much also mean to say "she/her/herself."

6. Franciscans are also called Friars Minor and Minorites because they consider themselves to be minor, that is, of lesser rank than members of other religious orders. I use any of these three terms throughout the book to refer to members of the religious order founded by St. Francis of Assisi in 1210.

7. In this decree Philip II ordered to seize chronicles written about the "superstitions and way of life" of the natives, and to prohibit further production of ethnographic treatises (Baudot, *Utopia*, 500–504).

8. See, among many other works and authors, Walter Mignolo, *Local Histories/Global Designs* (2000); Hernán Vidal, "The Concept of Colonial and Postcolonial Discourse: A Perspective from Literary Criticism" (1993); Aníbal Quijano, "Modernity, Identity, and Utopia in Latin America" (1995); Fernando Coronil, "Más allá del occidentalismo: hacia categorías geohistóricas no-imperialistas"(1998); Jorge Klor de Alva, "The Postcolonization of the (Latin) American Experience: A Reconsideration of 'Colonialism,' 'Postcolonialism,' and 'Mestizaje'" (1995).

9. As one of its most notable theorists has poignantly observed, postcolonialism as a criticism in the aftermath "acknowledges that it inhabits the structures of Western domination that it seeks to undo" (Prakash, "Subaltern," 1476).

Chapter 1 | The *Colloquios y doctrina cristiana* and the Emergence of the Nahua Christian Subject in Sixteenth-Century Mexico

1. See the introduction for a more detailed representation of the Twelve.

2. Whenever possible, I quote from Arthur J. O. Anderson and Charles Dibble's monumental translation of the complete Nahuatl version of the *Historia general de las cosas de la Nueva España* into English. Following the lead of two prominent Mexican scholars, Francisco Paso y Troncoso and Joaquín García Icazbalceta, Anderson and Dibble decided to entitle their version *Florentine Codex*. Although Sahagún's Spanish version was usually the ultimate authority for the American scholars (Anderson, "Variations," 1:5), it is not a literal rendition of the Nahuatl. However, except for Sahagún's prologues and interpolations, which have no counterpart in the Nahuatl version and which have thus been translated from Spanish into English by Dibble, their translations into English are from the Nahuatl version, not from the Spanish. Thus at times throughout this book, when I have considered that Sahagún's particular rendition in Spanish supports my argument better than the English translation from the Nahuatl, I have used it and later translated it into English. I am using the Spanish edition of Sahagún's *Historia general* prepared by Josefina García Quintana and Alfredo López Austin. This is the first edition in which the complete Spanish text of the *Florentine Codex* appears (López Austin and García Quintana, "Introducción," 1:26). For a detailed history of the manuscripts of Sahagún's *Historia*, see Dibble, "Sahagún's Historia" in *Florentine Codex* 1:9–23.

3. The Colegio de Santa Cruz was founded in 1536 in Tlatelolco in order to educate the sons of the Nahua elite and any other youth that showed outstanding intellectual abilities. The boys were taught to read and write Latin, Nahuatl, and Spanish. They served as cultural brokers between the Franciscans and their own communities. Many of the boys educated at the colegio became great grammarians, without whose help the friars would have been unable to produce their distinguished record of works in Nahuatl.

4. The Spanish version of Book Twelve of Sahagún's *Historia general* was published in 1829. It was the very first work to appear in the new Mexican Republic. Its editor was Carlos María de Bustamante, a Mexican patriot who fought fiercely for the cause of Mexican Independence. Book Twelve narrates the fall of Tenochtitlan from the Mexica point of view, and, not surprisingly, it offers a negative view of the Spaniards. As Ascención León-Portilla points out, "The fact that Sahagún's twelfth book was the first source published in independent Mexico clearly illustrates how nationalism and anti-Hispanism were born together in modern Mexico" (*Tepuztlahcuilolli*, 1:111; translation is mine).

5. Indeed, this was the *Historia de los indios de la Nueva España.*

6. I will be using Klor de Alva's translation in this chapter.

7. Ángel Garibay believes that because the friars would have hardly known any Nahuatl, the notes should have been written in Spanish or perhaps even in Latin (*Historia,* 2:241). Miguel León-Portilla proposes that they were written in Nahuatl but offers no evidence or explanation as to why he thinks this may be the case ("Estudio," 20). Klor de Alva states that Sahagún never specified the language in which the notes were written. However, he conjectures that most likely Spanish was the language used ("Historicidad," 163).

8. Obviously, the Spanish version, which Sahagún undertook, is also a linguistic and cultural re-creation, since it is not a literal rendition of the notes he presumably found about these conversations.

9. For Sahagún's Spanish version of the *Colloquios,* I will be using Miguel León-Portilla's edition of 1986 entitled *Coloquios y Doctrina Cristiana.* All translations of this version into English are mine.

10. For a thorough discussion on Sahagún's repudiation of the myth of the miraculous conversion of Indians to Christianity effectuated by the Twelve, see Klor de Alva, "Sahagún's Misguided Introduction to Ethnography and the Failure of the *Colloquios* Project." Klor de Alva states that although it is impossible to establish the date at which Sahagún became disillusioned or "desengañado" by the Indians' Christianity, after the death of Motolinía in 1569 he started to denounce openly the self-congratulatory pronouncements about the success of the Twelve. It should be noted that Motolinía had hastily claimed in the closing sentence of his *History of the Indians of New Spain* that the Indians "have forgotten the idols as if a hundred years had elapsed since they abandoned them" (337).

11. Sahagún does not allude to the thorny issue of the *patronato real.* On the one hand the Spanish monarchs claimed to subject themselves to the papal theocratic theory that the Pope ruled over the world as God's representative on Earth. The Catholic Kings, Isabella and Ferdinand, had based their right to rule over the islands and mainland discovered through Pope Alexander VI's donation on the 1493 *Inter Caetera* bulls. But on the other hand, and as a condition for carrying out the evangelization of the Amerindian gentiles, the Catholic Kings demanded full control of the Indian Church. This was the patronato real, a legal practice that had originated "in the Middle Ages as a means of supporting the churches by endowment" (Poole, 23). Among the powers that the patronato granted the Spanish monarch were the right to appoint bishops and other ecclesiastical functionaries, the collection and distribution of the tithe, the power to intervene in conflicts between bishops and religious orders, the right to delimit dioceses, and the like (La Hera, 58). Thus, the patronato real actually entailed the subjection of a significant part of the ecclesiastical sphere to the political, the opposite of what Sahagún praises in the prologue.

12. José Rabasa's notion of "love speech" as a "powerful mode of subjection and effective violence" may be deemed a constant motif in this text, since through-

out the *Colloquios* the tlatoque and the tlamacazque are "bound by the implicit obligation to accept the offering" of salvation and thus expected to repudiate their notions of divinity in favor of the Christian ones ("Writing," 6).

13. Written by Juan López de Palacios Rubios in 1513, the *requerimiento* derived its authority from the *Inter Caetera* bulls of 1493, in which Pope Alexander VI had given the lands discovered by Columbus to the Spanish (and Portuguese) kings in order to have them preach the word of God in these territories. The Indians were thus exhorted to accept the entrance of the Spaniards into their lands and to recognize the Spanish Kings as their superiors, by virtue of the aforesaid papal decision. If the Indians resisted, the Spaniards would be authorized to wage war against them as "vassals who do not obey and do not want to receive their legitimate lord, and who resist and contradict him" and to declare that "all the death and harm that will be suffered on account of this resistance will be your fault and not that of the Spanish kings or ours" (Palacios Rubios in Las Casas, *Historia*, 2:275–76; translation mine).

14. Cortés's pretext to burn Tenochtitlan to the ground was that the Mexica had rebelled against the Spanish king whom they had accepted as sovereign under Montezuma. In his Third Letter Cortés claims that since they had no intention of surrendering, he was left with no other alternative than to destroy them and the city: "When I saw how determined they were to die in their defense I deduced...*that they gave us cause, and indeed obliged us, to destroy them utterly*" (Cortés, 222–23; emphasis is mine). López de Gómara also claims insubordination and that the rebellious Aztecs thus forced Cortés to destroy them and the great city of Tenochtitlan (2:43–44). Bernal Díaz recounts how Cortés repeatedly sought to make peace with Cuauhtemoc, promising that Charles V would forget all the deaths and harm that they had perpetrated against the Spaniards, and would hold them in great esteem. But Cuauhtemoc did not yield. Cortés insists, arguing that "ya ha visto tantas muertes como en las batallas que nos dan les ha venido, y tenemos de nuestra parte todas las ciudades y pueblos de toda aquella comarca, y que cada día vienen más contra ellos, que se conduela de tal perdimiento de sus vasallos y ciudad" [he has seen already so many deaths as have befallen them in the battles that they have waged against us, and we have on our side all the cities and towns of the district, and that every day there are more people against them, that he may feel sorry for the loss of his vassals and city] (Díaz del Castillo, 360). The claims by these three chroniclers run contrary to the Twelve's representation in the *Colloquios*. As we have seen, in the latter text the destruction of the Nahuas by the Spaniards is explained as a divine punishment to their pre-Hispanic idolatrous practices.

15. There is God the Father, the Son, and the Holy Spirit, both one and three simultaneously. For a thorough discussion of the extreme complexity of the Christian Trinity, see Saint Thomas Aquinas's "Treatise on the Trinity," questions 27–43 of the first part of the *Summa Theologica* (1:153–237).

16. Sahagún and his Nahua aides follow the grades of angelic order assigned by Gregory the Great. For a comparison between Gregory and Dionysius the Pseudo-

Areopagite's hierarchy of the nine choirs of angels see Saint Thomas Aquinas's question 108, article 6, in the first part of the *Summa Theologica* (1:558–60).

17. According to Read, some of these powers were the capacity to change their forms and identities, and closely linked to these transformations, the power to reverse the aging process. In this way, the gods were not subject to one life span only, as were human beings (150).

18. See Nicholson, 401n8, for a list of the primary accounts of this myth.

19. In Nahuatl not only nouns, pronouns, adjectives, and adverbs can be used to indicate honorific speech, verbs can also become reverential "by only altering and changing a bit their roots" (Carochi, *Del arte*, 66; translation is mine). The usual way of making a verb reverential is by adding a reflexive prefix and an applicative suffix (Lockhart, *Nahuatl*, 15–16). Reflexive verbs in turn take the suffix *–tzinoa* to become honorific. One can indicate respect or tenderness about almost anyone or anything by adding the suffix *–tzin* to the names of persons, their titles, or to the revered objects (Campbell and Kartunnen, *Foundation*, 1:192–94; Soustelle, *Daily*, 223), *-tzinco* is the reverential mode of all prepositions (Carochi, 17), and so on.

20. It should be pointed out that Sahagún makes the Nahua lord of the Spanish version list a number of precious stones that do not appear in the Nahuatl version. These are sapphires, emeralds, rubies, and pearls. In the Nahuatl version, only turquoise and jade are mentioned, because the others were unknown in Mexico. Thus, it is clear that Sahagún wants to represent the tlatoani's polite reception of the friars' speech to the Spanish reader by emphasizing that the words of the friars are compared by the Nahua speaker to the most valued precious stones for Europeans. Klor de Alva alludes to this process of cultural translation when he writes about Sahagún's *Historia general* that "[Sahagún] understood that the interpretation of his findings, in ways that made them accessible to his Spanish-speaking peers, necessitated translations that identified native ways of being, doing, and experiencing as equivalent to European counterparts" ("Sahagún," 38).

21. For the humanists, eloquence and rhetoric were indispensable to the study of human nature "because of the necessity of moving the will to action" (Struever, 59). Eloquence's fundamental characteristic was richness, "and richness is not only copiousness, but a fluidity, a flexibility of form to correspond with the infinite variety of human nature to which one must appeal" (Struever, 57). Thus, eloquence was conceived as a most valuable instrument because it was able to sway the emotions of an audience: "The purpose of rhetoric is to persuade its audience through form; the rhetor is occupied with the phenomenal reality of the idea for the audience, not the 'pure' idea. Eloquence, not knowledge, is power" (Struever, 72).

22. According to León-Portilla, the *Códice Matritense de la Academia* also lists more than thirty (*Aztec*, 19).

23. Klor de Alva's translation of the passage in question reads as follows: "If you desire to enter there, into heaven / there where He resides / He by Whom All Live, Jesus Christ / it is very necessary for you/ that you detest them / that you

despise them, / that you hate them, / and you spit on them,/ these whom you have continually regarded as gods" ("Aztec," 99–100).

24. The idea of Christ's humanity is represented in chapter four of the Spanish and Nahuatl versions of the *Colloquios*.

25. "Indeed they give us / our supper, our breakfast, / and all that is drinkable, edible / this is our meat, the corn, the bean / the wild amaranth, the lime-leaved sage" (Klor de Alva, "Aztec," 121).

26. James Lockhart makes much the same point when he declares about the *Colloquios* that "whatever their degree of factual authenticity, the speeches presented correspond to our general understanding of religious interaction between two peoples in that the indigenous priests, instead of casting doubt on the new doctrine, insist on the necessity of retaining the core of their own traditions" (*The Nahuas*, 205–06).

27. "Altepetl" literally means, "the waters, the mountains." The altepetl was a territory controlled by an ethnic group, with its own dynastic ruler. Perhaps its closest comparable European formation was the city-state. See Lockhart's thorough treatment of the altepetl and the calpolli in *The Nahuas after the Conquest*, especially 14–58.

28. The position of the Catholic Church regarding other religions has changed dramatically in the twentieth century. Although still arguing that the Catholic Church has the obligation to proclaim that Christ is "the way, the truth and the life" (*Council*, 831; translation is mine), the Second Vatican Council (1965) declared that other religions also may "reflect a spark of that Truth which illuminates all men" (*Council*, 831; translation is mine). In the Vatican Council's view the Catholic Church is still deemed the privileged site of religious truth but now acknowledges that other religions may partially possess it. The asymmetry of truth and knowledge is then kept in place, but significantly tempered by the admission that there are roads to engage divinity other than Christianity.

29. "Mucho holgaremos de que nos digáis quiénes son éstos que adoramos, reuerenciamos y seruimos, porque de saberlo reciberemos gran contentamiento" (We will be glad to hear from you who are these whom we adore, revere, and serve, for by knowing we shall receive great contentment [Sahagún, *Coloquios*, 90; translation is mine]).

30. I use the term "long performance" and its scope following Dennis Tedlock. He uses it to refer to one of the roles of the implied readers of the *Popol Vuh*, who appear represented in the text. These readers, who at times take on the role of divinator or astronomer, on some occasions offer "'a long performance and account' whose subject is the emergence of the whole *cahuleu* or 'sky-earth' which is the Quiché way of saying 'world'" ("Introduction," 32).

31. As Read points out, "Mexican deities had split personalities, multiple identities they could take off and put on, combine and recombine like so many articles of clothing, all depending on the powers required for the moment" (15).

32. Among more than sixteen titles, Tezcatlipoca was called Moquequeloa, "the Mocker," and Nezahualpilli, "the Angry Prince." For a detailed list of names and characteristics of Tezcatlipoca, see Davies, *The Aztec Empire*, 256–63.

33. In the Spanish version, the following is stated about God: "Este solo verdadero Dios jamás se absenta, en todo lugar y a todas las cosas está presente; su magestad y divinidad a todas las partes alcança, nunca duerme, siempre vela para nuestra guarda y amparo. Lo visible y lo invisible todo lo tiene en la palma, todo lo sustenta, conserva y govierna, y de todo tiene actual cuidado; de ninguna cosa se descuida, ni de las cosas más pequeñas del mundo; es todo poderoso, todo su beneplácito se haze y nadie le puede yr a la mano" [This one and only true God is never absent, He is always present in every place and in everything; His majesty and divinity reach everywhere, He never sleeps, He always keeps vigil in order to protect us and care for us. He holds the visible and the invisible in the palm of His hand, He gives sustenance, He conserves and governs everything, and He actively pays heed to everything; He does not neglect anything, not even the smallest things in the world; He is all-powerful, His will is always done and nobody can challenge Him] (Sahagún, *Coloquios*, 91).

34. Christianity has always struggled with the problem of evil in a universe created by an all-loving God. In his *Summa Theologica*, Saint Thomas Aquinas, the Angelic Doctor of the Catholic Church, attempts to explain how good and evil can both be under the providence of an omnipotent, All-merciful God. Aquinas writes:

"It is otherwise with one who has care of a particular thing and one whose providence is universal, because a particular provider excludes all defects from what is subject to his care as far as he can, whereas one who provides universally allows some defect to remain, lest the good of the whole should be hindered. Hence, corruption and defects in natural things are said to be contrary to some particular nature; yet they are in keeping with the plan of universal nature, since the defect in one thing yields to the good of another, or even to the universal good; for the corruption of one is the generation of another, by which means the species is conserved. Since God, then, provides universally for all being, it belongs to His providence to permit certain defects in particular effects, that the perfect good of the universe may not be hindered, for if all evil were prevented much good would be absent from the universe" (*Summa*, 1:129–30).

According to Aquinas's passage, evil is an inextricable part of God's universal plan. Without it, goodness could not be whole. This is not too far away from seeing positive and negative forces in the world not as opposites or contraries, but as part of a higher scheme of things. In this sense, it can be argued that there is an intersection between the Christian theological concept of evil and the pre-Hispanic's concept of negativity and disorder as something not of an entirely moral origin, but as something that partakes of nature itself.

35. It should be pointed out, however, that the friars' claim about God's infallible

protection to His believers could not be honored by history. For one thing, the Twelve and the Spanish readers had to be aware that more than half of their own country had been under the rule of Moorish "infidels" for almost seven hundred years.

36. Gerónimo de Mendieta also comments in his *Historia eclesiástica indiana* that sacrifices and the worship of "idols" went on in secret after the arrival of the Twelve (227). By the time Sahagún edited the *Colloquios*, this must have been known. He does not bring it out, however. This would seem to support Klor de Alva's thesis that at least the purpose or objective of the Nahuatl version of the *Colloquios* was the continuing effort to edify and instruct the Nahuas in things Christian, not the recording of reality.

Chapter 2 | Introduction to Some Cultural Performance Practices in Medieval Spain and Pre-Hispanic Mexico

1. For the use of scriptural plays for evangelical purposes in Italy during the thirteenth century, see Arnaldo Fortini, *La Lauda in Assisi e le origini del teatro italiano* (1961). For the influence of Franciscan spirituality in drama and lyric, see Lawrence G. Craddock, "Franciscan Influences on Early English Drama" (1950) and David L. Jeffrey, *The Early English Lyric and Franciscan Spirituality* (1975).

2. In the *Cancionero* of Juan de la Encina, published in 1496, there are two Easter plays called *églogas* that were represented in the private chapel of the Dukes of Alba (Shergold, 26). There are three other vernacular plays from the second half of the fifteenth century. These are a short Nativity play entitled *Representación del nasçimiento de Nuestro Señor* by Gómez Manrique and believed to have been written between 1467 and 1481 (Shergold, 40). The second play is the anonymous *Auto de la huida a Egipto*, and the third is the also anonymous *Auto del día de la Asunción*. Interestingly, two important aspects that these plays share is the fact that all three were composed for convents of Franciscan nuns and that they treat "a devotional or theological motif popularized by the Franciscans" (Surtz, "'Franciscan,'" 141). These common aspects serve as evidence of the significant role the Franciscans may have played in the development of vernacular theater in Spain as well as in Europe during the Middle Ages.

3. Hermenegildo Corbató has emphasized the popularity and splendor achieved by the Valencian tradition of Corpus Christi festivities and has established suggestive connections between the Valencian mystery plays and some Nahua autos or neixcuitilli of the sixteenth century in Mexico. See his "Misterios y autos del teatro misionero en México durante el siglo XVI y sus relaciones con los de Valencia."

4. Ruiz Ramón is of this opinion and quotes extensively from two documents that bear witness to a Spanish religious theatrical tradition. These are the well-known and much quoted Alfonso El Sabio's *Siete Partidas* and the other is a canon of the Concilium of Aranda in 1473 (Ruiz Ramón 1:19–22).

5. The *calmecac* was usually reserved for the sons of the aristocracy, though some talented sons of merchants might be admitted. The education imparted in this type of school prepared the students for the priesthood or important state positions, and the discipline was extremely severe (Soustelle, 169).

6. See a detailed description of this feast in Sahagún, *Florentine*, 3:64–68.

7. Nevertheless, though apparently only in very exceptional cases, there are Crucifixion plays in Europe that have come down on record as having the person playing the role of Christ literally executed. In a passion play in Brussels where an actual crucifixion took place, the person playing Christ was a criminal sentenced to death (Stern, *Medieval*, 273–74). The significant differences with the habitual sacrifice of the ixiptla would be that the person executed in the European context was not believed to have been "possessed" by Christ, nor was the putting to death of the character a customary thing to do.

8. Such problems of identification between the representing and the represented were also tackled in sixteenth-century Spain. We should recall that one of the arguments zealous clergymen utilized at that time, in order to have the "pernicious" theatrical representations banished from the land, was precisely the immorality of the actors playing holy characters and the scandals to which this gave rise among the audience. One of the most famous anecdotes in this respect is narrated by José Lupercio de Argensola in 1598. In a play about the Annunciation, when the actress representing the Virgin Mary coyly asked the angel "*Quo modo fiet istud?*" (that is, how would she be able to conceive the baby Jesus), the whole audience burst into laughter, for everybody knew that she was the *manceba*, or concubine, of the actor playing Joseph (Cotarelo y Mori, 67).

9. The *locus* was the illusionary or mimetic space set up on platforms or pageant wagons, delimiting a relatively fixed, localized scenic unit; whereas the *platea* was the nonrepresentational setting where the communal festivities were held and in which the actors commingled with the audience. For a detailed discussion of these complementary medieval notions of locus and platea, see Weimann, 73–85.

10. Othón Arróniz believes that the students of the Colegio de Tlatelolco were allowed to take over gradually the translation of the friars' Spanish dramatic scripts from 1546 on, as well as the administration of the Colegio (101–106). In her study *Holy Wednesday* Burkhart dates the transcription of the playlet between 1582 and 1590 (52); Arróniz's hypothesis, therefore, would seem to support that of Lockhart.

11. Patrice Pavis cogently explains what the translation process means in the specific context of a dramatic text: "The theatre translation is a hermeneutic act: in order to find out what the source text means, I have to bombard it with questions from the target language's point of view.... This hermeneutic act—interpreting the source text—consists of delineating several main lines translated into another language, in order to pull the foreign text toward the target culture and language, so as to separate it from it source and origin" (138).

12. See *The Dialogical Theatre* (1993), in which Harris uses Bakhtin against the

grain in order to argue for the dialogical possibilities of theater and performance in general, and of the Nahua in particular, as a "meeting place for a plurality of ethnic and cultural voices" (81). In his more recent work *Aztecs, Moors, and Christians* (2000), Harris turns to anthropologist James Scott's concept of "hidden transcripts of resistance" inscribed in official and/or public performances in order to uphold the thesis that Nahua colonial theater was laden with subversive messages to be understood only by the indigenous audience.

13. This represents Richard C. Trexler's position; in no ambiguous terms he deems the religious and military theater of the Franciscans as perfidious insults to the indigenous culture and as humiliating enactments of their defeat. He writes: "Thus the 'triumph of the cross' that all missionary theater was intended to vaunt sooner showed the victory and defeat of different ways of life. It was manifested not only in the many Spanish dances that accompanied this military theatre but by the fixed *autos* as well, which could be still more pointed in what one author calls their 'calumniation of the indigenous pagan heritage'" ("We Think," 200). For Trexler, missionary theater was an imitation or reproduction of the theatrical acts of the conquest, geared toward displaying the subjection of "demons and Indians through a 'moving' theater" (ibid., 193). Trexler's observations about the political and cultural subtexts of the autos and military theater are undoubtedly insightful; yet, new research in this theater is starting to view this dramatic practice more as a hybrid. To think about this colonial dramatic practice only as a reenactment of subjection totally controlled by the colonizer might very well be underestimating the capacity of the native culture to accommodate, transform and preserve itself under the new, and no doubt, dismal colonial circumstances.

14. This is Scott's widely used concept of subversive hidden messages woven by subordinated groups into public and/or official representations displaying hegemonic discourses of domination. Scott developed this valuable decoding tool in *Domination and the Arts of Resistance: Hidden Transcripts* (1990).

15. In "Colonizing Souls" Jorge Klor de Alva points out that the friars, in order to produce a proper Christian subject, were very aware of the necessity of going beyond mere bodily control of the other: "But an effective proselytizing strategy had to go far beyond violent or physical coercion, the performance of baptisms, or the teachings of the rudiments of the Christian doctrine. It had to penetrate into every corner of native life, especially those intimate spaces where personal loyalites were forged, commitments were assessed, and collective security concerns were weighed against individual ambitions. Thus, the 'invasion within' could not be done by scare tactics, but rather by shifting the moral gears to produce social and political effects that favored the interests in stability and productivity of those in power" (15–16). Without disavowing the invasiveness and impositions of the friars' tactics that Klor de Alva so well describes in this passage, the need to procure the full consent of the other in the evangelization process also reveals the agency conferred upon him/her. Besides the fact that such interventions cannot be predicated only on the colonial

context (though there are some that are), if mere performance of the external rituals was not considered enough for a proper Christian subject, it was understood that the acquiescence of the other could not be secured against his or her will. That is to say, there was a recognition on the part of the spiritual colonizer of the limits of his power to impose and of the possibilities of resistance.

Chapter 3 | Performing the Limits of Colonialist Power: Evangelization, Irony, and Resistance in the *Neixcuitilli Final Judgment*

1. All quotations from the neixcuitilli *Final Judgment* will be taken from Barry D. Sell and Louise Burkhart's first of a four-volume series on Nahuatl theater, published by the University of Oklahoma Press. This volume is entitled *Nahuatl Theater: Life and Death in Colonial Nahua Mexico.*

2. As has been expounded in earlier chapters, in Nahua cosmological conceptions there were only five possible ages or suns, the present one being the fifth and last. Each sun had been brought into being by the self-immolation of a deity who was then transfigured into the sun of that age. Each age was independent and separate from the preceding one, and its end was markedly violent. There are different theories about the regent god of the fifth sun and about the way the ages were brought about (Brundage, 27–29; León-Portilla, *Aztec*, 25–61). In any case, when the Spaniards arrived, the Mexica were already expecting an end to their present age, which the cataclysm of the Conquest would only seem to have confirmed.

3. In his study on allegory, Angus Fletcher represents the figure as follows: "In the simplest terms, allegory says one thing and means another. It destroys the normal expectation we have about language, that our words 'mean what they say.' When we predicate a quality X of a person Y, Y really is what our predication says he is (or we assume so); but allegory would turn Y into something other (*allos*) than what the open and direct statement tells the reader" (2). Regarding the specific allos of the allegorical personification of concepts such as Death, Time, and Penance, Paolo Valesio explains that when they are allegorized, these concepts become something located outside of history, "that is, there is not, has not been, and will not be any other . . . [Death, Time, and Penance] next to this one" (Valesio, "Esquisse," 11; translation mine). The allos, or something other, will reside in the fact that Time, Death, and/or Penance never appear in historical reality as the absolute, tangible entities in human form that we see on stage or read in a text.

4. I believe that the use of allegory in *Final Judgment* most likely points to the hand of a friar, whether Andrés de Olmos or any other, at least for this part of the play.

5. Perhaps because of the ambivalence of European allegory and the difficulties of interpretation that it could present to an alien culture, the use of the figure would be infrequent in the Nahua theater of evangelization. According to Fernando de Horcasitas, "La personificación de ideas o cualidades abstractas que se encuentra en *El juicio final* (la muerte, el tiempo, etcétera) no es común en el teatro náhuatl, por

lo menos en las obras que han sobrevivido hasta nuestros tiempos" [The personification of ideas or abstract qualities that we find in *Final Judgment* (death, time, etc.) is not common in Nahua theater, at least in the works that have survived up to our times] (*Teatro*, 565).

6. Needless to say, I am not claiming that the author (or coauthor) of *Final Judgment* read and then dismissed Azpilcueta's manual in writing the original version of the neixcuitilli or part of it. I am just referring to the influential Portuguese theologian's manual in order to demonstrate that in his widespread opinion, accepting to hear confession without considering possible impediments (such as enough time to show the fruits of a reformed life) was improper.

7. Let us recall that in the Apocalypse, John declares that even after witnessing the sixth plague let loose by the angel (Apoc. 9:20–21) and suffering the vials of wrath spilled over the sun and over the throne of the beast (Apoc. 16:8–11), the obdurate sinners did not repent of their offenses, as if there still existed an opportunity of reconciliation or at least a last chance to glorify God. Though in the midst of so much eschatological horror, the sinners of the Apocalypse were so blind to their evils that they were incapable even of attrition or repentance because of fear of the evils that will befall the sinner. Not so Lucía, whose soul was greatly afflicted by her sins when she went to look for her confessor (Sell and Burkhart, 197), even though perhaps she did not know her time was up.

8. Here the text of the Apocalypse is followed closely: "And they were judged every one according to their works" (20:13).

9. See chapter 1, note 2 for clarification on my use of the English and Spanish versions of Sahagún's *Historia general*.

10. It should be pointed out that this is not the only play in which the irony of satanic gratitude is employed. The last scene of *In Animastin Ihuan Alvacaesme*, or *Souls and Testamentary Executors*, also represents the end of the world. Here, very ironically too, the Devil is the character beseeching divine justice. He demands punishment for those who had squandered money left to the Church by the dying for masses in order to aid them out of purgatory. After a wrathful, apocalyptic Christ condemns the guilty to hideous punishments in hell, a lesser devil manifests gratitude for such a sentence in much the same terms as in our play *Final Judgment*: "Your dear heart has done us a favor! You have heard our request; we thank You!... Let us be off to our eternal dwelling place" (Ravicz, 231). The sinners in *Souls and Testamentary Executors*, however, were represented as being much more obdurately evil and perverse than Lucía. In this sense, the sentence of the implacable Christian deity could be thought of as being equally harsh, though more deservedly so.

11. In the *Colloquios y doctrina cristiana* discussed in chapter 1, for instance, this connection is clearly made: "Indeed, of all these, which you regard as gods, / absolutely no one is a god, / no one is He by Whom All Live, / indeed, all are devils" (Klor de Alva, "Aztec," 152).

12. It is relevant to point out that after one hundred years of exposure to Chris-

tianity, all sorts of "idolatrous" practices would still be in place in the lands of Anahuac. Hernando Ruiz de Alarcón's 1629 *Tratado de las supersticiones y costumbres gentílicas que hoy viven entre los indios naturales desta Nueva España* [Treatise on Superstitions] and Jacinto de la Serna's *Manual de ministros de indios, para el conocimiento de sus idolatrías y extirpación de ellas* [Manual for the Ministers of Indians] finished in 1656 stand as invaluable evidence of this fact.

13. I concur with Sell in this opinion. He points out in note 24: "The implication is that the play is the mirror. What happened to Lucía is what they are supposed to see in the mirror, applied to themselves" (Sell and Burkhart, 207).

14. Though the images in the Apocalypse are far more dreadfully impressive than any in our neixcuitilli, Satan is never depicted as being grateful to God for having "cast into the pool of fire" (Apoc. 20:15) all those who had sinned against the Lord, as he would now have gained the condemned creatures. Satan and his allies are portrayed in the Book of Revelation as hideous and abominable antagonists finally crushed by the power of God

15. The irony of the alliance effect between Christ and Satan in the idea of the eternal condemnation of unhappy souls is not a unique product of the Spanish colonial discourse of the sixteenth century, however. It is true that there seems not to have been any fifteenth- or sixteenth-century European textual models for the neixcuitilli *Last Judgment* (Arróniz, 22–23). However, in Pedro Calderón de la Barca's 1641 auto sacramental *Lo que va del Hombre a Dios*, there is a similarity to the irony we have been pointing out. Having condemned Man to eternal punishment because of his incorrigible dissoluteness, Christ the Prince orders the allegorical characters of Guilt and Death (allied in this auto to the forces of evil) to execute his terrible sentence (Calderón 295b). Guilt and Death quite readily obey the Prince's orders to carry Man off to hell. For a more detailed discussion of how such irony is partially, though still unsatisfactorily, resolved in this auto, see Viviana Díaz Balsera, *Calderón y las quimeras de la Culpa*, 149–74. What is specific to the Mexican colonial context of the sixteenth century, however, is that an important aspect of the unwitting alliance between Christ and the devils is articulated in the auto in terms of nourishment and food. It is likely that such terms would point toward the missionaries' representations of pre-Hispanic gods and the sacrificial practices to feed them as satanic. In this sense, in the specific Mexican colonial context the ironies of the Apocalypse translate as the preservation of the Nahuas' demonized deities.

16. This position would be very much in accordance with that of Ramón A. Gutiérrez. In the evangelization of the Pueblo Indians of New Mexico, Gutiérrez has shown that the Franciscans also employed dramatic representations. Writing about the didactic autos, the author reproves historians and literary critics for having overlooked the strong political values they were communicating to the audiences: "The text of every *auto* had a subtext concealed in the costumes, generational casting, and dramatic actions. Every text had its context. Drama was not pure entertainment but a moving, pedagogical instrument. The explicit purpose of the *auto*

was to inculcate the Indians with a highly ideological view of the conquest, simultaneously forging in their minds a historical consciousness of their own vanquishment and subordination as the Spaniards wanted it to be remembered" (*When Jesus Came*, 83). Though with much more subtlety and sensitivity, Gutiérrez still shares Richard Trexler's position expounded in note 13 of chapter 2. The monolithic notion of "Spaniards," however, is already very problematical because the missionaries, the military, and the Crown bureaucrats were often at odds in their positions vis-à-vis the indigenous peoples. This would make it difficult to forge a common image of how all these sectors would like vanquishment and subordination to be remembered. Gutiérrez's arguments are most compelling when applied to the military theater. But, as Max Harris and other critics have shown, even these plays, known as *moros y cristianos* (Christians and Moors) were usually performed by the natives themselves. Thus, the latter were in a position to produce meanings for the indigenous audience that Spanish priests, officials, and/or soldiers may not have been culturally aware of. In the case of *Final Judgment*, as we have been trying to show, there are many contradictions and reversals taking place that could also be thought of as subtexts, disrupting or intefering with the subtextual meanings of domination that Gutiérrez suggests hover beneath the linguistic surface of the text.

Chapter 4 | A Judeo-Christian Tlaloc or a Nahua Yahweh? Domination, Hybridity, and Continuity in the Nahua Evangelization Theater

1. A version of this chapter appeared in *Colonial Latin American Review* 10, no. 2 (2001): 209–27. The Web site of the journal is *http://www.tandf.co.uk*.

2. In this chapter I will be using Sell's translation into English of *The Sacrifice of Isaac*, which appears in the first volume of a four-volume series on Nahuatl theater, edited and translated by Barry D. Sell and Louise M. Burkhart, published by University of Oklahoma Press. I will adopt the abbreviated title *The Sacrifice of Isaac* (or at times, the shorthand *The Sacrifice*) rather than the long form that appears in the eighteenth-century extant text.

3. The *Códice de autos viejos* is a collection of ninety-six dramatic pieces, all copied by one scribe during the second half of the sixteenth century. The first eight folios are missing, so it has been impossible to determine the provenance and chronology of the plays figuring in the collection. However, there is a consensus that the collection as such was formed between 1570 and 1578. Miguel Ángel Pérez Priego hypothesizes that the majority of the plays as they appear in the *Códice* must have been composed between 1559 and 1560 and 1577 and 1578. He clarifies, however, that the plays of the collection may have been reworkings or *refundiciones* of earlier plays (introduction to *Códice de autos viejos* [1988], 10).

. 4. There is a play in the *Códice* dealing with this episode entitled *Aucto del destierro de Agar*. However, the perspective and disposition of the elements of the story are very different from those in the Nahua play. Thus, the structure of the plot of the

Aucto del destierro de Agar makes it very unlikely that it may have been used as a source for *The Sacrifice of Isaac,* even if the *Aucto del destierro* was a reworking of an earlier text.

5. The friars' struggle against polygamy has been widely documented by chroniclers of the period. See Motolinía, *Historia,* 97–100; Grijalva, 38, 99–101; Mendieta, 296–306; Torquemada, 3:190–97, among others.

6. Horcasitas, on the other hand, proposes that the expulsion of Hagar and Ishmael by the chosen one of God might have been the best biblical episode the missionaries could have dramatized in order to promote the eradication of polygamy (*El teatro náhuatl,* 189). Since callous indifference toward the fate of a son, whether legitimate or natural, could hardly be held up as a nonproblematic Christian example for the Nahuas to follow, Horcasitas's unusually hard line on this issue does not seem to be well founded.

7. The altepetl was the "ethnic state" (Lockhart, The *Nahuas,* 14) or "corporate town" (Gibson, 267) usually consisting of four, six, seven, or eight *calpolli.* The calpolli was a Nahua unit of communal formation consisting of a group of families living in a single locality (Gibson, 34). The head of the altepetl was a dynastic ruler called the tlatoani.

8. The popular 1996 Bill Moyers series *Genesis* was yet another exegetical wrestling with the patriarch of patriarchs at a national level. See "The Test" (219–47), in the companion book to the series, which treats the episode of the Akedah: *Genesis: A Living Conversation.*

9. Though in the biblical story Isaac is supposed to be an adult, most probably in the indigenous auto the Isaac of the second part of the play is the same boy as in the first.

10. According to Burkhart, Nahuas believed that within solar ages there were shorter, alternating cycles of order and disorder. See *Slippery,* 72–77.

Chapter 5 | Performing Otherness and Identity in *The Fall of Our First Parents*

1. Critics have traditionally assumed that the author of the letter to fray Antonio de Ciudad Rodrigo was Motolinía. Edmundo O'Gorman disagrees, claiming that in March of 1539, when the feasts took place, Motolinía was in Atlihuezia, informing himself about the circumstances of the martyrdom of the child Cristóbal twelve years earlier. This explains for O'Gorman Motolinía's reason for transcribing the anonymous friar's letter, rather than offering his own direct account of the festivities (Motolinía, *Historia,* 63n11).

2. Although the auto does not receive any specific title in Motolinía's *History,* I am following critical convention in using as title the phrase with which he conveyed the auto's theme, namely, "the Fall of Our First Parents."

3. The religious confraternities in New Spain were closely modeled on those of

the Iberian Peninsula in terms of their social functions. The confraternities organized festivals, occasionally took up the staging of autos and other dramas, and were very involved in charitable activities. Confraternities were very popular among the Nahuas because of their social prestige and their communal nature (Burkhart, *Holy*, 82–84; Lockhart, *The Nahuas*, 218–29; Lavrin, "Confraternities," 30–32). They were introduced in the 1530s, but did not spread until the 1550s and 1560s. By 1585, Church authorities had recognized more than 300 Indian confraternities (Lavrin, "Confraternities," 25).

4. In his Second Letter to Charles V, Cortés writes, "Touching Mutezuma's service...there is so much to describe that I do not know how to begin even to recount some part of it; for as I have already said, can there be something more magnificent than that this barbarian lord should have all the things to be found under the heavens in his domain, fashioned in silver and gold and jewels and feathers; and so realistic in gold and silver that no smith in the world could have done better?" (Cortés, 108).

5. This possibility would seem to be confirmed by the friar's later observation in the letter to fray Antonio that boys dressed up as animals "acted as if they were domesticated and Adam and Eve teased and laughed at them" (Motolinía, *History*, 158).

6. According to Jacques Soustelle, "The term *tonalli* embraced the genius peculiar to each person, his good fortune and his 'star', in the sense of his predestination" (192). Alfredo López Austin writes that in contemporary Indian beliefs, the tonalli is a fragmentary animistic entity, part of which is continuously left behind in all places where one has lived. For some as yet unknown reason, the tonalli must reintegrate themselves after death by taking a journey to retrieve its lost parts. López Austin estimates that pre-Hispanic Indians may have believed something similar about this spiritual entity (López Austin, *Human*, 1:321–23).

7. Jerry Williams points out that this somewhat lascivious gesture would seem to evoke the "baile cosquilloso o de comezón" [ticklish or itching dance] registered by Diego Durán and considered by the Dominican friar as immodest and very provocative (*Teatro*, 62).

8. In another huehuetlatolli collected by Gerónimo de Mendieta, daughters were admonished by their mothers to obey their husbands joyfully and to avoid making them angry: "No le seas fiera como águila ó tigre, ni hagas mal lo que te mandare, porque harás pecado contra los dioses, y castigarte ha con razon tu marido" [Do not be fierce like an eagle or tiger to him, nor falter in what he commands you, because you will have sinned against the gods, and your husband will punish you with good reason] (Mendieta, HEI, 119). According to this huehuetlatolli, we may surmise that Eve's demeanor toward her husband would not be interpreted as a sign of proper behavior by the Nahua audience. For a discussion of the place allotted to women in Nahua society, see Inga Clendinnen, "Wives" and "Mothers" (*Aztecs*, 153–205).

9. See particularly book 6, chapters 20–22 of the *Florentine Codex* in this respect.

10. See Paul Ricoeur and his lucid discussion of guilt as opposed to fear of retribution in *Symbolism*, 102–57.

11. See Clendinnen (*Aztecs*, 167) for a reflection on the cautionary tale of the woman-as-cavern, represented in the huehuetlatolli appearing in book 6, chapter 21 of the *Florentine Codex*.

12. For a more detailed explanation of the tonalpohualli, see Sahagún, *Florentine*, 5:1–133; Soustelle, 109–12; Vaillant, 183–90; Krickeberg, 179–85; Nicholson, 439–40.

13. *Hidden Messages* is the title of Raquel Chang-Rodríguez's book on colonial Andean theater in which, using Scott's concept of hidden transcripts, she argues persuasively for the existence of such transcripts in four key plays, two written in Quechua and two in Spanish.

14. According to José M. Kobayashi, the first schools were established in Mexico, Tetzcoco, Tlaxcala, and Huexotzinco. Motolinía and Mendieta estimate that these monastery-schools could house from 300 to 600 students. The first school was built in Tetzcoco, but the most reputed one was in Mexico City, founded in 1525, eleven years before the famous Colegio de Tlatelolco (*La educación como conquista*, 232–59).

15. French nahuatlato George Baudot is also of the opinion that the aristocratic students of the Colegio de Tlatelolco became bicultural: "The way in which the Franciscans chose the students of Tlatelolco already contributed and offered a very fertile terrain for inquiries and research. Sons of the Mexican nobility, most of them had relatives who had occupied important positions in the pre-Hispanic political and religious organization, and probably kept a very vivid memory of pre-Hispanic traditions, only twelve years after the Conquest" (Baudot, introduction to *Tratado de hechicerías y sortilegios*, by Andrés de Olmos, xiii; translation is mine).

16. Jerry Williams points out that according to the friar's letter, the dramatic production should be considered multilingual, since the *Circumdederunt me* was sung in Latin (*Teatro*, 62). The friar's passage reads as follows: "Three angels carried Adam and three others carried Eve; they all left the place, singing to the accompaniment of the organ *Circumdederunt me*" (Motolinía, *History*, 159).

Chapter 6 | Confession in the Old and New Worlds

1. I use the term "contact zone" as coined by Mary Louise Pratt. In *Imperial Eyes*, she uses the term "to refer to the space of colonial encounters, the space in which peoples geographically and historically separated come into contact with each other and establish ongoing relations, usually involving conditions of coercion, radical inequality, and intractable conflict" (6).

2. According to several sources, it may be assumed that every baptized Indian, man or woman, had to confess at least once a year, as was required from every Chris-

tian (Motolinía, *History,* 192–97; Mendieta, HEI, 281–93; Ricard, 209–10; Gómez Canedo, 183–85; Gibson, 101; Lopetegui and Zubillaga, 406). Exceptions to the annual confession were marrying couples, the sick, and the overly scrupulous, who received the sacrament more than once a year. Since there was a shortage of friars during the sixteenth century, it is unlikely that frequent confession would be encouraged, at least among the *macehuales,* or common people.

3. Throughout this chapter I will make repeated references to this massive *Manual de confessores y penitentes.* Its eighty-two editions in five languages between 1553 and 1620 (Haliczer, 9) attest to its importance and influence in the conception of the proper practice of the sacrament of penitence during the sixteenth century. Needless to say, consulting this widely circulating, authoritative manual will allow me to consider how the European confessors were instructed to interrogate their penitents. This in turn will help me to map out more adequately the specificities of the practice of confession in colonial New Spain during the same period.

4. Recent scholars of Nahua studies have agreed with Sahagún's general assessment that the explanation for the success of confession among the Nahua masses was that they were able to link it to one or several of their own pre-Hispanic practices. Confession was rendered in Nahuatl as *neyolmelahualiztli* or *neyolcuitiliztli.* According to Louise Burkhart, these two terms "refer to some sort of operation upon the heart, a physical rather than a purely spiritual or mental behaviour" (*Slippery,* 182) that was more in accordance with Nahua pre-Hispanic notions of sin as bodily sickness and weariness than with the Christian one of sin as moral diminishment. In other words, the Nahuas may have also conceptualized confession as a way to rid themselves of physical ailments brought about by their improper behavior.

5. Juan Bautista also wrote the *Doctrina christiana muy cumplida, donde se contiene la exposicion de todo lo necessario para doctrinar a los Yndios, y administralles los Sanctos Sacramentos. Compuesta en lengua Castellana y Mexicana* (1565) and the *Confessionario en Lengua Mexicana y Castellana. Con mucha advertencias muy necessarias parla los Confessores* (1599).

Chapter 7 | Molina's *Confessionario mayor* and the Impossible Nahua Christian Subject

1. "Y por esto acorde,de te escrivir estos dos confessionarios,que ayuden a la memoria. El primero algo dilatado para ti, con el qual...ayude a salvar[te] a ti que eres christiano.... Y el segundo confessionario pequeño y breue,para tu confessor, por el qual sepa y entienda tu lenguaje y manera de hablar." [And this is why I resolved to write for you these two confessional guides, that will aid memory. The first one, somewhat detailed for you, with which...I help to save you, who are Christian.... And the second confessional manual, short and brief, for your confessor, so that he may know and understand your language and way of speaking] (*Confessionario,* 6v).

2. Interestingly in this regard, Fray Juan Bautista insists in the 1599 prologue to his *Confessionario* much more on the power of God to carry out the "negocio," or business, of producing the necessary efficacy and on engravings that would remind the penitents of their sins, than on a thorough knowledge of the native tongue of the penitent ("Prólogo," B2). And as we will see in his *Advertencias,* Fray Juan Bautista comforts the confessor who is not very proficient in Nahuatl and who has been obliged by circumstances to confess a dying person, arguing that the sacrament will yield its fruits even if there had been a much less than perfect communication between penitent and confessor.

3. I write "reshape" and not "produce" because the Nahuas had three concepts for psychic entities, the *tonalli,* the *ihiyotl,* and the *teyolia.* The one sometimes referred to as "alma" in the different ethnographical sources was the teyolia, which was believed to leave the body four days after death and to emanate from the heart. See Alfredo López Austin, *Human,* 1:203–36, 313–24.

4. As stated earlier in this book, in order to avoid cumbersome repetitions, I have adopted, under protest, the Western Judeo-Christian patriarchal convention of privileging the male gender as synecdoche of humanity. Thus, when I use "he/him/himself" to refer to men and women penitents, I very much also mean to say "she/her/herself." This is not a superfluous reminder, since Molina's confessional manual is also directed toward female penitents.

5. For an overview of the admonitions to confessors on the language and proper attitude they should assume toward their penitents, see Jean Delumeau, *Aveau,* 25–41. For a specific instance in Spain of such admonitions, see Martín de Azpilcueta, *Manual,* 55–59. The admonitions to the confessor as to how to behave appropriately in order to encourage the penitent to speak implies a recalcitrance in the latter to confess. The church's mandate to every Christian who had reached "the age of discretion" to confess at least once a year also points toward its difficulty. But such resistance, albeit more or less generalized, was not the case for everyone. Obviously, many Christians would confess more readily than others. The church, while always willing to confess anyone who felt the desire, made a distinction between those whose desire was well founded and those who were simply unduly obsessed with their sinfulness. The technical term for the latter was *scrupulosity.* For cases in point of scrupulosity, see Tentler, particularly 134–40, 153–65, 220–32. Our analysis of confession as an onerous redressing of the forgetfulness of the subject to itself refers more to the majority of Christians than to the pious few who demanded to speak endlessly about their faults.

6. The Jesuit missionary Francisco Xavier went so far as to admonish the confessors to confess their own "miseries" to the obdurate penitents in order to establish a reciprocity that would encourage the penitent to admit his own sins (Delumeau, 36). In the *Códice Franciscano,* believed to be authored by Gerónimo de Mendieta, the author in fact complains that in order to persuade a Spaniard to confess his sins, the priest must almost do so himself first (89).

7. See Azpilcueta for questions to be asked to confessors about the propriety and rectitude of their administration of penance (573), as well as about the relationship they should establish with the penitent after confession (598–618). All of these questions of course imply that the confessor is also in a position to sin as confessor. His exercise of pastoral power in the confessional situation is thus limited by conscience and ecclesiastical law. Needless to say, this does not mean that sinful abuse of pastoral power may not have occurred frequently. On the other hand, it may be overstating the case that such abuses were institutionalized and approved by a power-hungry church in a voracious quest to control and dominate.

8. Discussing the "just causes" why someone who did not confess a mortal sin might not be required to repeat the whole confession, Azpilcueta writes that if a penitent did not know an act was a mortal sin, ignorance of divine law did not excuse him from sinfulness, but it did not make him liable for not having confessed it (53). Albeit not openly stated in the *Confessionario mayor*, Azpilcueta's conclusion necessarily implies that someone may have unknowingly committed mortal sin. Thus, one of the tasks of confession is to make the sinner aware of the extent of his sinfulness, which is achieved, among other ways, with the imposition of an adequate penance (Azpilcueta, 58).

9. In another central text to the evangelization venture, the *Doctrina cristiana*, printed in Mexico in 1544, the Dominican Fray Pedro de Córdoba also asks questions about pre-Hispanic Nahua religious cults, under the first commandment (90–93). This use of the first commandment to ask questions about idolatry is not confined to the Mexican or Peruvian colonial contexts, however. In his 1534 *Arte de bien confesar*, Pedro de Ciruelo advises confessors to ask under the first commandment whether their Spanish penitents have had recourse to idolatrous practices such as nigromancy, divinations, witchcraft, and the decoding of omens (B7r–C6r). The same can be said for Martín de Azpilcueta, who, under the first commandment, also asks questions of the Spanish penitent about witchcraft and other idolatrous practices (71–80), and of Hernando de Talavera, who declares that those who adore creatures as if they were God are idolaters and therefore sin against the first commandment (E8v–Fr). Let us recall relative to this issue that one of the most important manuals used by the Franciscans for the extirpation of pre-Hispanic idolatrous practices, Andrés de Olmos's *Tratado de hechicerías y sortilegios* (1553), was a translation into Nahuatl of a work he had coauthored in 1527 with another Franciscan, Fray Martín de Castañega. Both had been involved, along with Fray Juan de Zumárraga, in trying to extirpate the widespread practice of witchcraft in the Basque countries. For an excellent comparison between Spanish confessional manuals and Mexican penitence as exemplified in Don Bartolomé de Alva's *Confessionario mayor* of 1634, see Homza, "The European Link to Mexican Penance."

10. Gruzinski quotes this very same passage in order to illustrate the Western concept of free will that the spiritual colonizer was wanting to instill in the Nahuas, a position with which I strongly agree. Gruzinski points out that such a concept

had the political effect of immediately corroding ancient Nahua communal structures, from which the confessor derived considerable advantage (Gruzinski, "Confesión," 185). Because of the specificity and constraints of pastoral power discussed
above, however, I disagree with the positing of the personal interests of the confessor as the main structural motive in the promotion of the concept of free will.

11. Time from the world of the gods was constantly irrupting in human time.
The Nahua had to be aware of the periods and sequence of these irruptions in
order to be able to proceed in a way that would protect him from its onslaughts or,
if beneficial, to be able to use them accordingly. Thus, for instance, an hour of the
day would have specific characteristics for being either diurnal or nocturnal, for
being under the influence of one of the twenty signs that gave a name to the days and
one of the thirteen numerals in a cycle of 260 days, for being a specific month among
18, and for its position within it, as well as for the year among the unit of 52, and
so on (López Austin, *Human*, 1:65; Vaillant, 186–90). All of these things needed to
be taken into account whenever a favorable time had to be selected for a specific
event. The Nahua had to avoid pregnant women, very old people, etc., because the
strength of their *tonalli*, or life force, could be harmful. In addition, certain animals
at certain times should be kept away. The negative energy of other people could
bring upon a person sickness and disgrace. Wandering spirits of the dead had to be
avoided, lest they steal one's tonalli.

12. However, to illustrate just how difficult it is to talk about different cultural
boundaries or thresholds of selfhood, it is appropriate to quote a passage from Natalie Zemon Davis's essay on the boundaries and the sense of self in sixteenth-century France: "One could be possessed by someone else's soul; a magician or a sorcer-
ess could affect one's thoughts, feelings, and bodily movements, sometimes even
without physical contact; indeed, the simplest little woman could change other people's loves and hates by breaking a thread in her daily spinning or by preparing herbs
from her garden" (56). Zemon Davis's depiction of the nonclosure or permeability
of the contours of the self in sixteenth-century France, particularly in popular discourses, is not entirely other than the boundaries posited for the Nahuas by López
Austin and other anthropologists. The mentality of magic in Europe during the
sixteenth century, the hermetic theories of sympathies, aversions, and the influences of the stars on the behavior of individuals would not have made the different
boundaries of the person constructed by the Nahuas wholly incomprehensible. For
an overview of the hermetic tradition during the Renaissance in sixteenth-century
Europe, see the classic studies by Frances Yates, *The Art of Memory* and *Giordano
Bruno and the Hermetic Tradition*.

13. In this sense, I cannot fully concur with historian Sabine MacCormack who
in an important article states that Christian instruction was overly simplified because
the missionaries thought that otherwise the Indians would not be able to understand:
"Such teaching, however, anchored almost exclusively in the exercise of authority
and force, precluded such inner assent as is postulated by the necessary coexistence

of faith and reason in Christian thought" (457). We see that this is certainly not the case in Molina's widely circulating *Confessionario mayor.* The Nahua Christian subject posited here is capable of assuming full responsibility for his acts, that is, of having fully consented out of his free will. Thus (just like in Spain), while many of the catechisms and abbreviated confessional manuals were in fact "dry and depressing reading" as MacCormack correctly points out (455), this was by no means always the case, at least in the Mexican highlands.

14. Prominent among these was the exclusion of the Nahua Christian subject (as well as blacks and mestizos) from priesthood by the Second Mexican Council of 1555. In his *Crónica de la Nueva España,* Francisco Cervantes de Salazar had bitterly criticized the Colegio de Tlatelolco founded by Bernardino de Sahagún. He said that the Indians were incapable of being ordained and that as soon as they went back to their towns they did not use what they had learned with the friars (1:320; also quoted in Ricard, 347). The Dominicans also thought so, and even Mendieta, who dreamed of an Indian church, poignantly admitted something quite incompatible with the ecumenical ideology of Christianity: "Hay en ellos mas causa que en otros descendientes de infieles para no los admitir á la dignidad del sacerdocio ni á la de la religion...y esta es un natural extraño que tienen por la mayor parte los indios, diferente del de otras naciones...que no son buenos para mandar ni regir, sino para ser mandados y regidos" [There is more cause in them than in other descendants of infidels not to admit them to the rank of priests or to religious orders ...and this is a strange nature that the majority of Indians have, different from other nations...that they are not good to rule or govern, but to be ruled and governed] (Mendieta, HEI, 448). These categorizations of the Nahua other as incapable of being ordained as a priest because of his "natural disposition" clash with Molina's demands for a fully responsible and accountable Nahua penitent subject, who was expected to resist to the death any temptation and even the Devil himself.

15. In order to enable both the colonial and noncolonial Christian subjects to confess themselves properly, they were admonished to know the following: the fourteen articles of faith, the Ten Commandments, the five commandments of the church, the seven sacraments, the definition of venial sin and the nine ways in which it may be forgiven, the definition of mortal sin, the three theological and four cardinal virtues, the fourteen acts of mercy, seven of which are spiritual and seven of the flesh, the seven gifts of the Holy Spirit, the five corporal senses, the three faculties of the soul, the three enemies of the soul, the eight blessings that the souls will enjoy in heaven, and the four attributes of the glorified body (Molina, *Doctrina,* 34–49)

16. In this sense, Bhabha's generalization about colonial domination being achieved "through a process of disavowal that denies the chaos of its intervention as *Entstellung,* its dislocatory presence in order to preserve the authority of its identity" (*Location,* 111), is a theoretical essentialization. There is not one but innumerable ways and structures of colonial domination that need to be studied in their

specificity. In the context of the Spanish colonial experience, there is not one colonial subject, but many, often in open opposition and contradiction to each other. The disquieting topic of a more civil and orderly pre-Hispanic past than that of the Christian colonial present recognizes the failure of colonial intervention and subverts the teleological narrative of progress under colonial rule. Such a topic circulated among many friar-ethnographers, though evidently it was not shared equally by all sectors of colonial discourses.

17. One can appreciate this paradoxical position well into the seventeenth century in Bartolomé de Alva's *Confessionario mayor* of 1634. Barry Sell, editor and translator into English of this confessional manual, points out that "the view that the pre-Hispanic past was in some respects superior to the colonial present was commonly accepted, at least among specialists in Nahuatl and Nahua culture" ("Classical," 29).

18. Bartolomé de Alva raises this very same point about the wisdom of Nahua pre-Hispanic vigilance and social control. Consider his praise for the extreme severity with which drunkenness was punished in pre-Hispanic times: "And even though the ancients your elders drank, it was with moderation and restraint.... And if by chance they sometimes used to discover some drunkard, they immediately took away his life for it. And now in our times it exists because nobody restrains you with the death penalty" (Alva, 16v).

19. This is an opinion many friar-ethnographers shared. The Dominican Fray Diego Durán posits in his *History of the Indies* that the Nahuas were one of the lost tribes of Israel precisely because of what he perceived or construed as their innumerable ceremonies.

20. In the *Instrucción* and the *Obediencia* addressed to the first Twelve destined to evangelize the Nahuas, the minister general of the Franciscan order, Fray Francisco de los Angeles, exhorted them to a battle to the death against the Devil at the eleventh hour of the world. For the texts of the *Instrucción* and the *Obediencia*, see Torquemada, *Monarquía*, 3:10–16.

21. Thus, I concur with Jonathan I. Israel when he affirms that: "Seeing in this meekness the essence of the Christian spirit, the mendicants believed that they had found a people uniquely fitted to receive the new faith. All the missionaries, however much they differed on other matters, agreed on this; Indian meekness, not the ill-gotten plunder of the Conquistadores, was the true treasure of the Indies, the material from which a pure Apostolic Church might be formed again on earth" (8–9). These virtues (meekness, obedience, humbleness) are also listed among the ones possessed by those who will deserve to enjoy the eight blessings in heaven (Molina, *Doctrina*, 48–9).

22. For the Franciscan millenarianism in sixteenth-century Mexico, see Georges Baudot, *Utopia and History in Mexico* and *La pugna franciscana por México*; John E. Phelan, *The Millenial Kingdom of the Franciscans in the New World*; Christian Duverger, *La conversión de los indios de Nueva España*; José Antonio Maravall, "La

utopía político-religiosa de los franciscanos en la Nueva España"; and Robert Ricard, *La conquista espiritual de México*; among others.

23. This does not mean, however, that Bautista's long confessional makes no demands on the Nahua penitent. Particularly in the questions to be asked in relation to the first, sixth, and seventh commandments, there are many that require the penitent's unqualified devotion to God as well as a significant control over his desire. But since Bautista's manuals are much less detailed and accomplished than Molina's *Confessionario,* it may be argued that they do not probe the penitent as deeply as the latter and thus do not shape his Christian subjectivity as thoroughly.

Chapter 8 | Juan Bautista's *Advertencias para los confessores de los Naturales* and the *Malaises of Domination*

1. For the most important seventeenth-century source documenting the prevalence of pre-Hispanic beliefs and practices among the Indians of central Mexico, see Hernando Ruiz de Alarcón's *Treatise on the Superstitions of the Natives of this New Spain* (1629). See also Bartolomé de Alva's *Confessionario mayor* of 1634, particularly his questions on idolatry, concerning the first commandment (8v–13r).

2. Any act committed against the Ten Commandments was usually considered to be a mortal sin (Azpilcueta, 60). Thus, because there was such a thing as general, "objective sins" defined by the church, Christians had to know these in order to form an adequate judgment of good and evil conduct. Serious interest in catechism instruction began to grow in Spain in 1480 when the Alcalá synod established new, stricter guidelines for the catechesis of the faithful. Every Sunday during Lent the priest had to read to the parishioners the Articles of Faith, the Commandments, and the seven sacraments, vices and virtues, as well as the works of charity, the gift of the Holy Spirit, the five corporal senses, and the list of cases reserved for the pope and the bishop (Dedieu, 3). By 1540, a minimum requirement of proving knowledge of the four prayers of the church (i.e., *Pater Noster, Ave Maria, Salve,* and *Credo*) at least once during the lifetime was established (Dediue, 6). By the beginning of the seventeenth century, the requisite was knowledge of the Ten Commandments and of the Five Commandments of the church (Dediue, 6). All this means a more rigorous treatment of the issue of consent from the end of the fifteenth century on. It would, therefore, be difficult for a Christian who had to memorize the Decalogue to claim that he was unaware that an adulterous act could be sinful and thus had not consented to evil. The massive bibliography of catechisms and doctrines for the indigenous groups in New Spain (Contreras García, *Bibliografía*) indicates that catechism instruction was one of the most important functions of the friars.

3. In *La universalidad del conocimiento de Dios en los paganos, según los primeros teólogos de la Compañía de Jesús, 1534–1648,* Pedro de Achutegui concludes that out of the twenty-six Jesuit theologians he had examined, at least five admitted the possibility of invincible ignorance of God in the "pagans." Not surprisingly, the two

most prominent theologians who defended the possibility of invincible ignorance of God, Luis de Molina and Francisco Suárez, had worked in Spain and Portugal and were thus in close contact with the missionary activity in America.

4. See Molina's questions regarding the five specific circumstances under which the Christian is obliged to baptize as an example of this point about the efficacy of the sacraments (*Confessionario*, 22r–25v).

5. Or as an old Nahua had flatly declared to a priest who complained about the ·Indian's incapacity to become Christian: "Pongan tanto cuydado los padres en hazer los yndios christianos, como ponian los ministros de los Idolos en enseñarles sus ceremonias y ritos, que con la mitad de aquel cuydado seremos los yndios muy buenos christianos [Let the fathers put as much diligence and care in christianizing the Indians, as the ministers of the idols used to put in teaching them their ceremonies and rites, for with half that diligence we Indians will be very good Christians] (*Advertencias*, 12v).

Chapter 9 | *Historia eclesiástica indiana* or Writing the Crisis of Providentialism

1. The HEI was published in 1870 by Joaquín García Icazbalceta during the so-called Mexicanist Renaissance, a cultural and scholarly movement that searched for the roots of the new Mexican nation in its pre-Hispanic civilizations (Ascensión León-Portilla, *Tepuztlahcuilolli*, 1:104–19) and therefore took a critical stance against the three centuries of Spanish colonization. Juan Ruiz de Larrínaga ("Fray Jerónimo de Mendieta") and Georges Baudot (*Utopia*) believed that the HEI had remained unpublished because of its strong, bitter critique against the corruption of the Spanish colonization enterprise in the New World. In this sense, it must have fit well into the identity and nationalistic pursuits of the Mexicanist Renaissance movement.

2. Notable exceptions are José de Acosta's *Historia natural y moral de las Indias*, published in 1590, and Fray Juan de Torquemada's *Monarquía indiana*, published in 1615. Both chroniclers would appropriate materials from censored works, the former from Diego Durán and the latter from the HEI. It should be noted that historians in the sixteenth and seventeenth centuries drew freely from other sources, particularly when they belonged to the same religious order. Some, however, were less willing than others to reveal their intellectual debts, and therein grew the controversy over Torquemada's excessive and at times not sufficiently disguised borrowings form Mendieta. A great controversy also arose over Acosta's borrowings at the end of the eighteenth century (O'Gorman, "Prólogo," xi–xxiii). Even more relevant to our study than these authors' imputed plagiarism are the reasons why Acosta and Torquemada's works about the Indian past were published while so many others were not. Georges Baudot is of the opinion that Torquemada's history was licensed because it was not as potentially dangerous as his Franciscan predecessors' work

(*Utopia*, 522–23) and because the Indians were no longer a threat due to the demographic catastrophe of the sixteenth century in which millions of Indians perished (*Utopia*, 523). To my knowledge, not much has been said about the publication of Acosta's *Historia*. The history of the censorship of these narratives (and exceptions to the rule) is extremely revealing about the crown's worried constructions (and appraisals) about the political volatility of representations of the Amerindian pre-Hispanic past. For an account of the confiscation and prohibition of mendicant ethnographic chronicles, see Baudot, *Utopia*, 491–524. See also Brading, 120–21; and Bakewell, 303–04. For other hypotheses about the non-publication of the HEI, see Solano y Pérez-Lila, "Estudio preliminar," lxxxiv–lxxxvi.

3. On this reversal of the *Historia*'s initial objective of propagating European culture, see also Todorov, 219–37.

4. For a look into the well-known debate about the problems of the linear temporality implied in the term "post-colonial," see Vijay Mishra and Bob Hodge, "What is Post(-)Colonialism?"; Anne McClintock, "The Angel of Progress"; Stephen Slemon, "The Scramble for Post-Colonialism"; Jorge Klor de Alva, "Post-colonization"; and Kwame Anthony Appiah, "Is the Post in Postmodernism the Post in Postcolonial?"; among others.

5. For scholars questioning a Joachimite eschatological mindset among the Twelve, see Robert Ricard, *Conquista*; José A. Maravall, "Utopía"; M. Bataillon, "Evangelisme"; and more recently Delno West, "Medieval"; and M. A. Martín "Nuevo." Standard studies advocating such Joachimite millenarian schema are George Baudot's *Utopia* and John L. Phelan's *Millenial Kingdom*, which actually concentrates on Mendieta's HEI. Other more recent studies supporting this position are L. Weckmann, "Esperanzas"; P. M. Watts, "Prophecy"; José Rabasa, *Inventing*, 151–64; and José Sala Catalá and Jaime Vilchis Reyes, "Apocalíptica."

6. In his *Testament*, St. Francis of Assis had commanded his friars to adhere to the vow of total poverty and not to seek papal permission under any condition or circumstance to contest it. The Spirituals would obey their founder's desire literally, but the Conventuals, as they came to be called, almost immediately after the death of St. Francis started soliciting a relaxation of the rule. At the bequest of certain friars, Gregory IX pronounced himself on the matter in 1230, declaring that St. Francis's *Testament* was not binding, since it had not been approved by the chapter general of the order. In addition, he declared that the friars were authorized to accept and spend some form of property when urgent need arose, and although they were not allowed to handle money directly, they could keep it under the custody of a representative (Hermann, 66). This was the first of many interpretations St. Francis's rule would receive and the beginning of the sad, bitter rift within the order. Both parties in the Franciscan conflict would henceforth be favored or opposed by popes, but the Spirituals were the ones who suffered the most persecution, with some of them even executed for refusing to renounce their strict vow of poverty.

7. As Columbus leaves the Dragon's Mouths at the northwestern tip of the island

of Trinidad, he writes, "I do not suppose that the earthly paradise is in the form of a rugged mountain, as the descriptions of it have made it appear, but that it is on the summit of the spot, which I have described as being in the form of the stalk of a pear; the approach to it from a distance must be by a constant and gradual ascent; but I believe that, as I have already said, no one could ever reach the top: I think also, that the water I have described may proceed from it, though it be far off, and that stopping at the place which I have just left, it forms this lake" (Columbus, 137).

8. By urging and promoting the Observantine reform Cisneros also paved the way for the emergence of *iluminismo*, or interior Christianity, among lay people. For the classic account of reformed Christian spirituality during the first three decades of the sixteenth century, see Marcel Bataillon's *Erasmo y España*. Such a history, however, lies beyond the scope of this study.

9. And possibly also influential family ties, for he was a relative of Charles V.

10. It must be said that the name of the Twelve as indicating the first missionaries ever to set foot on Mexican soil is a misnomer. Three Franciscan Flemish missionaries had already accompanied Cortés in his expedition to Mexico. These three were Pedro de Gante, Juan de Tecto, and Juan de Ayora.

11. Foremost among these was the famous Donation of Constantine, a document upon which the popes had traditionally founded the legitimacy of their political power in the West. According to the document, the Roman emperor Constantine had granted Pope Sylvester authority over the Western Empire, out of gratitude for having been cured of leprosy by the pope. Based on philological scrutiny of the document, the fifteenth-century Italian humanist Lorenzo Valla was able to prove the document of the Donation false. He demonstrated that the forger's Latin had been anachronistic, inconsistent with usage in the fourth century, when the document had supposedly been written (Zamora, *Language*, 18). Furthermore, with his philological artillery, Valla also challenged the translation into Latin of key passages in Saint Jerome's Vulgate, and consequently many exegetical interpretations of the Scriptures upon which the church had based its doctrines (Zamora, *Language*, 18–19; Breisach 161).

12. On the subject of Spain's tribulations in the sixteenth and seventeenth centuries, see Graziano, 31–34; Elliot, 281–380; Maravall, *Cultura*, 55–128; and Lynch 138–210.

13. The first culmination of history was considered to be the Incarnation of Christ.

14. This is not, however, entirely the case. Luther posts his 95 theses in Wittenberg in 1517, whereas Cortés starts "preaching" the Gospel in Mexico in 1519.

15. All translations of the HEI into English are mine.

16. In his book Graziano observes about millennial ideology and belief: "The commencement of the new age coincides with the appearance of a messiah and the inception of a movement or, in more apocalyptic visions, with an era beyond some cataclysmic punctuation—flood, holocaust, earthquake, total war, change of suns— that stops the clock and restarts it" (14).

17. Needless to say, representing Cortés as divinely inspired during the Conquest of Mexico also served the blatantly political purpose of exculpating him from his excesses. These were well documented by many not as sympathetic to him as the Franciscan missionaries, who traditionally had been defended and protected by Cortés.

18. For a suggestive description of the sacred aspects of the position of the supreme ruler, or tlatoani, as well as of his magico-political investment ceremony, see Clendinnen, *Aztecs*, 77–83. See López Austin, *Human*, 1:388–400, for an analysis of the Nahua pre-Hispanic beliefs in the superior nature of the noblemen and government officials; and Krickeberg, 79–85, for some comments on the ruling and military functions of the different dignitaries.

19. Montezuma is a clear case in point. His authority remained unchallenged even as a prisoner of the Spaniards, until the scandalous massacre of young pipíltin during the calendrical feast of the Toxcatl ordered by Pedro de Alvarado. When this terrible event happened, Cortés was off to the coast to capture Pánfilo de Narváez. The latter had been sent by the governor of Cuba, Diego de Velázquez, in order to arrest Cortés for having illegally undertaken the Conquest of Mexico.

20. In *sermones* and in *doctrinas*, the friars utilized the basic metaphor of sin as disease, in order to elevate it to the spiritual realm of the soul. Burkhart explains that their failure to do so explicitly enough had the effect of a literal understanding of the relationship sin-sickness on the part of the Nahuas, which was in accordance with their pre-Hispanic conceptions. The result was that the "Nahua etiological concepts could easily be retained" (*Slippery*, 183).

21. As stated in earlier chapters, the closest Nahua equivalent for the Western ánima was the teyolia, which was a life force located in the liver. When Mendieta refers to the Nahua pre-Hispanic belief that ejecting sin from the ánima was the best cure, it is not clear what he is assuming that the Nahuas understood by ánima.

22. I am using the Douay-Rheims version of the Latin Vulgate into English, produced by Roman Catholic scholars at Rheims (New Testament, 1582) and Douai (Old Testament, 1610). The Latin Vulgate was the first great translation of the Bible into Latin, attributed to Saint Jerome (c. 347–420?). The Council of Trent (1545–63) decreed that it was the most authentic version and the only one that should be used.

23. In the medieval exegesis of the Bible, episodes in the Old Testament were reinterpreted according to four levels of meaning: the literal, allegorical (which referred to the New Testament or the Christian church), moral or tropological (referring to the destiny of the individual soul), and anagogical (which pertained to universal history and the end of the world) (Baldick, 9, 232). Mendieta is making both an allegorical and anagogical interpretation of Psalm 58, when referring to the Christian church as well as to the end of the world.

24. The Latin in the Vulgate reads as follows: "Convertentur ad vesperam / et famem patientur ut canes / et circuibunt civitatem" (Ps. 58:7, 15). Mendieta trans-

lates "convertentur ad vesperam" as "convertirse han a la tarde" [will be converted in the afternoon]. The verb *convertere* means "to turn around, whirl around" or "to turn back." In Spanish, the verb for "to convert,"*convertirse*, indeed comes from the Latin *convertere*. Mendieta's translation is thus not incorrect, except when one takes into consideration the context of the phrase in the psalm.

25. Mendieta learned Nahuatl from Motolinía. Apparently, Mendieta was very deeply influenced by the latter's optimistic if not millenarian perspective, which was easier to believe in 1541 than by the end of the century. A significant part of Mendieta's information for books 3 and 4 was taken from Motolinía's *Historia*. However, in the latter, the Indian church is already represented as facing opposition.

26. "Nor is it fitting that the ministers become neglectful of this conversion by saying there are no sins among this people other than orgies, thievery, and lustfulness, because there are many other, much graver sins among them which are in great need of remedy. The sins of idolatry, idolatrous rituals, idolatrous superstitions, auguries, abuses, and idolatrous ceremonies are not yet completely lost.

To preach against these matters...it is needful to know how they practiced them in the times of their idolatry, for, through [our] lack of knowledge of this, they perform many idolatrous things in our presence without our understanding it" (Sahagún, *Florentine*, 1:45)

27. The doctrina was a colonial parochial jurisdiction that was composed of a principal town or *cabecera*, where the clerics would reside, and many adjacent towns called *visitas* (Gibson, 101). Obviously, the cabecera town was the most distinguished, and in choosing them the church had the tendency to respect as much as possible the pre-Hispanic system of cabeceras and *sujetos* (Gibson, 102–03). In this way, the indigenous labor draft overseen by the caciques was facilitated by the fact that it was founded on native custom, and pre-Hispanic native hierarchy would be appropriated to serve the interests of evangelization.

28. According to James Lockhart, the process of assigning parishes to the different orders has never been clear. Apparently, the Franciscans got a generous share of the doctrinas in central Mexico by virtue of having arrived first, while Dominicans and Augustinians were located in unoccupied, more faraway areas (Lockhart, *The Nahuas*, 206).

29. One notable case is the vegetable figure of Huitzilopochtli, carefully and impeccably dressed up for the feast of the Toxcatl, as registered in book 12 of Sahagún's *Historia general*. There are many other references to this phenomenon collected by Clendinnen, *Aztecs*. See "Ritual," 248–59. For the importance of costume in Nahua ritual and social life, see Burkhart, *Holy*, particularly 42–48.

30. Diego de Landa was appointed Custodian of the Franciscans in Yucatán in 1558. He confronted great opposition from the Spanish colonists who claimed the Friars Minor were resettling the Indians without their consent, and the latter were dying in large numbers as a consequence of the forced relocation. As provincial or head of the Franciscans later on, Landa dealt harshly with Maya Indians who had

been discovered to be hiding "idols" in caves. For a detailed history of this violent episode, see Clendinnen, *Ambivalent Conquests*.

31. This is not to say that the Indians relinquished all authority over the churches to the friars. According to Lockhart, the Indians considered the churches they had built in their altepetl their own, and they had an important say as to which mendicant order would administer them. Indian zeal with temples and with their proper maintenance was not only due to the ardor of their new faith, however, but also harked back to pre-Hispanic patterns of establishing prestige and displaying hierarchy among the altepetl according to the splendor of their religious buildings (*Nahuas*, 206–10).

32. On the issue of bringing up socially responsible children, see Motolinía, *Memoriales*, 311–23, 335–44; Bartolomé de Las Casas, *Apologética historia sumaria*, chapters 219–24. Sahagún writes about this matter:

> "With regard to what they were most capable of in times past in the administration of the state as well as in the service of the gods, it is the reason why they held the affairs of their administration in accordance with the need of the people. And therefore, they reared the boys and girls with great sternness until they were adults. And this was not in the home of their parents...they reared them conjointly under very careful and stern teachers, the men by themselves and the women by themselves. There they taught them how they were to honor their gods and how they were to revere and obey the state and its rulers. They occupied people under fifty in many exercises, by night and by day. And they reared them in great austerity so that the carnal activities and tendencies had no dominion over them, whether men or women" (*Florentine*, 1:74–75).

33. See book 6 of his *Historia general de las cosas de la Nueva España* or *Florentine Codex*.

34. See Roberto González-Echevarría, "The Law and the Letter," in *Myth and Archive*.

35. The humanist Domingo de Soto (1494–1570), for instance, was anti-imperialist precisely because he claimed that the king would not be able to irradiate his "warmth throughout a society which extends across all regions and all peoples" (quoted in Pagden, "Empire and its Discontents," 319). For de Soto, the proximity of the body of the king was essential for a legitimate exercise of his authority. Imperialism required supplements and substitutes for his presence (such as the letter) that would eventually undermine his rule.

36. Mendieta's concept of the monarchy is beautifully expressed by Fray Bartolomé de Las Casas in his 1552 Prologue to the *Brevísima relación de la destrucción de Indias*: "As Divine Providence has ordained that the world shall, for the benefit and proper government of the human race, be divided into kingdoms and peoples and that these shall be ruled by kings, who are fathers and shepherds to their people and are, accordingly, the noblest and most virtuous of beings, there is no doubt,

nor could there in all reason be any such doubt, but that these kings entertain nothing save that which is morally unimpeachable. It follows that if the commonwealth suffers from some defect, or shortcoming, or evil, the reason can only be that the ruler is unaware of it; once the matter is brought to his notice, he will work with utmost diligence to set matters straight and will not rest content until the evil has been eradicated" (5).

37. See Stafford Poole's *Pedro Moya de Contreras* for an excellent study on this power struggle between the episcopacy and the mendicant orders in Mexico during the last three decades of the sixteenth century, with Moya de Contreras at the center of it all.

38. The alcalde mayor was the highest-ranking Spanish officer of a province or district. The title was often used as the equivalent of corregidor.

39. See the scathing "Parecer del Dr. Alonso Zorita," in Cuevas, *Documentos* (331–44). Complains the auditor Zorita:

"Los clérigos casi en común no saben la lengua de los pueblos que tienen a su cargo, y algunos dicen que les sobra tiempo porque piensan que cumplen con sólo decirles misa....

En el recoger de la comida para los clérigos...hacen grandes agravios y robos en el pueblo los mandoncillos que las recogen...y les tienen los clérigos lo que les han de dar cada día y si se tardan y no son tan buenas las gallinas y tan gordas como ellos las quieren...maltratan de palabra y de obra a los que las recogen, y a los caciques y principales....

Los clérigos tienen consigo, como se ha dicho, parientes y amigos y allegados ...y para todos hacen que les den comida ay servicio y vino y especies que lo han de ir a buscar y comprar a otros pueblos donde lo venden o se lo venden ellos...Y cuando se van los huéspedes o pasajeros les hacen dar tamemes para que les lleven sus ropas...." (336–38)

[The clergymen almost as a whole do not know the language of the towns under their care, and some of them say that they have extra time because they believe that they fulfill their duties solely by saying mass to the Indians....

Regarding the issue of collecting food for the clergymen...the *mandoncillos* (church officials) wrong and grieve the town from which they collect it...and the clergy establish what must be given to them every day and if they do not hasten, or if the chickens are not as good and plump as they want them...they mistreat by word and deed those who collect them, and also the caciques and principales....

As has been said, the clergy have with them relatives and friends...and they demand that all of them receive food and service and wine and species that the Indians must get and buy from other towns where such things are sold ...And when the guests or travelers leave, they (the clergy) demand that the Indians provide *tamemes* (carriers) so that they carry their clothing....]

The list of indictments goes on and on. See also the short letter by Don Luis de Velasco I to Philip II in which the viceroy defends the mendicants and obliquely criticizes the seculars for not knowing the indigenous languages, for their lavish lifestyles, and for doing business with tribute surpluses (244–45).

40. The mendicants fiercely defended the privileges of administering sacraments reserved to ordained priests that were conferred extraordinarily to them by Leo X and Adrian VI for more effectively carrying out the task of converting the Indians to Christianity. After the Second Mexican Council in 1555 in which the spiritual conquest was deemed complete, the secular ecclesiastical authorities wanted those extraordinary powers revoked, since according to their view, the special missionary circumstances had already been superseded.

41. There were three major epidemics ravaging the Valley of Mexico during the sixteenth century. The first one, smaller in scale, came during the siege of Tenochtitlan in 1520–21, greatly helping the Spaniards to defeat the unyielding Mexica. The second cocolitzli, the most devastating (as well as disconcerting) of them all happened in 1545–48, wiping out at least three-fourths of the indigenous population, according to the friars' calculations (Israel, 13), or almost 14 million Nahuas. The third one came in the period between 1576and 1580, reducing the indigenous population to 2 million (Israel, 17).

42. Anthropologist Julian Pitt-Rivers defines the concept of honor in the following way: "Honour is the value of a person in his own eyes, but also in the eyes of his society. It is his estimation of his own worth, his *claim* to pride, but it is also the acknowledgment of that claim, his excellence recognized by society, his *right* to pride" (21). Thus, to have honor is to fulfill the imperative of being absolutely recognized by others both in word and deed. It is "to be who one is" ("ser quien se es") publicly, without any room for doubt. In a classic article about honor in sixteenth- and seventeenth-century Spain, Gustavo Correa observes that to dishonor someone is first and foremost "manchar a la persona" ("to stain the person"). The only way of gaining back lost honor was through the shedding of blood of the offender by the victim (102). Because of the social aspect of honor and the absolute public recognition it demanded, it could be easily marred by a mere linguistic act such as a mischievous comment or innuendo. Thus, I argue that in stating that the king's conscience was loaded on the issue of the repartimiento, Mendieta is putting into question the king's integrity, and, thus, the author is actually dishonoring him in his public linguistic act of writing history. Similarly, Mendieta blemishes the name and reputation of all of the king's colonial administrators by his accusations, whether justified or not.

43. I am using John Austin's concept of the speech-act and the distinction he makes between the constative function of language and the performative one, in which words, more than simply stating things or conveying information about an extra-linguistic world, actually perform acts. See *How to Do Things with Words*. Austin later changed his nomenclature from the binary opposition of constative/

performative into the triad of locution, illocution, and perlocution. However, his distinction between constative and performative is still widely used to distinguish utterances that say something about things from those that perform or reproduce with language acts to which they refer.

44. The visitador was a judge sent by the king to conduct an investigation of a civil or ecclesiastical case.

45. The Indians had to pay tribute to the king, to their own caciques and tlatoque, and had community obligations to fulfill (*Códice Mendieta,* 12). In addition, under the repartimiento they were obliged to work for the Spaniards a few weeks per year, although for pay. The Indians also constructed churches and monasteries for their altepetl and supported the resident friars, if they had any.

46. According to Ramón Iglesias, the visitador accused the friars of having spent too much money and "real hacienda," or royal treasury, on churches and monasteries, in silver and ornaments, in relatives, and in sending back goods to Castile (170). In addition, the visitador criticized the friars for employing Indians in excessive numbers to serve the monasteries in superfluous tasks such as singing and playing music, thus wasting their labor and encouraging vagrancy (170–71).

47. "Deus absconditus" means hidden God.

48. This is a rewriting of Psalm 79 by Mendieta.

Conclusion: The Pyramid under the Cross

1. Consider the following fragment:

"As you know, dear Father, the news reached this land a few days before Lent. The Tlaxcaltecas wanted first to see what the Spaniards and Mexicans would do. When they saw that they arranged and represented the conquest of Rhodes, the Tlaxcaltecas decided to stage the conquest of Jersualem, a prediction which, we pray, God may fulfill in our day. In Tlaxcallan, the city that they have begun to rebuild, they set aside, down in the center of the plain, a large and pleasant plaza. Here they constructed a Jerusalem on top of some houses which they were erecting for the town council. It was on the site where the buildings were an *estado* in height. They leveled off the buildings, filled the shell with earth, and on this erected five towers" (Motolinía, *History,* 160).

Works Cited

Achutegui, SJ, Pedro S. de. *La universalidad del conocimiento de Dios en los paganos, según los primeros teólogos de la Compañía de Jesús, 1534–1648*. Madrid: Consejo Superior de Investigaciones Científicas, 1951.

Acosta, José. *Historia natural y moral de las Indias*. 1590. 2nd ed. Edited by Edmundo O'Gorman. México, D.F.: Fondo de Cultura Económica, 1962.

Adorno, Rolena. "Colonial Reform or Utopia? Guaman Poma's Empire of the Four Parts of the World." In *Amerindian Images and Legacy of Columbus*, edited by René Jara and Nicholas Spadaccini, 346–74. Minneapolis: University of Minnesota Press, 1992.

———. "Cultures in Contact: Mesoamerica, the Andes, and the European Written Tradition." In *The Cambridge History of Latin American Literature*, edited by Roberto González-Echevarría and Enrique Pupo-Walker, 33–57. Vol. 1. Cambridge: Cambridge University Press, 1996.

———. "Reconsidering Colonial Discourse for Sixteenth- and Seventeenth-Century Spanish America." *Latin American Research Review* 28, no. 3 (1993): 135–45.

Alva, Bartolomé de. *A Guide to Confession Large and Small in the Mexican Language, 1634*. Edited by Barry D. Sell and John F. Schwaller. Norman: University of Oklahoma Press, 1999.

Anderson, Arthur J. O. "Variations on a Sahaguntine Theme." In Sahagún, *Florentine Codex*, 1:3–8.

Anguis, Luis de. "Carta del Doctor Luis de Anguis a Felipe II. México, 20 de febrero de 1561." In *Documentos inéditos del siglo XVI para la historia de México* (1914), edited by Mariano Cuevas, 250–67. México, D.F.: Porrúa, 1975.

Appiah, Kwame Anthony. "Is the Post in Postmodernism the Post in Postcolonialism?" *Critical Inquiry* 17 (1991): 336–57.

Aquinas, Thomas. *Summa Theologica*. Vols. 19–20. Translated by Fathers of the English Dominican Province. Chicago: Encyclopedia Britannica, 1952.

Arieti, Silvano. *Abraham and the Contemporary Mind*. New York: Basic Books, 1981.

Arróniz, Othón. *Teatro de evangelización en Nueva España*. México, D.F.: Universidad Nacional Autónoma de México, 1979.

Assisi, St. Francis. *Writings and Early Biographies*. Edited by Marion A. Habig. Chicago: Franciscan Herald Press, 1972.

Auerbach, Erich. *Mimesis: The Representation of Reality in Western Literature*. Translated by Willard R. Trask. Princeton: Princeton University Press, 1968.

Austin, John L. *How to Do Things with Words*. Cambridge: Harvard University Press, 1962.

Ayala, Martín de. *Breve compendio para bien examinar la conciencia en el juyzio de la confession sacramental.* Valencia: Joan Mey, 1567.

Azpilcueta, Martín de. *Manual de confessores y penitentes qve clara y brevemente contiene, la universal y particular decision de quasi todas las dudas, que en las confessiones suelen ocurrir de los pecados, absoluciones, restituciones, censuras, & irregularidades.* Salamanca: Andrea de Portonariis, 1556.

Bakewell, Peter. "Conquest after the Conquest: The Rise of Spanish Domination in America." In *Spain, Europe and the Atlantic World: Essays in Honor of John H. Elliot,* edited by Richard L. Kagan and Geoffrey Parker, 296–315. Cambridge: Cambridge University Press, 1995.

Baldick, Chris. *The Concise Oxford Dictionary of Literary Terms.* Oxford: Oxford University Press, 1990.

Bataillon, Marcel. *Erasmo y España. Estudios sobre la historia espiritual del siglo XVI.* Translated by Antonio Alatorre. México, D.F.: Fondo de Cultura Económica, 1950.

———. "Evangelisme et millénarisme au Nouveau Monde." In *Courants religieux et humanisme à la fin du Xve et au début de XVIe siècle in Colloque de Strasbourg (9–11 May 1957),* 25–36. Paris: Presses Universitaires de France, 1959.

Baudot, Georges. Introduction to *Tratado de hechicerías y sortilegios, by Andrés de Olmos.* México, D.F.: Universidad Nacional Autónoma de México, Consejo Nacional para la Cultura y las Artes, 1990.

———. *La pugna franciscana por México.* México, D.F.: Alianza Editorial Mexicana, 1990.

———. *Utopia and History in Mexico: The First Chronicles of Mexican Civilization, 1520–1569.* Translated by Bernard R. Ortiz de Montellano and Thelma Ortiz de Montellano. Niwot, CO: University Press of Colorado, 1995.

Bautista, Juan. *Advertencias para los confesores de los Naturales.* México, D.F.: Melchior Ocharte, 1600.

———. *Confessionario en lengua Mexicana y Castellana. Con muchas advertencias muy necessarias parla los Confessores.* Santiago de Tlatelolco: Melchior Ocharte, 1599.

Bell, Catherine. *Ritual Theory, Ritual Practice.* Oxford: Oxford University Press, 1992.

Benveniste, Emile. *Problems in General Linguistics.* Translated by Mary Elizabeth Meek. Coral Gables: University of Miami Press, 1971.

Bernand, Carmen, and Serge Gruzinski. *De la idolatría: una arqueología de las ciencias religiosas.* México, D.F.: Fondo de la Cultura Económica, 1992.

Bhabha, Homi K. *The Location of Culture.* London: Routledge, 1994.

———. "The Other Question: Difference, Discrimination and the Discourse of Colonialism." In *Literature, Politics and Theory,* edited by Francis Baker et al., 148–72. London: Methuen, 1986.

Boone, Elizabeth Hill, ed. *Ritual Human Sacrifice in Mesoamerica: A Conference at Dumbarton Oaks, 13–14 October 1979.* Washington D.C.: Dumbarton Oaks Research Library and Collection, 1984.

Brading, David A. *The First America. The Spanish Monarchy, Creole Patriots, and the Liberal State 1492–1867.* Cambridge: Cambridge University Press, 1991.

Breisach, Ernst. *Historiography. Ancient, Medieval, and Modern.* Chicago: University of Chicago Press, 1983.

Broda, Johanna. "Las fiestas aztecas de los dioses de la lluvia." *Revista Española de Antropología Americana* 6 (1971): 245–327.

Brundage, Burr C. *The Fifth Sun: Aztec Gods, Aztec World.* Austin: University of Texas Press, 1979.

Burkhart, Louise M. "Doctrinal Aspects of Sahagún's *Colloquios.*" In Klor de Alva, Nicholson, and Quiñones Keber, *Work of Bernardino de Sahagun,* 65–82.

———. *Holy Wednesday: A Nahua Drama from Early Colonial Mexico.* Philadelphia: University of Pennsylvania Press, 1996.

———. "Moral Deviance in Sixteenth-Century Nahua and Christian Thought: The Rabbit and the Deer." *Journal of Latin American Lore* 12, no. 2 (1986), 107–39.

———. *The Slippery Earth: Nahua-Christian Moral Dialogue in Sixteenth-Century Mexico.* Tucson: University of Arizona Press, 1989.

Calderón de la Barca, Pedro. *Autos sacramentales. Obras completas.* Vol. 3. Edited by A. Valbuena Prat. Madrid: Aguilar, 1987.

Campbell, R. Joe, and Frances Kartunnen. *Foundation Course in Nahuatl Grammar.* 2 vols. Missoula: University of Montana Press, 1989.

Canons and Decrees of the Council of Trent. 1941. St. Louis and London: B. Herder, 1960.

Carochi, Horacio. *Arte de la lengua mexicana con la declaración de los adverbios della.* México: Juan Ruiz, 1645. México, D.F.: Universidad Nacional Autónoma de Mexico, Instituto de Investigaciones Filológicas, Instituto de Investigaciones Históricas, 1985.

Carrasco, Davíd. *City of Sacrifice: The Aztec Empire and the Role of Violence in Civilization.* Boston: Beacon Press, 1999.

Castro-Gómez, Santiago, and Eduardo Medieta, eds. *Teorías sin disciplina. Latinoamericanismo, poscolonialidad y globalización en debate.* San Francisco and México, D.F.: University of San Francisco and Miguel Ángel Porrúa, 1988.

———. "Introducción: la translocalización discursiva 'Latinoamérica' en tiempos de la globalización." In Castro-Gómez and Mendieta, *Teorías,* 5–30.

Castro-Klarén, Sara. "Writing Subalterity: Guaman Poma and Garcilaso, Inca." *Dispositio/n* 46 (1994): 229–44.

Cervantes, Fernando. *The Devil in the New World: The Impact of Diabolism in New Spain.* New Haven: Yale University Press, 1994.

Cervantes de Salazar, Francisco. *Crónica de la Nueva España.* 1914. Edited by

Manuel Magallón. 2 vols. Biblioteca de Autores Españoles 244-245. Madrid: Atlas, 1971.

Cesareo, Mario. *Cruzados, mártires y beatos. Emplazamientos del cuerpo colonial.* West Lafayette, IN: Purdue University Press, 1995.

Chang-Rodríguez, Raquel. *Hidden Messages: Representation and Resistance in Andean Colonial Drama.* Lewisburg: Bucknell University Press, 1999.

Ciruelo, Pedro. *Arte de bien confesar.* 1534. Sevilla: Dominico de Robertis, 1548.

Clendinnen, Inga. *Ambivalent Conquests: Maya and Spaniard in Yucatan, 1517–1570.* Cambridge: Cambridge University Press, 1987.

———. *Aztecs: An Interpretation.* Cambridge: Cambridge University Press, 1991.

———. "Franciscan Missionaries in Sixteenth-Century Mexico." In *Disciplines of Faith: Studies in Religion, Politics and Patriarchy,* edited by Jim Obelkevich, Lyndal Roper, and Raphael Samuel, 229–45. London: Routledge and Kegan Paul, 1987.

Códice de autos viejos. Selección. Edited by Miguel Ángel Pérez Priego. Madrid: Castalia, 1988.

Códice Franciscano: Siglo XVI. Vol. 2, *Nueva colección de documentos para la historia de México,* edited by Joaquín García Icazbalceta. 2nd ed. México, D.F.: Salvador Chávez Hayhoe, 1941.

Columbus, Christopher. *Four Voyages to the New World.* 1847. Translated by R. H. Major. New York: Corinth Books, 1961.

Comaroff, Jean, and John Comaroff. *Of Revelation and Revolution: Christianity, Colonialism and Consciousness in South Africa.* Vol. 2. Chicago: University of Chicago Press, 1991.

Concilio Vaticano II. Constituciones. Decretos. Declaraciones. Legislación posconciliar. Madrid: Biblioteca de Autores Cristianos, 1967.

Contreras García, Irma. *Bibliografía sobre la castellanización de los grupos indígenas de la República Mexicana.* 2 vols. México, D.F.: Universidad Nacional Autónoma de México, 1986.

Corbató, Hermenegildo. "Misterios y autos del teatro misionero en México durante el siglo XVI y sus relaciones con los de Valencia." In *El teatro francsciano en la Nueva España,* edited by María Sten, 93–105. México, D.F.: Universidad Nacional Autónoma de México y CONACULTA, 2000. First published in *Anales del centro de cultura valenciana.* Valencia: Consejo Superior de Investigaciones Científicas, 1949.

Córdoba, Pedro de. *Doctrina cristiana y cartas.* 1544. Santo Domingo: La Fundación Corripio, 1986.

Coronil, Fernando. "Más allá del occidentalismo: hacia categorías geohistóricas no-imperialistas." In Castro-Gómez and Mendieta, *Teorías,* 121–46.

Correa, Gustavo. "El doble aspecto de la honra en el teatro del siglo XVII." *Hispanic Review* 26 (1958): 99–107.

Cortés, Hernán. *Letters from Mexico*. Translated and edited by Anthony Pagden. New Haven: Yale University Press, 1986.

Cotarelo y Mori, Emilio. *Bibliografía de las controversias sobre la licitud del teatro en España*. Madrid: Est. Tip. de la Revista de Archivos, Bibliografía y Museos, 1904.

Craddock, Lawrence G. "Franciscan Influences on Early English Drama." *Franciscan Studies* 10 (1950): 383–417.

Cuevas, Mariano, ed. *Documentos inéditos del siglo XVI para la historia de México*. 1914. México, D.F.: Porrúa, 1975.

Davies, Nigel. *The Aztec Empire: The Toltec Resurgence*. Norman and London: University of Oklahoma Press, 1987.

De Certeau, Michel. *The Writing of History*. Translated by Tom Conley. New York: Columbia University Press, 1988.

Dedieu, Jean Pierre. "'Christianization' in New Castile: Catechism, Communion, Mass and Confirmation in the Toledo Archbishopric, 1540–1650." In *Culture and Control in Counter-Reformation Spain*, edited by Anne J. Cruz and Mary Elizabeth Perry, 1–24. Minneapolis: University of Minnesota Press, 1992.

Delumeau, Jean. *L'aveu et le pardon. Les difficultés de la confession XIIIe–XVIII siècle*. Paris: Fayard, 1990.

de Man, Paul. "The Task of the Translator." *The Resistance to Theory*, 73–105. Minneapolis: University of Minnesota Press, 1986.

De Marinis, Marco. *The Semiotics of Performance*. Trans. Áine O'Healy. Bloomington and Indianapolis: Indiana University Press, 1993.

Dennis, Trevor. *Sarah Laughed. Women's Voices in the Old Testament*. Nashville: Abingdon Press, 1994.

Derrida, Jacques. "Donner la mort." In *L'Éthique du don. Jacques Derrida et la pensée du don*, edited by Jean-Michel Rabaté and Michael Wetzel, 11–108. Paris: Métailié-Transition, 1992.

Díaz Balsera, Viviana. *Calderón y las quimeras de la Culpa: alegoría, seducción y resistencia en cinco autos sacramentales*. West Lafayette: Purdue University Press, 1997.

Díaz del Castillo, Bernal. *Historia verdadera de la conquista de México*. México: Porrúa, 1960/1994.

Dibble, Charles E. "Sahagún's *Historia*." In *Florentine Codex*, by Bernardino de Sahagún, 1:9–23.

Donovan, Richard B. *The Liturgical Drama in Medieval Spain*. Toronto: Pontifical Institute of Mediæval Studies, 1958.

Douie, Decima L. *The Nature and the Effect of the Heresy of the Fraticelli*. Manchester: University Press, 1932/1978.

Dreyfus, Hubert L., and Paul Rabinow. *Michel Foucault: Beyond Structuralism and Hermeneutics*. 2nd ed. Chicago: University of Chicago Press, 1982/1983.

Dubois, Claude-Gilbert. *La Conception de l'Histoire en France au XVIe siècle (1560–1610)*. Paris: A. G. Nizet, 1977.

Durán, Diego. *Historia de las Indias de la Nueva España e islas de Tierra Firme.* 1867–1880. Edited by Ángel M. Garibay K. 2 vols. México, D.F.: Porrúa, 1967/1984.

———. *History of the Indies of New Spain*, translated by Doris Heyden. Norman: University of Oklahoma Press, 1994.

Duverger, Christian. *La conversión de los indios de Nueva España con el texto de los* Coloquios de los Doce *de Bernardino de Sahagún (1564)*. Translated by María Dolores de la Peña. México, D.F.: Fondo de Cultura Económica, 1993.

Elliot, John H *Imperial Spain: 1469–1716*. New York: St. Martin's Press, 1964.

Fletcher, Angus. *Allegory: the Theory of a Symbolic Mode*. Ithaca: Cornell University Press, 1964.

Flint, Valerie I. J. *The Imaginative Landscape of Christopher Colombus*. Princeton: Princeton University Press, 1992.

Fortini, Arnaldo. *La Lauda in Assisi e le origini del teatro italiano*. Assisi: 1961.

Foucault, Michel. Afterword to *Michel Foucault*, by Hubert L. Dreyfus and Paul Rabinow, 208–64.

———. *Discipline and Punish. The Birth of the Prison*. Translated by Alan Sheridan. New York: Vintage, 1979.

———. *The History of Sexuality*. Vol. 1, *An Introduction*. Translated by Robert Hurley. New York: Vintage, 1980.

Gage, Thomas. *A New Survey of the West Indies, 1648*. Edited by A. P. Newton. New York: Robert McBride, 1929.

García Icazbalceta, Joaquín. *Bibliografía mexicana del siglo XVI. Catálogo razonado de libros impresos en México de 1539 a 1600. Con biografías de autores y otras ilustraciones. Precedido de una noticia acerca de la introducción de la imprenta en México.* 1886. Edited by Agustín Millares Carlo. México, D.F.: Fondo de Cultura Económica, 1954.

Garibay K., Ángel M. *Historia de la literatura náhuatl*. 2 vols. México, D.F.: Porrúa, 1953.

Gates, Henry Louis, Jr. "Editor's Introduction: Writing 'Race' and the Difference It Makes." *Critical Inquiry* 12 (1985): 1–20.

Giard, Luce. "Epilogue: Michel de Certeau's Heterology in the New World." *New World Encounters*, edited by Stephen Greenblatt, 313–22. Berkeley: University of California Press, 1993.

Gibson, Charles. *The Aztecs under Spanish Rule. A History of the Indians of the Valley of Mexico, 1519–1810*. Stanford: Stanford University Press, 1964.

Gómez, Jesús. *El diálogo en el Renacimiento español*. Madrid: Cátedra, 1988.

Gómez Canedo, Lino. *Evangelización y conquista. Experiencia franciscana en Hispanoamérica*. México, D.F.: Porrúa, 1977.

González-Echevarría, Roberto. *Myth and Archive: A Theory of Latin American Narrative.* Durham: Duke University Press, 1998.

González Torres, Yólotl. *El sacrificio humano entre los mexicas.* México: Fondo de Cultura Económica, 1994.

Graziano, Frank. *The Millennial New World.* Oxford: Oxford University Press, 1999.

Grijalva, Juan. *Crónica de la Orden de N.P.S. Agustín en las provincias de la Nueva España. En cuatro edades desde el año de 1533 hasta el de 1592.* 1624. México, D.F.: Porrúa, 1924/1985.

Gruzinski, Serge. "Confesión, alianza y sexualidad entre los indios de la Nueva España: Introducción al estudio de los confesionarios en lenguas indígenas." In *El placer de pecar y el afán de normar,* 171–215. México, D.F.: Instituto Nacional de Antropología e Historia/Joaquín Mortiz, 1987.

——. *La colonización de lo imaginario. Sociedades indígenas y occidentalización en el México español. Siglos XVI–XVIII.* Translated by Jorge Ferreiro. México, D.F.: Fondo de la Cultura Económica, 1991.

——. *La guerre des images: De Christophe Colomb à "Blade Runner" (1492–2019).* Paris: Fayard, 1990.

——. "Individualization and Acculturation: Confession among the Nahuas of Mexico from the Sixteenth to the Eighteenth Century." In *Sexuality and Marriage in Colonial Latin America,* edited by Asunción Lavrin, 96–117. Latin American Studies Series. Lincoln: University of Nebraska Press, 1989.

Gutiérrez, Ramón A. *When Jesus Came, the Corn Mothers Went Away: Marriage, Sexuality, and Power in New Mexico, 1500–1846.* Stanford: Stanford University Press, 1991.

Haliczer, Stephen. *Sexuality in the Confessional. A Sacrament Profaned.* Oxford: Oxford University Press, 1996.

Hardison, O. B. *Christian Rite and Christian Drama in the Middle Ages: Essays in the Origin and Early History of Modern Drama.* Baltimore: Johns Hopkins University Press, 1965.

Harris, Max. *Aztecs, Moors, and Christians: Festivals of Reconquest in Mexico and Spain.* Austin: University of Texas Press, 2000.

——. *The Dialogical Theatre: Dramatizations of the Conquest of Mexico and the Question of the Other.* New York: St. Martin's Press. 1993.

Hartog, François. *The Mirror of Herodotus: The Representation of the Other in the Writing of History.* Translated by Janet Lloyd. Berkeley: University of California Press, 1988.

Hera, Alberto de la. *Iglesia y corona en la América Española.* Madrid: MAPFRE, 1992.

Hermann, OFM, Placid. Introduction and notes to *St. Francis of Assisi. Writings and Early Biographies. English Omnibus of the Sources for the Life of St. Francis.*

3rd ed. Edited by Marion A. Habig. London: The Society for Promoting Christian Knowledge, 1979.

The Holy Bible. Douay-Rheims Version. 1899. Rockford, IL: Tan Books and Publishers, 1971.

Homza, Lu Ann. "The European Link to Mexican Penance. The Literary Antecedents to Alva's *Confessionario*." In *A Guide to Confession Large and Small*, by Bartolomé de Alva, 33–48.

Horcasitas, Fernando. *El teatro náhuatl. Épocas novohispana y moderna*. México, D.F.: Universidad Autónoma de México, 1974.

Hosley, Richard. "England: The Middle Ages." In *The Reader's Encyclopedia of World Drama*, edited by John Gassner and Edward Quinn, 202–08. New York: Thomas Y. Crowell, 1969.

Iglesia, Ramón. "Invitación al estudio de Jerónimo de Mendieta." *Cuadernos Americanos* 22 (1945): 156–72.

Israel, Jonathan. *Race, Class and Politics in Colonial Mexico, 1610–1670*. London: Oxford University Press, 1975.

Jacquot, Jacques, and Elie Konigson, eds. *Les Fêtes de la Renaissance*. 2 vols. Paris: Centre National de la Recherche Scientifique, 1956–75.

JanMohamed, Abdul. "The Economy of the Manichean Allegory: The Function of Racial Difference in Colonialist Literature." *Critical Inquiry* 12 (1985): 59–87.

Jara, René, and Nicholas Spadaccini, eds. *Amerindian Images and the Legacy of Columbus*. Minneapolis: University of Minnesota Press, 1992.

———. "Introduction. The Construction of a Colonial Imaginary: Colombus's Signature." In Jara and Spadaccini, *Amerindian Images*, 1–95.

Jeffrey, David L. *The Early English Lyric and Franciscan Spirituality*. Lincoln: University of Nebraska Press, 1975.

———. "Franciscan Spirituality and the Rise of Early English Drama." *Mosaic* 8, no. 4 (1975): 17–24.

Kagan, Richard L., and Geoffrey Parker, eds. *Spain, Europe and the Atlantic World: Essays in Honor of John H. Elliot*. Cambridge: Cambridge University Press, 1995.

Kierkegaard, Soren. *Fear and Trembling/Repetition*. Edited and translated by Howard V. Hong and Edna H. Hong. Princeton: Princeton University Press, 1983.

Klor de Alva, Jorge. "The Aztec-Spanish Dialogues of 1524." *Alcheringa* 4 (1980): 52–193.

———. "Colonizing Souls: The Failure of the Indian Inquisition and the Rise of Penitential Discipline." In *Cultural Encounters: The Impact of the Inquisition in Spain and the New World*, edited by Mary Elizabeth Perry and Anne J. Cruz, 3–22. Berkeley: University of California Press, 1991.

———. "Contar vidas: la autobiografía confesionsal y la reconstrucción del ser nahua." *Arbor* 515–16 (1988): 49–78.

———. "El discurso nahua y la apropiación de lo europeo." In *De palabra y obra en el Nuevo Mundo. Imágenes interétnicas*, edited by Miguel León-Portilla et al., 339–68. Vol. 1. México, D.F.: Siglo Veintiuno, 1992.

———. "La historicidad de los *Coloquios* de Sahagún." *Estudios de Cultura Náhuatl* 15 (1982): 147–84.

———. "The Postcolonization of the (Latin) American Experience: A Reconsideration of 'Colonialism,' 'Postcolonialism,' and 'Mestizaje.'" In *After Colonialism: Imperial Histories and Postcolonial Displacements*, edited by Gyan Prakash, 241–75. Princeton: Princeton University Press, 1995.

———. "Sahagún and the Birth of Modern Ethnography: Representing, Confessing, and Inscribing the Native Other." In Klor de Alva, Nicholson, and Quiñones Keber, *Work of Bernardino de Sahagún*, 31–52.

———. "Sahagún's Misguided Introduction to Ethnography and the Failure of the Colloquios Project." In Klor de Alva, Nicholson, and Quiñones Keber, *Work of Bernardino de Sahagún*, 83–92.

Klor de Alva, Jorge, Henry B. Nicholson, and Eloise Quiñones Keber, eds. *The Work of Bernardino de Sahagún. Pioneer Ethnographer of Sixteenth-Century Aztec Mexico*. Albany: Institute for Mesoamerican Studies, State University of New York at Albany, 1988.

Kobayashi, José María. *La educación como conquista (empresa franciscana en México)*. México: El Colegio de México, 1974.

Kolve, V. A. *The Play Called Corpus Christi*. Stanford: Stanford University Press, 1966.

Krickeberg, Walter. *Las antiguas culturas mexicanas*. Translated by Sita Garst and Jasmín Reuter. México: Fondo de Cultura Económica, 1961/1993.

Kuschel, Karl-Josef. *Abraham. Signs of Hope for Jews, Christians and Muslims*. New York: Continuum, 1995.

Lafaye, Jacques. *Quetzalcóatl and Guadalupe: The Formation of Mexican National Consciousness 1531–1813*. Translated by Benjamin Keen. Chicago: University of Chicago Press, 1976/1987.

Las Casas, Fray Bartolomé de. *Apologética historia sumaria*. 1909. Edited by Edmundo O'Gorman. 2 vols. México: Universidad Autónoma de México, Instituto de Investigaciones Históricas, 1967.

———. *Historia de las Indias*. 2 vols. Edited by José M. Vigil. México, D.F.: I. Paz, 1877.

———. *A Short Account of the Destruction of Indies*. 1552. Edited and translated by Nigel Griffin. London: Penguin, 1992.

Lavrin, Asunción. "Confraternities in Colonial Spanish America." In Sell, *Nahua Confraternities*, 23–40.

Lázaro Carreter, Fernando. *Teatro medieval*. Madrid: Castalia, 1965.

Lehmann, Walter, ed. and trans. *Sterbende Gotter und Christliche Heilsbotschaft*

[Study and translation into German of Sahagún's *Colloquios* (1564)]. Stuttgart: W. Kohlhammer Verlag, 1949.

León-Portilla, Ascención H. *Tepuztlahcuilolli. Impresos en náhuatl. Historia y bibliografía.* 2 vols. México: Universidad Autónoma de México, 1988.

León-Portilla, Miguel. *Aztec Thought and Culture: A Study of the Ancient Nahuatl Mind.* Translated by Jack E. Davis. Norman: University of Oklahoma Press, 1963.

———. "Estudio introductorio." In Sahagún, *Coloquios, 15–29.*

———. "¿Insertos en la 'historia sagrada'? Respuesta y reacomodo de los mesoamericanos." *Estudios de Cultura Náhuatl* 26 (1996): 187–209.

———, ed. and trans. *Literatura del México antiguo: los textos en lengua náhuatl.* Caracas: Ayacucho, 1978.

———. Prologue to *Adiciones, apéndice a la postilla y ejercicio cotidiano,* by Bernardino de Sahagún.

Lockhart, James. *The Nahuas after the Conquest: A Social and Cultural History of the Indians of Central Mexico, Sixteenth through Eighteenth Centuries.* Stanford: Stanford University Press, 1992.

———. *Nahuatl as Written. Lessons in Older Written Nahuatl, with Copious Examples and Texts.* Stanford: Stanford University Press and UCLA Latin American Center Publications, 2001.

Lockhart, James, and Frances Kartunnen. *The Art of Nahuatl Speech. The Bancroft Dialogues.* Los Angeles: UCLA Latin American Center Publications, 1987.

Lopetegui, León, and Félix Zubillaga. *Historia de la Iglesia en la América Española. Desde el Descubrimiento hasta comienzos del siglo XIX. México. América Central. Antillas.* Madrid: Biblioteca de Autores Cristianos, 1965.

López Austin, Alfredo. *Hombre-Dios. Religión y política en el mundo náhuatl.* Mexico: Universidad Nacional Autónoma de México, Instituto de Investigaciones Históricas, 1973.

———. *The Human Body and Ideology: Concepts of the Ancient Nahuas.* 2 vols. Translated by Thelma Ortiz de Montellano and Bernard Ortiz de Montellano. Salt Lake City: University of Utah Press, 1988.

———. *Tamoanchan, Tlalocan, Places of Mist.* Translated by Bernard Ortiz de Montellano and Thelma Ortiz de Montellano. Niwot: University Press of Colorado, 1997.

López de Gómara, Francisco. *Historia de la Conquista de México.* 2 vols. México, D.F.: Pedro Robredo, 1943.

Lynch, John. *Spain 1516–1598. From Nation State to World Empire.* Malden, MA: Blackwell, 1992.

MacAloon, John J., ed. "Introduction: Cultural Performances, Culture Theory." In *Rite, Drama, Festival, Spectacle: Rehearsals toward a Theory of Cultural Performance,* 1–15. Philadelphia: Institute for the Study of Human Issues, 1984.

MacCormack, Sabine. "'The Heart Has Its Reasons': Predicaments of Missionary Christianity in Early Peru." *Hispanic American Historical Review* 65 (1985): 443–66.

Maravall, José Antonio. *La cultura del Barroco. Análisis de una estructura histórica.* Barcelona: Ariel, 1980.

———. "La utopía político-religiosa de los franciscanos en la Nueva España." *Estudios Americanos* 2 (1949): 199–227.

Martín, Melquíades A. "Nuevo planteamiento de la utopía franciscana en México." In *Extremadura en la evangelización del Nuevo Mundo. Actas y Estudios*, edited by Fray Sebastián García, O.F.M., 269–89. Madrid: Turner, 1990.

Matos Moctezuma, Eduardo. "The Templo Mayor of Tenochtitlan: Economics and Ideology." In Boone, *Ritual,* 133–64.

McClintock, Anne. "The Angel of Progress: Pitfalls of the Term 'Postcolonialism.'" In *Colonial Discourse / Postcolonial Theory*, edited by Francis Barker, Peter Hulme, and Margaret Iversen, 253–66. Manchester: Manchester University Press; New York: St. Martin's Press, 1994.

McGinn, Bernard. *The Calabrian Abbot. Joaquim of Fiore in the History of Western Thought.* New York: MacMillan, 1985.

Mendieta, Gerónimo. *Historia eclesiástica indiana.* 1870. México, D.F.: Porrúa, 1993.

Mendoza López, Margarita. "Un problema inicial en la historia del teatro americano." *Rueca* 5 (1942–43): 5–11.

Menegus, Margarita. "La destrucción del señorío indígena y la formación de la república de indios en la Nueva España." In *El sistema colonial en la América española*, edited by Heraclio Bonilla, 17–49. Barcelona: Crítica, 1991.

Mignolo, Walter D. *Local Histories/Global Designs. Coloniality, Subaltern Knowledges, and Border Thinking.* Princeton: Princeton University Press, 2000.

Ministerio de Fomento. *Cartas de Indias.* 1877. *Biblioteca de Autores Españoles.* Vol. 264. Madrid: Manuel G. Hernández, 1974.

Mishra, Vijay, and Bob Hodge. "What is Post(-)Colonialism?" *Textual Practice* 5, (1991): 399–415.

Molina, Alonso de. *Confessionario mayor en la lengua mexicana y castellana.* 1569. Edited by Roberto Moreno. México, D.F.: Universidad Nacional Autónoma de México, 1984.

———. *Doctrina Christiana breve traduzida en lengua Mexicana.* In *Códice Franciscano: Siglo XVI,* 29–54.

———. *Vocabulario en lengua castellana y mexicana.* 1551–1571. México, D.F.: Porrúa, 1992.

Motolinía, Toribio de Benavente. *Historia de los indios de la Nueva España.* 1858. Edited by Edmundo O'Gorman. México: Porrúa, 1990.

———. *Memoriales o Libro de las cosas de la Nueva España y de los Naturales de ella.*

1903. Edited by Edmundo O'Gorman. México: Universidad Autónoma de México, Instituto de Investigaciones Históricas, 1971.

———. *Motolinía's History of the Indians of New Spain*. Translated by Francis Borgia Steck. Washington: Academy of American Franciscan History, 1951.

Moyers, Bill. *Genesis: A Living Conversation*. New York: Doubleday, 1996.

Muñoz Camargo, Diego. *Historia de Tlaxcala: crónica del siglo XVI*. 1892. Edited by Alfredo Chavero. México, D.F.: Innovación, 1978.

Nicholson, Henry B. "Religion in Pre-Hispanic Central Mexico." In *Archeology of Northern Mesoamerica*, edited by Gordon F. Ekolm and Ignacio Bernal, 395–446. Vol. 10, *Handbook of Middle American Indians*, edited by Robert Wauchope. Austin: University of Texas Press, 1971.

Olmos, Andrés de. *Tratado de hechicerías y sortilegios*. Edited by Georges Baudot. México: Universidad Nacional Autónoma de México, 1990.

O'Gorman, Edmundo. "Estudio crítico." In Motolinía, *Historia,* ix–xix.

———. "Prólogo." In Acosta, *Historia natural,* xi–liii.

Ong, Walter. *Orality and Literacy: The Technologizing of the Word*. London: Methuen, 1982.

Pagden, Anthony. *The Fall of Natural Man: The American Indian and the Origins of Comparative Ethnology*. Cambridge: Cambridge University Press, 1982.

———. "Heeding Heracles: Empire and Its Discontents." In Kagan and Parker, *Spain,* 316–33.

Parker, Alexander A. "Notes on the Religious Drama in Medieval Spain and the Origins of the 'Auto sacramental.'" *Modern Language Review* 30 (1985): 170–82.

Parker, Geoffrey. "David or Goliath? Philip II and his world in the 1580s." In *Spain, Europe and the Atlantic World*, edited by Richard L. Kagan and Geoffrey Parker, 245–66. Cambridge: Cambridge University Press, 1995.

Paso y Troncoso, Francisco. "Advertencia." In *Del Sacrificio de Isaac: auto en lengua mexicana (anónimo) escrito en el año 1678*, 3–8. Florence: Salvador Landi, 1899.

Pavis, Patrice. *Theatre at the Crossroads of Culture*. Trans. Loren Kruger. London: Routledge, 1992.

Pelikan, Jaroslav. *The Christian Tradition. Reformation of Church and Dogma (1300–1700)*. Vol. 4. Chicago: University of Chicago Press, 1984.

Pérez Priego, Miguel Ángel. "Introducción crítica." In *Códice de autos viejos,* 7–41.

Phelan, John Leddy. *The Millenial Kingdom of the Franciscans in the New World*. Berkeley: University of California Press, 1970.

Pitt-Rivers, Julian. "Honour and Social Status." In *Honour and Shame and the Unity of the Mediterranean*, edited by J. G. Peristany, 221–77. Chicago: University of Chicago Press, 1966.

Poole, Stafford. *Pedro Moya de Contreras: Catholic Reform and Royal Power in New Spain, 1571–1591*. Berkeley: University of California Press, 1987.

Prakash, Gyan. "Subaltern Studies as Postcolonial Criticism." *The American Historical Review* 99 (1994): 1475–90.

Pratt, Mary Louise. *Imperial Eyes: Travel Writing and Transculturation.* New York: Routledge, 1992.

Quijano, Aníbal. "Modernity, Identity, and Utopia in Latin America." In *The Postmodernism Debate in Latin America,* edited by John Beverley, Michael Aronna, and José Oviedo, 201–16. Durham, London: Duke University Press, 1995.

Rabasa, José. "Franciscans and Dominicans under the Gaze of a Tlacuilo: Plural-World Dwelling in an Indian Pictorial Codex." *Morrison Library Inaugural Lecture Series 14.* University of California at Berkeley, 1998.

———. *Inventing America. Spanish Historiography and the Formation of Eurocentrism.* Norman: University of Oklahoma Press, 1993.

———. "Writing and Evangelization in Sixteenth-Century Mexico." In *Early Images of the Americas: Transfer and Invention,* edited by Jerry M. Williams and Robert E. Lewis, 65–92. Tucson: University of Arizona Press, 1993.

Ravicz, Marlyn E. *Early Colonial Religious Drama in Mexico: From Tzompantli to Golgotha.* Washington: Catholic University of America Press, 1970.

Read, Kay Almere. *Time and Sacrifice in the Aztec Cosmos.* Bloomington and Indianapolis: Indiana University Press, 1988.

Reeves, Marjorie. *Joachim of Fiore and the Prophetic Future.* New York: Harper and Row, 1977.

Ricard, Robert. *La conquista espiritual de México. Ensayo sobre el apostolado y los métodos misioneros de las órdenes mendicantes en la Nueva España de 1523–1524 a 1572.* Trans. Ángel M. Garibay. México, D.F.: Fondo de Cultura Económica, 1986/1991.

Ricoeur, Paul. "'Original Sin': A Study in Meaning." In *The Conflict of Interpretations: Essays on Hermeneutics,* edited by Don Ihde, 269–86. Evanston: Northwestern University Press, 1974.

———. *The Symbolism of Evil.* Translated by Emerson Buchanan. New York: Harper and Row, 1967.

Rivers, Elías L., ed. *Poesía lírica del Siglo de Oro.* Madrid: Cátedra, 1989.

Rodríguez de Bibanco, Diego. "Carta de Diego Rodríguez Bibanco, defensor de los indios, al Rey Don Felipe II, suplicándole se dignara expulsar de las Indias á los frailes de la orden de San Francisco.—Mérida, 8 de marzo de 1563." Ministerio 392-96.

Román Berrelleza, Juan Alberto. "Offering 48 of the Templo Mayor: A Case of Child Sacrifice." In *The Aztec Templo Mayor: A Symposium at Dumbarton Oaks, 8th and 9th October 1983,* edited by Elizabeth Hill Boone, 131–43. Washington, D.C.: Dumbarton Oaks, 1984.

Ruiz de Larrínaga, Juan. "Fray Jerónimo de Mendieta, historiador de la Nueva España." *Archivo Ibero-Americano* 1 (1914): 290–300, 488–99; 2 (1914): 188–201, 387–404; 4 (1915): 341–373.

Ruiz Ramón, Francisco. *Historia del teatro español.* 2 vols. Madrid: Alianza Editorial, 1967–71.

El sacrificio de Abraham. In *Autos sacramentales desde su origen hasta fines del siglo XVII*, edited by Eduardo González Pedroso, 16–22. Biblioteca de Autores Españoles. Madrid: Atlas, 1952.

Sahagún, Bernardino de. *Adiciones, Apéndice a la Postilla y Ejercicio cotidiano.* Paleography and translation by Arthur J. O. Anderson. México, D.F.: Universidad Nacional Autónoma de México, 1993.

———. *Coloquios y doctrina cristiana.* Edited by Miguel León-Portilla. México, D.F.: Universidad Autónoma de México, Fundación de Investigaciones Sociales, 1986.

———. *Florentine Codex. General History of the Things of New Spain.* Edited and translated by Arthur J. O. Anderson and Charles E. Dibble. 12 vols. Santa Fe, NM and Salt Lake City: School of American Research and University of Utah, 1953–82.

———. *Historia general de las cosas de la Nueva España.* 2 vols. Edited by Alfredo López Austin and Josefina García Quintana. México, D.F.: Alianza Editorial Mexicana, 1989.

Said, Edward. *Orientalism.* New York: Vintage, 1979.

Sala Catalá, José, and Jaime Vilchis Reyes. "Apocalíptica española y empresa misional en los primeros franciscanos de México." *Revista de Indias* 45 (1985): 421–47.

Schechner, Richard. *Between Theater and Anthropology.* Philadelphia: University of Pennsylvania Press, 1985.

Scott, James C. *Domination and the Arts of Resistance: Hidden Transcripts.* New Haven: Yale University Press, 1990.

Sell, Barry D. "The Classical Age of Nahuatl Publications." In Alva, *Guide*, 17–32.

———, trans. and ed. *Nahua Confraternities in Early Colonial Mexico: The 1552 Nahuatl Ordinances of Fray Alonso de Molina, OFM.* Berkeley: Academy of American Franciscan History, 2002. See esp. "The Molina Confraternity Rules of 1552."

———. "Nahuatl Plays in Context." In Sell and Burkhart, *Nahuatl Theater*.

Sell, Barry D., and Louise Burkhart, eds. and trans. *Nahuatl Theater: Life and Death in Colonial Nahua Mexico.* V 1. *Nahuatl Theater.* Norman: University of Oklahoma Press, 2004.

Shergold, Norman D. *A History of the Spanish Stage: From Medieval Times until the End of the Seventeenth Century.* Oxford: Clarendon Press, 1967.

Siker, Jeffrey S. *Disinheriting the Jews: Abraham in Early Christian Controversy.* Louisville: Westminster/John Knox Press, 1991.

Slemon, Stephen. "The Scramble for Post-Colonialism." In *De-Scribing Empire. Post-Colonialism and Textuality*, edited by Chris Tiffin and Alan Lawson, 15–32. London: Routledge, 1994.

Smith, Michael E. *The Aztecs.* Oxford, UK; Cambridge, Mass.: Blackwell Publishers, 1996.

Solano y Pérez-Lila, Francisco. "Estudio preliminar." In *Historia eclesiástica indiana* by Gerónimo de Mendieta, ix–cxi. Biblioteca de Autores Españoles, v. 260. Madrid: Atlas, 1973.

Soustelle, Jacques. *Daily Life of the Aztecs on the Eve of the Spanish Conquest.* Translated by Patrick O'Brian. Stanford: Stanford University Press, 1970.

Stern, Charlotte. *The Medieval Theater in Castile.* Binghamton, NY: Center for Medieval & Early Renaissance Studies, 1996.

———. "The Medieval Theater: Replacing the Darwinian Model." *La Corónica* 24, no. 2 (1996): 166–78.

———. "Reassessing the Nahua Autos: A Propos of Jerry M. Williams's *El teatro del México colonial: poca misionera.*" *Bulletin of the Comediantes* 52, no. 2 (2000): 113–65.

Struever, Nancy. *The Language of History in the Renaissance.* Princeton: Princeton University Press, 1970.

Subirats, Eduardo. *El continente vacío: la conquista del Nuevo Mundo y la conciencia moderna.* Barcelona: Anaya & Mario Muchnik, 1994.

Surtz, Ronald E. "The 'Franciscan Connection' in Early Castilian Theater." *Bulletin of the Comediantes* 35, no. 2 (1983): 141–52.

———. *Teatro castellano de la Edad Media.* Madrid: Taurus, 1992.

Talavera, Hernando de. *Breve y muy provechosa doctrina de lo que deve saber todo cristiano, con otros tratados muy provechosos, compuestos por el arzobispo de Granada.* Granada, n.d.

Taylor, William B. *Magistrates of the Sacred: Priests and Parishioners in Eighteenth-Century Mexico.* Stanford: Stanford University Press, 1996.

Tedlock, Dennis, trans. Introduction to *Popol Vuh. The Mayan Book of the Dawn of Life,* 23–65. New York: Simon and Schuster, 1985.

Tentler, Thomas N. *Sin and Confession on the Eve of the Reformation.* Princeton: Princeton University Press, 1977.

Tiffin, Chris, and Alan Lawson, eds. *De-Scribing Empire. Post-colonialism and Textuality.* London: Routledge, 1994. See esp. "Introduction: The Texuality of Empire," 1–15.

Todorov, Tzvetan. *The Conquest of America: The Question of the Other.* Translated by Richard Howard. New York: Harper Perennial, 1992.

Torquemada, Juan. *Monarquía indiana.* 1614. 3 vols. México, D.F.: Salvador Chávez Hayhoe, 1943.

Townsend, Richard F. *The Aztecs.* London: Thames and Hudson, 2000.

Trexler, Richard. "We Think, They Act: Clerical Readings of Missionary Theatre in 16th-Century New Spain." In *Understanding Popular Culture: Europe from the Middle Ages to the Nineteenth Century,* edited by Steven Kaplan, 189–227. Berlin: Mouton, 1984.

Turner, Victor. "Rokujo's Jealousy: Liminality and the Performative Genres." In *The Anthropology of Performance*, 99–122. New York: PAJ, 1988.

Vaillant, George. *The Aztecs of Mexico*. Baltimore: Penguin, 1956.

Valesio, Paolo. "Esquisse pour une étude des personnifications." *Lingua e stile* 4 (1969): 1–21.

Velasco el Primero, Luis de. "Carta de Don Luis de Velasco, el primero, a Felipe II.—México, 1ro de febrero de 1558." In *Documentos inéditos del siglo XVI para la historia de México*, edited by Mariano Cuevas, 244–45. México, D.F.: Porrúa, 1914/1975.

Vidal, Hernán. "The Concept of Colonial and Postcolonial Discourse: A Perspective from Literary Criticism." *Latin American Research Review* 23, no. 3 (1993): 113–19.

Watts, Pauline M. "Languages of Gesture in Sixteenth-Century Mexico: Some Antecedents and Transmutations." In *Reframing the Renaissance: Visual Culture in Europe and Latin America, 1450–1650*, edited by Claire Farago, 140–51. New Haven: Yale University Press, 1995.

———. "Prophecy and Discovery: On the Spiritual Origins of Christopher Colombus's 'Enterprise of Indies.'" *American Historical Review* 90 (1985): 73–102.

Weckmann, Luis. "Las esperanzas milenaristas de los franciscanos de la Nueva España." *Historia Mexicana* 32 (1982): 89–105.

Weimann, Robert. *Shakespeare and the Popular Tradition in the Theater: Studies in the Social Dimension of Dramatic Form and Function*. Edited by Robert Schwartz. Baltimore: Johns Hopkins University Press, 1978.

West, Delno. "Medieval Ideas of Apocalyptic Mission and the Early Franciscans in Mexico." *The Americas* 45 (1989): 293–313.

Williams, Jerry M. *El teatro del México colonial. Época misionera*. New York: Peter Lang, 1992.

Yates, Frances A. *The Art of Memory*. Chicago: University of Chicago Press, 1966.

———. *Giordano Bruno and the Hermetic Tradition*. Chicago: University of Chicago Press, 1964.

Zamora, Margarita. *Language, Authority and Indigenous History in the Comentarios reales de los Incas*. Cambridge, New York: Cambridge University Press, 1988.

———. *Reading Colombus*. Berkeley: University of California Press, 1993.

Zemon Davis, Natalie. "Boundaries and the Sense of Self in Sixteenth-Century France." In *Reconstructing Individualism: Autonomy, Individuality and the Self in Western Thought*, edited by Thomas C. Heller, Morton Sosna, and David E. Wellbery, 53–63. Stanford: Stanford University Press, 1986.

Zorita, Alonso de. "Parecer del Dr. Alonso Zorita acerca de la doctrina y administración de los sacramentos a los naturales—Granada, 10 de marzo de 1584." In *Documentos inéditos del siglo XVI para la historia de México*, edited by Mariano Cuevas, 331–54. México, D.F.: Porrúa, 1914/1975.

Acosta, José de, 237n2
Adorno, Rolena, 7, 35–36, 163
Adrian VI, 4, 148
Adventus, 5, 213n3
Advertencias para los confessores de los Naturales (Bautista), 9, 123, 147–58, 208–9, 211, 231n2; confessors' position in, 154–57; hybridity in, 157–58; ignorance in, 152–54; insufficient remorse in, 149–50; mortal vs. venial sins in, 150–53; objectives of, 147–48, 155–56; racial constructions in, 149, 156–57
Agency, 135–37, 222n15
Alexander VI, 166, 168, 215n11
Allegory, 223n3; in *Final Judgment*, 67–69, 223n5
Altepetl, 38, 184, 218n27, 227n7
Alva, Bartolomé de, 235n17, 235n18
Alvarado, Pedro de, 240n19
Ángeles, Francisco de los, 166
Angels: in *Colloquios*, 28, 43–45; in *The Fall of Our First Parents*, 106, 109–10; in *Final Judgment*, 66–67; in *The Sacrifice of Issac*, 88, 91
Anger: divine, 24, 25–26, 36, 45
Anunciación, Juan de la, 123
Apocalypse, 224n7, 225n14
Argensola, José Lupercio de, 221n8
Arróniz, Othón, 65, 111, 221n10
Attrition, 120, 138–39, 140, 149
Audience: for *Colloquios y doctrina cristiana*, 19, 34; for *Confessionario mayor en la Lengua Mexicana y Castellana*, 126, 127; for *The Fall of Our First Parents*, 111
Austin, John, 244n43
Auto del sacrificio de Abraham, 82, 90
Auto of the Reyes Magos, 55

Azpilcueta, Martin de, 70, 73, 121–22, 135, 232n7, 232n8, 232n9

Baptism, 176–77, 181, 182, 184, 186
Baudot, Georges, 165, 169, 229n15, 237n1, 237n2
Bautista, Juan, 7, 9, 81, 144, 147–58. See also *Advertencias para los confessores de los Naturales* (Bautista)
Benveniste, Émile, 128
Bhabha, Homi, 5–6, 78, 95, 118, 137, 149, 155, 234n16
Blasphemy, 29
Brevísima relación de la destrucción de Indias (Las Casas), 199, 242n36
Burkhart, Louise, 18, 26, 44, 59, 61, 78, 100, 102, 139, 207, 221n10, 223n1, 226n2, 227n10, 230n4

Cabecera, 183, 241n27
Calendrical rituals, 58–59
Calmecac, 57, 177, 221n5
Calpolli, 38
Calpulteotl, 148
Cancionero (Encina), 220n2
Cantares mexicanos, 57
Carrasco, Davíd, 58
Castañega, Martín de, 232n9
Castro-Gómez, Santiago, 11
Catechism instruction, 236n2
Chang-Rodrígues, Raquel, 229n13
Charles V, 192
Christian deity: carved representation of, 28–29; in *Colloquios y doctrinia cristiana*, 26–27, 31–32, 42–47; in *The Fall of Our First Parents*, 106; in *Final Judgment*, 72–74, 77; ixiptla of, 36; Nahuatl terms for, 26–27; universality of, 38–39

Christian priesthood: and Nahuas, 234n14

Cihuacoatl, 31

Cipactonal, 107–8, 207

Ciruelo, Pedro, 71, 72, 232n9

Cisneros, Jiménez de, 166

Clapión, Juan, 166

Clendinnen, Inga, 59, 99, 176, 185

Coateocalli, 40

Cocolitzli (epidemics), 195–96, 244n41

Codes, 98

Codex Telleriano Remensis, 107, 184

Códice de autos viejos, 57, 82, 226n3

Códice Franciscano, 141–42, 231n6

Códice Matritense de la Real Academia, 40

Colegio de Santa Cruz de Tlatelolco, 17, 108–9, 214n3, 229n14, 229n15, 234n14

Colloquios y doctrina cristiana (Sahagún), 7–8, 15–20, 203–5; audiences for, 19, 34; bilingualism of, 18–20, 37–38; Christian deity's representation in, 26–27, 31–32, 42–47; disappearance of, 18; discovery of, 18; discursive terror in, 41; epistemic domination in, 39–40; epistemic violence of, 24–26; expressive styles of, 19–20; first book of, 17; foreword to, 18; fourth book of, 17; genre of, 20–21; historicity of, 20–21; Holy Spirit allusions in, 22–23; hybridity in, 21, 49–50; missionaries' counter reply in, 38–41; missionaries' long performance in, 42–47; missionaries' representation in, 26, 36, 40, 41; Nahua dieties' representation in, 27–31, 35, 36–37, 47–48; Nahua lords and priests' representation in, 32–38; Nahuatl version of, 18–20, 37–38; papal authority in, 23–24; plan for, 17; prologue to, 21–23, 47–48; providential discourse of, 22; second book of, 17; Spanish conquest's representation in, 24–26;

Spanish version of, 18–19, 37–38; terror in, 41; third book of, 17; tlamacazque's representation in, 34, 41, 48; tlatoani's representation in, 32–34, 41; translations of, 18

Columbus, Christopher, 165, 216n13, 238n7

Comedia de los Reyes, 54

Concrete-relational society, 104–5

Confession, 69–72, 117–24; annual, 119, 229n2, 231n5; attrition and, 120, 138–39, 140; contrition and, 120, 138–39, 140; in *Historia eclesiástica indiana*, 178–80; insufficient remorse and, 149–50; Nahua parallels to, 120–21, 178–80; Nahua pursuit of, 121–22; power relations and, 117–19, 128–29; as pre-Hispanic practice, 122–23, 178–80, 230n4; speech act of, 128–29; subjectivity and, 128

Confessionario mayor (Alva), 235n17

Confessionario mayor en la Lengua Mexicana y Castellana (Molina), 8–9, 123–24, 125–45, 208–9, 211; agency and, 135–37; audience for, 126, 127; charity and, 138–39; Christian subjectivity of, 135–41; circumstances in, 134–35; evil's acknowledgement in, 130; failure of, 144–45; idolatry in, 132–33; linguistic competence and, 127, 128–29; mitigating circumstances and, 134–35; Nahua agency and, 135–37; Nahua virtue and, 142–44; objectives of, 126–27, 143–44; penitent's responsibility in, 133–37, 222n15; prologue of, 127; ritual observances and, 137; self-knowledge in, 130–32

Constructed deficiency, 3

Contact zone, 229n1

Contrition, 120, 122, 138–39, 140, 149–50, 154, 178–79

Corbató, Hermenegildo, 97, 220n3

Córdoba, Pedro de, 91–92, 101, 102, 232n9
Cornyn, John, 66
Corpus Christi: feast of, 55–56, 57, 60, 87, 100
Cortés, Hernán, 4–5, 23, 25, 170, 171, 172, 216n14, 228n4, 239n10, 239n14, 240n17, 240n19
Cosmology: Nahua, 32, 45–46, 223n2
Council of the Indies, 17, 18, 162
Council of Trent, 138–39, 193
Counter-narrative of continuity, 112–13
Counter-Reformation, 177
Cuezal, 43

Derrida, Jacques, 89
Desire: sins of, 92, 132
Despair: sin of, 71–72
Devils: in *Colloquios y doctrinina chris-tiana,* 43–45, 46–47; in *Final Judg-ment,* 74–76, 77; in *Souls and Testa-mentary Executors,* 224n10
Díaz del Castillo, Bernal, 25, 216n14
Diezmo, 200–201
Difrasismo, 19
Diminished self, 132
Disease: sin as, 240n20
Divination, 107–8
Doctrina (parochial jurisdiction), 241n27
Doctrina Cristiana (Córdoba), 91–92, 101, 232n9
Donation of Constantine, 239n11
Drunkenness, 100–101
Duns Scotus, John, 120, 149–50
Durán, Diego, 156, 179, 235n19
Duverger, Christian, 20

Eloquence: Western conception of, 33, 217n21
El sacrificio de Abraham, 82, 90
Encina, Juan de la, 220n2
Enríquez, Martín, 9, 161, 197
Epistemic domination: *Colloquios*'s rep-resentation of, 39–40

Epistemic violence: in *Colloquios y doctrina cristiana,* 24–26; in *Final Judgment,* 66–68, 206
Escalona, Alonso de, 139
Eucharist (consecrated host), 55, 144, 155–56, 157, 189
Evangelization, 5–6
Evil, 105–6, 111–12, 130, 219n34, 224n7; and knowledge, 105, 106
Exponi Nobis, 4

Fall of Our First Parents, The (Motolinía), 8, 97–113, 207; angels in, 106, 109–10; animals in, 100–101; audience's representation in, 111; dat-ing of, 97; earth's representation in, 109; Eve's representation in, 102–3, 105, 106; evil's representation in, 105, 106, 111–12; hidden message in, 98, 108; hybridity in, 102, 107–8, 112–13; mise-en-scène of, 98–102, 112; ocelots in, 101; paradise's repre-sentation in, 99–102; primal couple in, 106–8; rabbits in, 100–101; stum-bling in, 102; villancico in, 109–10
Feast of Corpus Christi, 55–56, 57, 60, 81, 87, 100
Fifth sun, 32, 46, 67, 96, 223n2, 227n10
Filth, 25, 30–31, 37, 104
Final Judgment, 8, 65–79, 206; allegory in, 67–69, 223n4; authorship of, 66, 223n4; Christ's demands in, 72–74, 77; confession in, 69–72; dating of, 65–66; devils' interests in, 74–76, 77, 78; didactic goal of, 68–69; direct address in, 76; epistemic violence of, 66–68; hybridity in, 77–79; priest's behavior in, 69–72; resistance in, 78; Saint Michael in, 66–67; subverting rhetoric of, 72, 74–76, 77–78
Fiore, Joachim de, 23, 164–65
Fletcher, Angus, 223n3
Foucault, Michel, 117, 118, 150
Fourth Lateran Council, 119

France, 55, 233n12
Francis of Assis, Saint, 22, 166, 213n6, 238n6
Free will, 5, 103, 108, 112, 134–37, 181, 232n10
Friars Minor, 6, 213n5
Fuente, Agustín de la, 81

Gage, Thomas, 60
García Icazbalceta, Joaquín, 214n2, 237n1
Garibay, Ángel, 18, 19, 20, 104, 215n7
Gender, 213n5, 231n4; body language and, 103; division of labor and, 106–7; wives and, 103, 228n8
Genesis, 42–47, 227n8
Gibson, Charles, 196
González-Echevarría, Roberto, 242n34
Gruzinski, Serge, 123, 133, 212, 232n10
Guadalupe, Juan de, 166
Gutiérrez, Ramón, 225n16

Hardison, O. B., 56
Harris, Max, 63, 78, 207, 221–22n12, 226n.16
Hidden messages, 63, 66, 108, 222n14, 229n13
Himmelstrasse (Lanzkranna), 151–52
Historia de los indios de la Nueva España (Motolinía), 81, 87, 97, 181, 196, 241n25
Historia eclesiástica indiana (Mendieta), 9, 161–201, 209–10, 237n1; abuse scandal in, 192–99; baptism in, 176–77, 181, 182; books of, 167; Christian disputes in, 181, 182–84; Christian marvelous in, 189–90; confession in, 178–80; eulogetic discourse of, 173–77; fifth book of, 167; fourth book of, 167, 186–201; hybridity in, 172–73, 187; linguistic issues in, 173–76; Nahua virtue in, 190–92; providential agency in, 169, 170–73, 180–81, 186; publication of, 161–62;

repartimiento in, 196–98; resident friars in, 182–86; rhetoric of scandal in, 199; second book of, 167; third book of, 167, 170–86; tithe in, 200; universal history and, 167–69
Historia general de las cosas de la Nueva España (Sahagún), 16–17, 18–19, 22, 34, 122, 162, 171, 181, 191, 214n2
Historia moral y natural de las Indias (Acosta), 237n2
History of the Indians of New Spain (Motolinía), 97. See also Fall of Our First Parents, The (Motolinía); Historia de los indios de la Nueva España (Motolinía)
Holy Spirit: the age of, 23, 164, 186; Colloquios's representation of, 22–23
Honor: concept of, 244n42
Horcasitas, Fernando de, 53, 57, 65, 66, 69, 81, 88, 103, 223–24n5, 227n6
How to Do Things with Words (Austin), 244n43
Huitzilopochtli, 241n29
Humanism, 21, 167–68
Human sacrifice, 29–30, 58–60, 75, 87, 88, 93, 206; Christian deity's demand for (See Sacrifice of Isaac, The); in Crucifixion plays, 221n7
Hybridity, 5–6, 119; in Advertencias para los confessores de los Naturales, 157–58; in Colloquios y doctrina cristiana, 21, 49–50; in The Fall of Our First Parents, 102, 112–13; in Final Judgment, 77–79; in Historia eclesiástica indiana, 172–73, 187; in The Sacrifice of Isaac, 84–85, 86–87, 91, 93–96; in theater of evangelization, 77–79

Idolatry, 43, 44, 132–33, 162, 173, 189, 203, 220n36, 224n12, 232n9, 236n1
Ihiyotl, 231n3
Iluminismo, 239n8
Imitatio Christi (St. Francis), 22

Implied receiver, 82–83, 88
In Animastin Ihuan Alvacaesme, 224n10
Inter Caetera bulls, 168, 215n11, 215n13
Israel, Jonathan I., 235n21
Ixiptla, 30, 36, 58–60, 185, 221n7

Jacobita, Martín, 7, 18, 35, 203
John XXII, 55

Kierkegaard, Søren, 89
Klor de Alva, Jorge, 10, 18, 20, 24, 33,
    35, 37, 38, 42, 43, 112, 131, 136,
    215n10, 217n20, 222n15
Kobayashi, José M., 229n14
Kolve, V. A., 56

Landa, Diego de, 189, 241n30
Lanzkranna, Stephan, 151–52
Las Casas, Bartolomé de, 65, 97, 156,
    162, 199, 242n36
Lehmann, Walter, 18, 27
Leonardo, Andrés de, 7, 18, 35–36, 203
León-Portilla, Ascención, 125
León-Portilla, Miguel, 18, 20, 58, 78,
    108, 207, 215n7
Leo X, 166
*Libro de los Colloquios. See Colloquios y
    doctrina cristiana* (Sahagún)
Liminality, 59–60
Lockhart, James, 28, 34, 58, 61–62, 78,
    184
Locus: medieval theater notion of, 221n9
Long performance, 42–47, 218n30
López Austin, Alfredo, 45, 104, 107,
    214n2, 228n6, 231n3
López de Gómara, Luis, 25, 216n14
Lo que va del Hombre a Dios, 225n15
Love speech, 215n12
Lucifer, 43, 44, 211; identification of
    Nahua deities with, 43–44

MacCormack, Sabine, 233n13
Macehualtin, 107
Manual de confessores y penitentes (Martin

de Azpilcueta), 70, 73, 135, 230n3,
    231n5
McAfee, Byron, 66
Medieval religious drama, 53–57
Mendieta, Eduardo, 11
Mendieta, Gerónimo de, 5, 7, 9, 120–22,
    123, 141–42, 161–202, 209–10, 212,
    228n8, 229n14, 231n6. *See also Histo-
    ria eclesiástica indiana* (Mendieta)
Mendoza López, Margarita, 66, 71
Metonymic substitution, 184–85
Michael, Saint, 43, 66–67, 72
Mictecacihuatl, 30–31, 75
Mictlan, 43, 74, 76, 206
Mictlantecuhtli, 30–31, 75
Millenarianism, 21–22, 235–36n22
Millennial ideology, 239n16
Minorites, 213n5
Molina, Alonso de, 7, 8–9, 123–24,
    125–45, 147, 154, 208, 211, 237n4.
    *See also Confessionario mayor en la
    Lengua Mexicana y Castellana* (Moli-
    na)
Monarquía indiana, 97, 235n20, 237n2
Montezuma, 31, 171, 240n19
Montúfar, Alonso de, 126, 195
Mortal sin, 137, 150–53, 232n8
Motolinía, Toribio de, 8, 97, 100,
    142–43, 144, 162, 163, 181, 195,
    215n10, 227n1, 227n2, 229n14,
    241n25
Mount Moriah, 89, 94
Moya y Contreras, Pedro, 193, 196,
    243n37

Nahua, 213n4; altepetl of, 38; calendrical
    rituals of, 58–59, 89; children's
    instruction by, 83–84, 242n32;
    daughters' instruction by, 228n8;
    dieties' relationships with, 25, 30, 37,
    104–5; divination by, 107–8; ecclesi-
    astic exclusion of, 191–92; educated
    elite of, 108–9; human sacrifice by,
    29–30, 58–60, 75, 87, 88, 93; individ-

ual's status among, 104–5; painting
by, 40; pious representation of,
142–43, 190–91, 235n1; priests of,
33–34; prophecies of, 171–73; repli-
cation skills of, 99–100; ritual practices of, 57–61, 148; social relations
among, 104–5; songs of, 57–58; time
for, 233n11; writing by, 40; young
girls' instruction by, 103
Nahua deities: anger of, 25–26; capriciousness of, 29, 43–44; capture of,
40, carved representation of, 28–29;
Colloquios's representation of, 27–31,
35, 36–37; as devils, 43–44, 46–47;
human forms of, 31–32; human sacrifice to, 29–30, 58–60, 75, 87, 88, 93;
local character of, 38–39; mankind's
creation by, 32, 45–46; multiple identities of, 29, 43–44; multiplicity of,
27–28, 35; nocturnal rituals and,
73–74; origins of, 39–40; self-sacrifice
of, 32
Nahuatl: eloquence in, 33; honorific
speech in, 217n19; Nahua grammarians of, 18, 35–36; oral rhetoric of,
19–20, 24; politeness in, 32–33; songs
in, 57–58; speech of elders in, 84,
103; theological terms of, 26, 27
Nanahuatzin, 32
Narváez, Panfilo de, 240n19
Neixcuitilli: definition of, 61 (*See also*
Theater of evangelization)
*Nexcuitilmachiotl motenehua Juicio Final.
See Final Judgment*
Nutall, Zelia, 20

Observantine branch, 165–66
Observantine reform, 165–66, 239n8
Old Testament: Medieval interpretation
of, 240n23
Olmos, Andrés de, 66, 68, 103, 223n4,
232n9
Oxomoco, 107–8

Palacios Rubios, Juan López de, 216n13
Pastoral power, 117–19, 232n7, 232n10
Patronato real, 215n11
Pavis, Patrice, 221n11
Penance, 119–20, 232n7, 232n8
Pérez de Marchena, Antonio, 165
Philip II, 6, 9, 17, 147, 161–62, 168,
192–94
Philo of Alexandria, 89
Pitt-Rivers, Julian, 244n42
Plenitudo intellectis, 23, 164
Polygamy, 68, 84, 227n5, 227n6
Pope: *Colloquios*'s representation of,
23–24
Postcolonial theory, 10–12
Pratt, Mary Louise, 229n1
Presumption, 71–72
Psalmodia cristiana, 17, 18
Punishment: Spanish conquest as, 24–26

Quem quaeretis?, 54
Quetzalcoatl, 32, 38, 45–46

Rabasa, José, 184, 215n12
Ravicz, Marlyn E., 65, 69, 88
Read, Kay A., 46, 104
Real hacienda, 245n46
Relaciones (Cortés), 25
Repartimiento, 196–98, 244n42, 245n45
Requerimiento, 25, 216n13
Rouqueitallade, Jean de, 165
Ruiz Ramón, Francisco, 220n4

Sacrifice of Isaac, The, 8, 81–96, 206–7;
Abraham's obedience in, 86–89,
92–93; addressee of, 82–83; angel in,
88, 91; animal sacrifice in, 88–89, 95;
children's disobedience in, 83–84;
Christian deity's demand in, 86–89,
94–95; dating of, 81–82; didactic goal
of, 90–91; first part of, 83–85; hybridity in, 84–85, 86–87, 91, 93–96; identities in, 94–95; linguistic features of,

83–84; second part of, 85–90; weaning feast in, 83

Sahagún, Bernardino de, 7–8; censorship of works by, 161–62; ethnographic studies of, 16–17, 22, 39, 48, 73–74, 84, 86, 87, 88, 103, 122–23, 171, 179, 191, 214n2, 230n4, 242n32; on evangelization, 144–45, 156, 181; modernity of, 16; on vice, 140–41. *See also Colloquios y doctrina cristiana* (Sahagún)

Saura, Pascual, 18

Scott, James C., 98, 108, 221n12, 222n14

Scrupulosity, 231n5

Sell, Barry D., 65–66, 69, 78, 81, 223n1, 225n13, 226n2, 235n17

Sermones en mexicano (Escalona), 139

Sins, 25–26, 92–93, 150–53; confession of (*See* Confession); of desire, 92, 132; as disease, 240n20; of idolatry, 132–33, 232n9; impoverished self and, 105, 106; mortal, 150–53, 232n8; Nahua parallels to, 120–21

Songs: in *The Fall of Our First Parents,* 109–10; Nahua, 57–58

Soto, Domingo de, 242n35

Souls and Testamentary Executors, 224n10

Soustelle, Jacques, 74, 228n4

Spain: historiography of, 167–69; religious drama in, 54–57

Speech-act, 128, 244n43

Stern, Charlotte, 56–57

Stumbling, 101

Subjectivity: Christian, 151, 154, 158, 208, 236n23; definition of, 127–28; European, 192; Nahua, 190; Nahua Christian, 158, 174, 177, 204

Summa Theologica (St. Thomas Aquinas), 71–72, 153, 216n15, 216n16, 219n34

Tamoanchan, 32, 35, 107

Tecciztecatl, 32

Tedlock, Dennis, 40, 218n30

Testament (St. Francis of Assis), 238n6

Teyolia, 231n3, 240n21

Tezcatlipoca, 26–28, 30, 211–12; capriciousness of, 29, 87–88, 94, 95; feast of, 59; human form of, 31; negative attributes of, 44, 87–88, 95, 106, 219n32; skunk and, 30

Theater of evangelization, 5, 8, 53–54, 205–8; characters and plot in, 61; language of, 61–62; mise-en-scène of, 61; Nahua forms and, 57–58, 60–61, 73–74, 75; nobility in, 108–9; objectives of, 53–54; power relationships and, 62–63; prohibition of, 78; resistance in, 78; script production for, 61–62; self-legitimation through, 100. *See also Fall of Our First Parents, The; Final Judgment; Sacrifice of Isaac, The*

Third age of the world, 22–23

Third Mexican Council, 6–7, 147–48

Thomas Aquinas, Saint, 71–72, 120, 128, 153, 157, 164, 216n15, 216n16, 219n34

Tithe, 200–201

Tlacamictiliztli, 94, 96

Tlalchitonatiuh, 75

Tlaloc, 88, 94, 95; feast of, 87

Tlamacazqui: *Colloquios*'s representation of, 34–38, 41, 48

Tlamatinime, 40, 95

Tlapialli, 147–48

Tlatlacolli, 25–26, 132

Tlatoani (tlatoque), 4, 24, 74, 240n18; *Colloquios*'s representation of, 32–34; *Historia eclesiástica indiana*'s representation of, 177–78

Tlazolli, 25

Tlazolmiquiztli, 104, 132

Tlazolteotl, 31

Todorov, Tzvetan, 208

Tonalli, 228n6, 231n3, 233n11

Tonalpohualli, 107, 109

Tonalpouhque, 107–8
Torquemada, Juan de, 97, 237n2
Translation, 62, 221n11
Tratado de hechicerías y sortilegios (Olmos), 232n9
Trexler, Richard C., 222n13, 225n16
Trinity: Christian, 216n15
Twelve, the, 4, 166–67, 239n10. *See also Colloquios y doctrina cristiana* (Sahagún)
Tzitzimime, 43
Tzontemoc, 43

Vade mecum in tribulatione (Rouqueitallade), 165
Valderrama, 200–201
Valeriano, Antonio, 7, 18, 35–36, 203
Valesio, Paolo, 223n3
Vegerano, Alonso, 7, 18, 35–36, 203
Velasco, Luis de, 195, 197

Velázquez, Diego de, 240n19
Venial sin, 150–53
Villancico: in *The Fall of Our First Parents*, 109–10
Visitador, 141, 200, 245n44, 245n46
Visitas, 241n27
Visitatio sepulchri, 54

Watts, Pauline M., 5, 213n3
Weaning, 83
Wiesel, Eli, 89
Williams, Jerry, 88, 228n7, 229n16

Xavier, Francisco, 231n6

Zamora, Margarita, 165
Zemon Davis, Natalie, 233n12
Zorita, Alonso de, 195, 243n39
Zumárraga, Juan de, 232n9

About the Author

VIVIANA DÍAZ BALSERA is Associate Professor of Spanish at the University of Miami. She received her Ph.D. from Yale University in 1989 in Hispanic Literatures, with emphasis on the early modern period. Díaz Balsera is the author of *Calderón y las quimeras de la Culpa: alegoría, seducción y resistencia en cinco autos sacramentales* (Purdue University Press, 1997), a book that questions the widely held assumption that Calderón's *autos* harmonize the dramatic and religious discourses that constitute them. Rather than the dogmatic champion of the Catholic Church, the auto that emerges in this book is conflictive, ambivalent, yet profoundly moving, participating in the very dangers of sensual pleasure it so earnestly seeks to warn against. Díaz Balsera has also published on the drama and prose of sixteenth- and seventeenth-century Spain and Colonial Spanish America by a wide-range of authors such as Cervantes, Lope de Vega, Hernán Cortés, Alonso de Ercilla, Toribio de Benavente Motolinía, and Sor Juana Inés de la Cruz, establishing transatlantic connections in their work. Her articles have appeared in journals such as *Colonial Latin American Review, Revista de Estudios Hispánicos, Bulletin of the Comediantes, Journal of Spanish Cultural Studies,* and others.